The Acquisition of Creole Languages

How do children acquire a Creole as their first language? This relatively underexplored question is the starting point for this first book of its kind; it also asks how first language acquisition of a Creole differs from that of a non-Creole language. Dany Adone reveals that in the absence of a conventional language model, Creole children acquire language and go beyond the input they receive. This study discusses the role of input, a hotly debated issue in the field of first language acquisition, and provides support for the nativist approach in the debate between nativism and input-based models.

The Acquisition of Creole Languages will be essential reading for those in the fields of First Language Acquisition and Creole Studies. Adone takes an interdisciplinary approach, and uses insights from the acquisition of language in the visual modality, making this of great interest to those in the field of Sign Linguistics.

DANY ADONE is a Professor of Applied English Linguistics, Director of the Australian Studies programme and Director of the Language Lab at the University of Cologne. She has also served as President of the Society for Pidgin and Creole Linguistics.

The Acquisition of Creole Languages

How Children Surpass Their Input

DANY ADONE

University of Cologne

CAMBRIDGE
UNIVERSITY PRESS

CAMBRIDGE UNIVERSITY PRESS
Cambridge, New York, Melbourne, Madrid, Cape Town,
Singapore, São Paulo, Delhi, Mexico City

Cambridge University Press
The Edinburgh Building, Cambridge CB2 8RU, UK

Published in the United States of America by Cambridge University Press,
New York

www.cambridge.org
Information on this title: www.cambridge.org/9780521199650

First published 2012

Printed in the United Kingdom at the University Press, Cambridge

A catalogue record for this publication is available from the British Library

Library of Congress Cataloguing in Publication data
Adone, Dany.
  The acquisition of Creole languages : how children surpass their input / Dany
  Adone.
    pages   cm
  Includes bibliographical references and index.
  ISBN 978-0-521-19965-0
  1. Creole dialects.   2. Language acquisition.   3. Children–Language.
  I. Title.
  PM7831.A74 2012
  417′.22019–dc23
  2012011696

ISBN 978-0-521-19965-0 Hardback

Pu tu ban dimun ki fin kit zot pei ek ki pa fin bliye zot langaz kreol

Contents

Figures

Tables

Acknowledgements

In some way this voyage of discovery started when I left my small island of Mauritius to study in Germany. I am very grateful to my parents, Karelina and Claude Adone, for constantly encouraging me over time and distance and for always believing in me, even when they wished I had never left my island.

I am deeply indebted to my mentor, Dieter Wunderlich. He has always been an invaluable source of inspiration for me since I began studying linguistics. I have gained much from Tom Roeper's intellectual generosity and deep interest in all my work on language acquisition. I am also greatly indebted to Noam Chomsky who made time to discuss my work on Mauritian Sign Language.

I acknowledge with gratitude the Deutsche Forschungs-gemeinschaft (DFG) for funding the habilitation project, parts of which have been included in this book. A special thank you to Dr Susanne Anschütz. The following people read all or parts of the draft of the book and made most valuable comments: Derek Bickerton, Harald Clahsen, Claudia Felser, Andrew Radford. I shared some of the findings discussed in this book during conferences with the following people: Lisa Green, Annie Senghas, Marie Coppola, Susanne Goldin-Meadow, Roland Pfau, Marlyse Baptista, Carol Myers-Scotton, Sarah Thomason, Juana Licieras, Virgina Yip and Stephen Matthews, and Harold Koch.

I also thank Maaike Verrips and Heather van der Lely for their material that I used in the experiments. A special thank you goes to Helen Barton, Sarah Green and Gillian Dadd from Cambridge University Press and to two anonymous reviewers. Special thanks to Professor Groth, who also encouraged me to finish the book in times of health problems.

I thank all the children, parents and adults involved in all the experiments carried out in Mauritius and the Seychelles. I would also like to thank Mary-Ann, Daniella and the staff of the St Joseph Pre-school in Mahé, Seychelles. I also acknowledge the invaluable support of Mrs Marie Therese Choppy from the Ministry of Culture, Mrs Penda Choppy of Lenstiti Kreol, Sister Jude of the Ministry of Education, Mr Jean Claude Mahoune from the Ministry of Culture, Mr Gabriel Essack and Mr Marcel Rosalie of the National Heritage in the Seychelles. Without their help and support, I would not have had a successful field trip. In Mauritius, I thank the children and their parents involved in the experiments. I also thank my colleagues and friends, Vinesh and Patricia Hookoomsing, for their support. A special thank you to Founa and Olga, who unfortunately is no longer among us to see the book.

In the Northern Territory, Australia, I thank Paul Black, Brian and Nancy Devlin and Anne Lowell for their support. I am also very grateful to several members of the Ngukurr, Galiwin'ku and Yirrkala communities. I am grateful to the Joshua family and my extended family throughout Arnhemland, especially Gertie Joshua, Angela Huddlestone and Justine Rogers.

In Germany, I would like to thank Iman Laversuch for her comments, Sigrid Newman for proofreading the manuscript, Anthony Bülow, Sarah Krauß, and Ipek Krutsch for reading through the chapters. I am endlessly indebted to Timo Klein, Matt Davies and Marjory Bisset for their help in revising and formatting the manuscript. Finally, and most importantly, I thank Shaun, who had a lot of patience over the last years while I concentrated on this task.

Abbreviations

Object language is italicised in the text with a translation in English in single quotation marks. Additionally, italics are used for emphasis. To highlight parts of examples I use underscoring.

Technical terms are in small capitals. Grammatical categories are printed in full capitals, usually in abbreviations. Indications of children's ages have the following format: (years; months).

ABBREVIATIONS

A	Adjective
AP	Ambiguous passives
ASL	American Sign Language
AsPP	Aspect phrase
AsP$_E$	Aspect (eventive)
AT	Active transitive
AUX	Auxiliary
BT	Binding Theory
C(OMP)	Complementiser
CP	Complementiser phrase
CT	Computed tomography
D(ET)	Determiner
DOC	Double-object construction
DP	Determiner phrase
FVP	Full verbal passives
GB	Government and Binding framework
I(NFL)	Inflection
IP	Inflectional phrase

IL	Interlanguage
L1	First language acquisition
L2	Second language acquisition
LAD	Language acquisition device
LLH	Lexical learning hypothesis
MDG	Minimal default grammar
N	Noun
NP	Noun phrase
PPET	Positron emission tomography
PM	Passive morpheme
Op	Empty operator
OV	Object verb
PDC	Prepositional ditransitive construction
PLD	Primary linguistic data
PP	Prepositional phrase
SPEC	Specifier
SVC	Serial verb construction
t	Trace
TP	Tense phrase
UG	Universal grammar
V	Verb
V2	Verb second
VO	Verb object
VP	Verb phrase
XP	X phrase (X=N, V, A, etc.)
Y/NJ	Yes/No judgment

ABBREVIATIONS USED IN INTERLINEAR GLOSSES

Ø	Empty category
1PL	First person plural
1POS	First person possessor
1SG	First person singular
2PL	Second person plural

2POS	Second person possessor
2SG	Second person singular
3PL	Third person plural
3POS	Third person possessor
3SG	Third person singular
ADJ	Adjective
HAB	Habitualis
INST	Instrumental
LOC	Locative
MOD	Modality
NEG	Negation
PAST	Past tense
PL	Plural
PP	Prepositional phrase
ADV	Adverb
AGR	Agreement
ASP	Aspect
AUX	Auxiliary
BEN	Benefactive
CAUS	Causative
CLI	Clitic
COMP	Complementiser
DET	Determiner
EXIST	Existential
FUT	Future
PROG	Progressive aspect
REDUP	Reduplication
REFL	Reflexive
REL	Relativiser
SG	Singular
TMA	Tense, mood, aspect
TNS	Tense
V	Verb

An asterisk (*) before an example indicates that the example is not grammatical. Furthermore, when the asterisk is used with children's sentences, it indicates that the sentences are not correct according to the adult grammar. A question mark (?) before an example indicates that the example is marginally acceptable.

I   Creole languages

INTRODUCTION

This study focuses on how Creole-speaking children acquire their native language. Like other children acquiring their first language (L1), they show creativity and ingenuity through which we get some insight into the acquisition of complex structures. Before I address the acquisition issue, I will briefly define and describe Creole languages.

Creole languages came into existence under specific circumstances of language contact, that is, during colonisation, and they are closely associated with Pidgins. It is generally accepted that Pidgins represent speech forms that are essentially used as a means of communication among people who do not speak the same language. As such, Pidgins do not have native speakers. Mühlhäusler (1986), among others, distinguishes three basic forms of Pidgin (jargons, stable Pidgins and expanded Pidgins) to account for the various degrees of sophistication and development that a Pidgin can reach in its life cycle before it develops into a Creole, as in the case of Tok Pisin in New Guinea. However, a Pidgin does not always develop into a Creole. The fundamental difference between Creole languages and Pidgins is that Creole languages have native speakers. At this point I refer the reader to Arends *et al.* (1994), and Holm and Michaelis (2008) for an overview of Creole studies.

CREOLISATION REVISITED

When a Pidgin turns into a Creole language, we refer to this process as creolisation (Hall 1966, Todd 1990, among others). In the discussion on creolisation, which without doubt is one of the most controversial issues in the field, the genesis of Creole languages per se, and their 'exceptional' status have been addressed.

The classical view that creolisation is a process that takes place when a Pidgin becomes the mother tongue of its speakers assumes that a Pidgin is a structurally and lexically simplified system which emerges in a language contact situation and eventually develops into a fully fledged language, that is, a Creole. As a simplified system, a Pidgin typically has the following characteristics: a very restricted lexicon, no inflectional morphology, no functional categories and a highly variable word order. In contrast, a Creole system typically shows an elaborate lexicon, derivational and some inflectional morphology, functional categories and an underlying word order. The Creole system is less variable than the Pidgin one. The creolisation process here takes place as soon the first generation of children acquires the Pidgin as a first language.

Another view is that creolisation takes place when Pidgins expand into Creole languages without nativisation. Scholars such as Sankoff (1979), Chaudenson (1992), Singler (1992, 1996), Arends (1993) and McWhorter (1997) have argued against the nativisation-based view of creolisation. Through detailed historical reconstruction, scholars have pointed out that creolisation can be a gradual process taking place over several generations of speakers (see Arends 1993, Plag 1993, Roberts 1995 for Hawaiian Creole, Baptista 2002 for Cape Verde Creole, and Bollée 2007 for Reunion Creole). In this view, creolisation equates to language change. It implies continuity in the linguistic systems between the superstrate/substrate languages and the Creole systems formed. Case studies presented by Plag (1993) and Mufwene (1996), as well as several papers in Baker and Syea (1996), show that the development of grammatical structures in the formation of Creoles can be accounted for by universal principles of grammaticalisation operative in languages in the same way. This view of creolisation is plausible and can be assumed to account for the emergence of some Creoles. More recently, some scholars have discussed grammaticalisation and creolisation as processes that are not mutually exclusive (Plag 1998, Adone 2009, among others).

Bickerton (1981 and subsequent work), taking a universalist stand, rejected this view and proposed that there is a break in the transmission between the lexifier languages and the Creoles. This has led Bickerton (1984, 1990 and subsequent work) to argue that creolisation must be abrupt if there is a breakdown in transmission of language. In his Language Bioprogram Hypothesis (1984) Bickerton argues that Pidgin adult speakers passed on their Pidgin to their children. His hypothesis is that this first generation of Creole speakers, that is, children, must have been exposed to some 'macaronic form' of language since their parents were Pidgin speakers. These children (i.e. the first generation of Creole speakers) were exposed to deficient input. As a result, they had to rely on their 'language bioprogram' (a sort of default grammar that children bounce back on when the input is inadequate) to invent language. The basic idea here is that this type of creolisation, which is abrupt, is an instance of first language acquisition in the absence of input. It is nativisation which takes place as soon as a Pidgin becomes the first language for its speakers (cf. Bickerton 1974, Thomason and Kaufmann 1988, Adone and Plag 1994, Mufwene 1999, Adone 2001b, 2003).

Arends (1993) and Singler (1995, 1996), among others, on the basis of a series of well-documented socio-historical facts, questioned the plausibility of Bickerton's claim. Since then, the role of children and adults in the process of creolisation has become a subject of great debate within the field. In the current debate most scholars adhere to the view that adults rather than children must have been the ones creolising the system (Singler 1992, Lumsden 1999a, b, Lefèbvre 1998, Siegel 1999, Veenstra 2003, among others). For other scholars, such as Bickerton (1984, 1990), Adone and Vainikka (1999), Bruyn et al. (1999) and Mufwene (1999), Adone (2001b), children were the ones mainly responsible for creolisation. Nowadays, it is obvious that both adults and children must have contributed to the process of creolisation (cf. Plag 1998, DeGraff 1999, Baptista 2002, among others). As a result of an insufficient historical record on the development of most Creole languages, there is no reliable data available, especially for the early stages of formation in the seventeenth- and eighteenth-century colonial plantation communities. Also, most Creole languages emerged in the context of European colonial expansion, which was practised from the sixteenth century onwards, with rigid social stratification of the society, master–slave relationships and plantation environments (Arends *et al.* 1994). While it is not possible to reconstruct the creolisation process, experimental studies such as those conducted by Newport and colleagues contribute significantly to clarifying the unique role of children in creolisation. However, it is this socio-historical dimension that distinguishes Creole languages from non-Creole languages (see DeGraff 2003).

The second question regarding the exceptional status of Creoles has also been hotly debated. While scholars such as Muysken (1988) and, more recently, Mufwene (2000), DeGraff (2003) and Ansaldo and Matthews (2007) have argued that there is no such thing as Creole exceptionalism or uniqueness, other scholars such as McWhorter (2001) have presented arguments for a distinction between Creole and non-Creole languages. Furthermore, McWhorter argues that Creole grammars are 'the world's simplest grammars' (for similar views see Heine and Kuteva 2005). To discuss this issue at length would certainly go beyond the scope of this book. But at this point, I would like to add that the burden of proof is surely on those who argue that Creole languages have simple grammars. The dichotomy Creole and non-Creole languages is artificial. However, if we are to make a distinction among languages, the only relevant difference would be in terms of the age factor. Creole languages, like sign languages, for instance, are relatively 'young' languages, and are not established, given their recent genesis.

MORISYEN

Morisyen is the language spoken in the Republic of Mauritius, which has a population of roughly 1.5 million. The island is situated in the middle of the Indian Ocean, and its population consists of several ethnic groups of various origins, such as French, Chinese, Indian, African and 'mixed' types. Demographically speaking, the majority of Mauritians nowadays are of Indian descent (68%). The second group consists of the *'population génerale'* (27%), followed by Sino-mauritians (3%) and Franco-mauritians (2%) (cf. Baggioni and de Robillard 1990, Florigny 2010).

Morisyen is one of the languages spoken along with French and English. Officially it is the national language of the country. However, as the national language, it does not enjoy the prestige attributed to French and English. Morisyen, a French-based Creole, is still not regarded as a full-fledged language by many of its native speakers. According to the 2003 census conducted by the Bureau Central des Statistiques Mauricien, it is spoken as the first language by 80 per cent of the population (Florigny 2010).

SESELWA

Seselwa is one of the official languages of the Republic of Seychelles, along with French and English. The country is made up of over 115 islands in the southwest of the Indian Ocean. The main island is Mahé, located a few thousand kilometres east of Kenya. The population is concentrated on the islands of Mahé, La Digue and Praslin and was estimated to be 70,000 in 2000 (personal communication, Mahoune). Similar to Mauritius, the population consists of several ethnic groups (Chinese, Indian, African and French origins), but is predominantly African. According to Bollée (1993), 94 per cent of the population has Seselwa as its L1. At the same time, 97 per cent of the population speaks Seselwa fluently.

Seselwa was established as the national language with an official orthography in 1981. It is not considered to have the prestige status of French or English, but it is not subject to such invidious judgment as Morisyen. Bollée (1993) argues that Seselwa is accepted as the first national language of the Seychelles. It is also regarded as the most important element of national identity. According to M.T. Choppy (personal communication), there is a growing tendency to use English or French in public functions. Together with Morisyen, Rodrigue and Reunione (the Creole languages of the neighbouring islands) it forms the Isle de France Creole of the Indian Ocean. Similar to Morisyen, it is a French-based Creole. According to Ravel and Thomas (1985), instead of a continuum there are three main varieties seen: 'Créole populaire', Creole of the middle class and of the educated class and Creole of the media.

THE SCOPE AND GOALS OF THIS STUDY

In this study I investigate how Creole-speaking children acquire certain complex structures in their L1. The questions I address here are:

1. What is the nature of input in the Creole context and how does it affect acquisition?
2. How (dis)similar is the acquisition of Creole languages when compared to that of other 'established' languages?
3. What does the acquisition of Creole languages reveal of the part played by children in acquisition?

Previous work of mine focused on spontaneous data gathered on Morisyen and Ngukurr Kriol (Australia) (Adone 1994a, b, 1997). In this study, I focus on the acquisition of four complex structures, namely references (pronouns and reflexives), double-object, passive and serial verb constructions in Seselwa. Although both spontaneous and experimental data are analysed, the emphasis is on experimental data elicited from Seselwa-speaking children. I also included naturalistic data on Morisyen in the relevant chapters, for three reasons: first, because acquisition data on Creole languages in general is rare, second, because these two languages are sister languages, and third, because the combination of these different methods, though by no means complete, does give us some new insights into first language acquisition, for example, on the question of input and the question of how children acquire their first language.

This book has been written with the strong conviction that there is considerable value to be gained through interdisciplinary work. This is why I have included findings from other fields including sign languages, home signs and gesture, learning theories, computational theories of language learning and evolution, the emergence of language, and language typology, among others, and have tried to integrate them into the general discussion.

The study is organised as follows: Chapter 2 examines the theoretical issues involved in first language acquisition studies, especially innateness, and Universal Grammar. The discussion is centred on exposure to input and its consequences for acquisition. First, I define what language acquisition with a language model implies. I then look at several cases of language acquisition, starting with deprivation of input, as seen in the case of feral children and deaf children with hearing parents, and extending to cases of language invention (presumably, in the case of the first generation of children, to home signers). Finally, I focus on cases of language acquisition in which children do get a language model, as is the case with Creole-speaking children. Chapter 3 briefly describes some complex structures in adult Seselwa grammar and these are compared to Morisyen, which is a sister language of Seselwa. Chapter 4 analyses the methods of data collection used in this study. Chapters 5 to 8 examine the production of pronouns and reflexives, double-object, passive and, finally, serial verb constructions. These areas of grammar have been chosen because of the challenge they pose for acquisition. Cross-linguistic studies show that these structures are difficult to acquire. Chapter 9 embeds the acquisition findings of the previous chapters into the discussion on the role of children in acquisition. The overall results of this study strongly support the view that children surpass their input.

2 Issues in first language acquisition

The capacity for language is what makes our species different from other species. This statement has been made repeatedly since the 1950s and has provoked much controversial discussion since then. The assumption behind the statement above is that our species has a biological predisposition to acquire language, independent of its modality. At the core of the discussion within Linguistics are two concepts – Universal Grammar and innateness. Although these concepts have been at the heart of conceptual motives for grammatical studies, they have been typically used in different ways, misunderstood or even oversimplified. This chapter will thus first give an overview of some central issues within the generative field of language acquisition, such as innateness, Universal Grammar, the logical problem of first language acquisition and negative evidence, because they are crucial to the line of argument and understanding in this work. For the purpose of this chapter I will focus on relating these issues to the question of exposure to input affecting first language acquisition. Nonetheless, this chapter should serve as an overview of the state of the art in linguistic nativism.

INNATENESS

Innateness is one of the most controversial topics in Linguistics, especially among scholars of the formal and functional approaches. Although it is widely assumed that humans are the only species capable of acquiring language when exposed to it, there are a number of open issues related to this area. Children, under different circumstances, have been reported to acquire language when exposed to it. Animals, on the contrary, have not been successful in acquiring language, in spite of the amazing statistical learning capacities that some of them have demonstrated in experiments (Kanzi (Savage-Rumbaugh *et al.* 1993), for example). Some species seem to have means of communication but no species has demonstrated the form of the languages that humans acquire. The dance of the honeybees, the alarm calls of vervets or birdsong might all have structures but these systems do not seem to have structures resembling grammatical categories, word order, etc. (Valian 2009). This species-specificity argument has been taken to be the piece of evidence par excellence to argue for the innateness of language. In fact, both camps acknowledge this argument and it is not the source of disagreement between the formal and functional scholars.

Another point relevant in the innateness debate is the domain-specificity argument. According to the generative approach, the language faculty of humans is due to a specialised domain-specific organ in the brain. It is genetically endowed. In contrast, the functional view is that language is an inherent part of our cognitive make-up. It would certainly go beyond the scope of this study to focus on the debate between the functional and formal views. However, some arguments used by proponents of functionalism have been taken to cast serious doubts on the innate domain-specificity view. Findings on learning have been interpreted as counter-evidence to domain specificity. Studies such as Squire and Kandel (1999) have revealed that learning depends heavily on the connections between the activated neurons. Findings on the plasticity of brain tissue have been taken to provide evidence against the domain-specificity argument. Furthermore, studies have revealed that the impact of experience on the brain circuitry is bigger than previously assumed. Thus, this argument, together with others, speaks against the innateness view and for the equipotentiality hypothesis (Elman *et al.* 1996).

Connectionist neural network models account for learning in terms of networks of input–output related to each other by connections. These networks have been successful in tasks such as producing the English past tense for real and nonce verbs (Hinton 1992, Elman *et al.* 1996, Marcus 2001). It has become clear from these networks that several factors such as frequency distribution, similarity and statistical correlations are relevant to successful associative learning. The arguments from the connectionists have been refuted by formal linguists such as Chomsky (2002) and Pinker (2002), who presented strong evidence showing that the brain is organised in a domain-specific manner. More recently, findings can be taken to indicate that the organisation of the brain is genetically specified. Further, the dissociation between language and other cognitive capacities in genetic disorders such as Specific Language Impairment (SLI) or children with Williams Syndrome is another argument supporting the domain-specificity argument. In spite of normal cognitive development, children with SLI show deficits in core areas of grammar. Children with Williams Syndrome have excellent language skills despite severe mental retardation, as shown in several studies (Gopnik and Crago 1991, van der Lely 1996, Clahsen and Almazan 1998, Penke personal communication).

Another idea that seems equally important is to distinguish several levels of innateness, as Maratsos (1999) does. One level deals with the innate features common to many species, a second one refers to the species-specific innate features of humans in particular, and a third level applies to the faculty-specific innate features of grammar acquisition.

Eimas *et al.* (1971) found that young human infants perceive certain voiced–voiceless perceptual boundaries innately. These boundaries are seen in phoneme pairs like /p/–/b/, /t/–/d/, /k/–/g/. Experiments using the high-amplitude-sucking method show that newborns have the ability to discriminate their first language from other languages (Mehler *et al.* 1988, Venditti and Swerts 1996). Interestingly, Jusczyk (1997) suggests that prenatal hearing experience is a possible source of explanation for this early sensitivity to language-specific prosodic properties of speech in children. However, Kuhl and Miller (1975) found that chinchillas make similar auditory discriminations to children. Subsequent research also shows that rhesus monkeys as well as mink do the same. Taken together, we could argue that this discrimination is innate to many mammals. But one fundamental difference between the humans and non-humans lies in the ability of human infants to use prosodic features of their mother tongue (e.g. stress, rhythm, intonation) to acquire their syntactic regularities (Gleitman and Wanner 1982, Pinker 1984, Höhle and Weissenborn 1999).

The second level of innateness consists of two components, memory and off-line thinking. Working memory is part of the computational abilities of humans. Relevant for the argument of this chapter is the short-term memory, currently known as working memory, especially the system specialised for the processing of language-based information, allowing us to identify language-specific properties.

As far as the capacity of off-line thinking is concerned, it has been argued that it became possible with the emergence of protolanguage.[1] On-line thinking and off-line thinking both involve computations. The main difference between these two systems, however, is that in on-line thinking computations are carried out in terms of 'neural responses elicited by the presence of external objects'. Off-line thinking consists of 'computations carried out on more lasting internal representations of those objects' (cf. Bickerton 1996: 90). According to Gazzaniga (1985), while all creatures above a low level of brain organisation can perform on-line thinking, humans are the only species that can practise both on-line and off-line thinking.

With respect to the third level of definition, an example is knowledge in syntax. Such knowledge of syntax-specific properties such as innate knowledge that languages have nouns, verbs, control, command, etc., which has been mentioned earlier in this chapter. Although these three levels of innateness are probably mutually exclusive, I regard syntax as the product of faculty-specific innateness,

---

[1] See Bickerton (1995: 90).

for the reasons already provided above by Bickerton's scenario (1998, 1999). Innateness, following Bickerton's definition, consists of hard-wired 'principles or algorithms for assembling sentences'. Rules of the various languages come from the combination of principles and a language-specific vocabulary (Bickerton 1996: 631).

More recently, scholars such as Tomasello and Tenenbaum have argued that innateness may not be of relevance when we take into account other abilities such as general learning capacities and probabilistic analysis.

THE LOGICAL PROBLEM OF LANGUAGE ACQUISITION

The logical problem of language acquisition is another argument that has been put forward in favour of the assumption of the innate language faculty. It is based on the poverty-of-the-stimulus argument as proposed by Chomsky (1965, 1980). The poverty-of-the-stimulus argument is also known as 'Plato's problem'. This problem refers to the discrepancy between the poverty of the input and the complexity of acquired knowledge during language acquisition. Chomsky originally claimed that the input is impoverished and ungrammatical. This led to a discussion on the nature of the input that children receive, followed by a series of studies scrutinising input (cf. Gerken 1996, the overview by Eisenbeiss *et al.* 2002). Today we have a more realistic picture of the input data, in which several factors have been shown to play a role, such as child-directed speech, the frequency of certain elements and the context, all of which facilitate the acquisition process.

One important characteristic of the input is underdetermination. The input is both quantitatively and qualitatively underdetermined. Quantitatively means the child receives a small set of input data and is later capable of producing/comprehending an infinite number of data after s/he has acquired the target language. Qualitatively means that the child is exposed to certain types of sentences and has to extract rules of grammar that will allow him/her to produce/comprehend an infinite number of sentences later.

NEGATIVE EVIDENCE

There are several types of negative evidence. The most important one for the discussion here is the correction that adults or parents provide in response to children's utterances. Within the field of psycholinguistics it is generally assumed that negative evidence does not play a central role in first language acquisition (Hyams 1986, Pinker 1989, Marcus 1993, among others).

Saxton (1997) experimented with a series of novel irregular verb pairs following the English irregular verb paradigm (neak/noke (speak/spoke)), (pell/pold (sell/sold)), (sty/stought (buy/bought)), etc. Children had positive evidence in that adults described pictures or events with these verbs. Negative evidence was also provided through corrective feedbacks from the adults for one subgroup of the verbs only. The studies showed that children were significantly more inclined to produce the correct form after reformulations (i.e. negative evidence) than when they received only positive evidence. This result, together with others found in Saxton *et al.* (1998) and Chouinard and Clark (2003), have been taken to indicate that negative evidence can facilitate acquisition (Clark and Lappin 2011). That negative evidence can play a facilitating role in L1 acquisition is not denied. However, it is unrealistic to think that parents systematically give corrective feedback to their children at all times. If they did, then we would have to reconsider the role of negative evidence in L1 acquisition. As a matter of fact, we know that corrective feedback is not at all a strategy commonly used by parents. A look at several cultures with oral languages illustrates the point in question. In several Aboriginal communities of Australia I observed that parents do not give corrective feedback straight away. The situation with Creole-speaking children is no different. Based on my observations in three Creole-speaking communities (Mauritius, the Seychelles and Australia in the 1990s) I noted that conversations of parents with children are not frequent compared to the interaction between parents and children coming from a middle-class European background.

We know that there is a significant amount of cross-cultural variation in the way carers relate to children. Other factors such as level of education, social class of the parents, types of society/community (e.g. patrilineal) can also affect the situation.

Now let us turn to the implicit knowledge that a child brings to the task of language acquisition. It is the means by which the child learns and analyses the linguistic input (referred to as the primary linguistic data (PLD)). Based on this data, the child hypothesises a series of grammars with the help of the Language Acquisition Device (LAD) before s/he reaches the adult grammar or Final State. The process is represented schematically in (1):

(1)   Input (PLD) → **LAD** → Final State (Adult Grammar)

One of the tasks of generative grammar is to explain the course of language acquisition, which is remarkable for its universality, uniformity and rapidity. A distinguishing feature of this theory is that it postulates universal principles that are unique to the formation of grammar, instead of characterising the acquisition process in terms of general principles of cognitive growth. Languages do differ from each other, thus yielding cross-linguistic variation. There are aspects of Universal Grammar that distinguish the limits of variation in certain parts of the grammar. These aspects of the variation are grasped by parameters. Parameters specify all the possible choices that languages make. As such, parameters account for the obvious differences in the grammars of different languages as well as allowing for linguistic variation, including variation in language development. Children are exposed to particular languages, and have to set the parameters at the appropriate values (Radford 2006).

An example of a parameter is, let us say, the Null Subject Parameter. According to this parameter, there is cross-linguistic variation in terms of subject availability in languages. There are languages that are called null subject languages because they do not require a surface subject. Examples of such languages are Italian or Spanish because subjects in these languages are not expressed on the surface and the verbal morphology encodes person specification, for instance. Parameters are generally binary in nature, i.e. in this case +null subject languages and –null subject languages. However, there might be more than two parameter settings possible (see Manzini and Wexler 1987 discussing multivalued parameters concerning the binding domain for anaphors in a given language). In the discussion on parameters Meisel (1995) and others have drawn our attention to the problem of parameter resetting in first language acquisition, as Hyams (1986) proposes. The issue of resetting parameters is only relevant when one assumes that there is a preset default value determined by Universal Grammar (UG).

In a nutshell, the theory of UG is a theory of the internal mental capacity which enables human learners to process the very complex structures of language. It is the generative stance of how children acquire language. In contrast, functionalists have argued that children acquire language on the basis of input. One functionalist approach to language acquisition has been proposed by Tomasello (2003). He claims that language structure comes into existence through language use. Children hear utterances and then reconstruct the language. The crucial idea here is that this reconstruction of language is done by general cognitive processes such as intention-reading and pattern-finding. The intention-reading skill is the social cognitive skill found in the human species whereas the pattern-finding skill is found in primates.

LANGUAGE ACQUISITION MODELS

The question of how syntactic phrase structure emerges in child grammar is one of the central issues in language acquisition research. There are two major approaches within the field of first language acquisition that explain the development from child grammar to adult grammar. One approach is best known as the nativist, generativist, Universal Grammar approach and assumes that children's linguistic knowledge is innate rather than acquired. The other approach is known as the constructivist, usage-based approach.

The main assumption here is that children do not have any innate knowledge available. Instead the focus lies on input and it is argued that frequency, for instance, plays a role. Constructivist approaches are also referred to as emergentist (Ambridge and Lieven 2011). Interestingly the usage-based approach explains language acquisition by the desire of children to communicate and use language (for an up-to-date overview see Ambridge and Lieven 2011).

Within the nativist, Universal Grammar approach, there is a version that assumes UG principles to be operational from birth and, as a result, children's syntactic structures at all stages are compatible with the UG principles. If the language faculty contains a Uniformity Principle which determines that all sentences have a CP+TP+(NEGP+)VP, then children are born with this tacit knowledge. Thus there is continuity between the children's and adults' sentence structures. This means that children's sentences should contain functional layers such as CP/TP/DP.

A second version has been proposed by Rizzi (1994, 2000). He claims that children go through a stage in which they alternate between full adult-like functional structures and truncated structures (where CP/TP is omitted). Empirical support for the truncation hypothesis comes from the analysis of wh-questions in Adam's files on the CHILDES database.

A third version has been put forward by Hyams and others and is known as the Underspecification Model. Such a model posits that children omit grammatical features in their grammars. Empirical evidence for this comes from several areas including finite verb auxiliaries, negation and wh-questions. Poeppel and Wexler (1993), Schütze (1996), and Wexler, Schütze and Rice (1998) have analysed the so-called optional infinitive stage.

A fourth proposal has a factor in common with the two previous approaches, namely the assumption that all UG principles are available to the child from the beginning of the acquisition task. But the grammar of a particular language the child is acquiring develops gradually, through the interaction of abstract knowledge (such as X-bar principles) and the child's learning of the lexicon. This view does not violate the continuity assumption because the child's learning device does not change over time. Grammatical development can thus be regarded as a result of the child's lexicon. Proponents of this view are Radford (1990, 1996), Vainikka (1990), Adone (1994a), Clahsen *et al.* (1996) and Meisel and Ezeizabarrena (1996). Clahsen *et al.* (1996) call it the structure-building hypothesis plus lexical learning, also known previously as the weak continuity approach.

Although this study cannot offer any compelling evidence for one particular theory because of its cross-sectional nature, the data gathered here together with previous work (Adone 1994a) is compatible with the fourth language acquisition model, namely the structure-building hypothesis, as advocated by Radford, Clahsen and others.

CASES OF LANGUAGE ACQUISITION

In this section my primary interest is to discuss various cases of language acquisition especially with respect to exposure to input. Children acquiring a Creole language nowadays offer a very interesting case of language acquisition because most of the Creole languages are still oral languages. In looking closely at how the children acquire the language in question, we gain an insight into the creative extent of the language-learning capacity of children.

An increasing number of studies on input in L1 have been gathered up to now. So far we know that there are cases of language deprivation as seen in the case of feral children (Skuse 1994), Genie (Curtiss 1977) and Isabelle (Mason 1942), among others. We also have studies on deaf children with hearing parents (Feldman, Goldin-Meadow and Gleitman 1978, Goldin-Meadow 2003). Bickerton (1981, 1984) has argued that the first generation of Creole-speaking children who were exposed to Pidgins had to create or invent language because they did not have any input from their parents. Newport (1982) shows how deaf children in an environment with non-native models of American Sign Language, in particular the case of Simon, go beyond their input (Singleton and Newport 1987, Singleton 1989). Taken together, these cases represent an order of accumulative richness of linguistic exposure. Cases of language deprivation can be regarded as cases in which there is no input. This is followed by cases of home signers – deaf children growing up with minimal input from a hearing world. The case of Simon illustrates what children can do with language when their parents are L2 learners. Similar cases are Pidgin speakers and the first generation of Creole-speaking children, deaf children with L2 learners of ASL and the second generation of migrant children. At this point I assume that the case with children acquiring a Creole language represents language acquisition with a conventional language model as is the case with English and other established languages. So, to sum up, there are cases of language deprivation, language invention and finally cases of language acquisition under normal circumstances.

Language deprivation

Feral children are children who grow up without contact with humans, in the wilderness. They have no communicating experience with human beings. When discovered, they behave in a very similar way to animals. They snarl and growl (Skuse 1994).

As already pointed out in the literature, there is no knowledge of the conditions of these children before they were left in the wilderness. The reason for their abandonment is not known. However, the most important condition in these cases is that these children are without language, which means that they lack not only a language model but also an interlocutor. Several studies have shown that when these children were integrated into society, they received language instruction but without much success. Victor, the wild boy of Aveyron, is a typical example (Itard 1806, Lane 1976). In this respect it is worth mentioning Lenneberg (1967), who hypothesised that the ability to acquire language effortlessly disappears during the critical period in which biological changes take place as children reach puberty. The case of Genie is a strong piece of evidence in support of Lenneberg's hypothesis (1967). She was discovered in 1970 at the age of thirteen-and-a-half. Until then she had grown up left on her own in a small room, given minimal care and food and punished by her father when she made noises.

When she was discovered, she made whimpering and spitting noises and had the physique of a six-year-old girl. She made some encouraging progress in cognitive development and in learning vocabulary. At one stage she could produce short strings of words. But she never could step beyond a simple syntax and morphology. Furthermore, her speech was produced with great effort. This led Curtiss (1977) to the conclusion that the acquisition of simple morphology and syntax in the case of Genie was due to the fact that she had not acquired language before the critical period of language development. This conclusion is certainly a plausible one, but there could also be other reasons for her unsuccessful language acquisition.

The case of Isabelle (Mason 1942, reviewed in Skuse 1994) offers an interesting counter-example to Genie. She was exposed to language at the age of six-and-a-half. Her mother was deaf and did not speak. Isabelle was conceived illegitimately, and both mother and daughter were shut in a secluded room for seven years. The mother finally escaped and brought her daughter to the hospital. At first, Isabelle made noises like a wild animal and initially she was thought to be deaf. But by the age of eight she was evaluated to have normal intelligence and language skills and could talk. Her success in learning to talk is clearly due in large part to the fact that she learned to speak at an earlier age than Genie. Although details about the gestures she used with her mother are not known, it is clear that she did use some sort of gestures to communicate with her mother. This rough home sign system, it has been assumed, probably helped her to learn a spoken language (Senghas 1995a).

So far, we have seen three cases of language deprivation. In the case of feral children, as well as Genie, there was no language model and no interlocutor. In the case of Isabelle there was a small amount of input that seems to have contributed to her success in learning a language at a later stage.

Language invention

The case of deaf children of hearing parents is a different type of language deprivation because the children involved here have a healthy and supportive home life, as compared to the three previous cases. However, they do not have access to the language model spoken around them.

Of all deaf children in the USA, 90 to 95 per cent are born to hearing parents. Most of them do not have access to a sign language. Instead, many parents concentrate on teaching them to speak and read lips (Hoffmeister and Wilbur 1980). Few children deaf from infancy succeed at learning spoken language, since a great degree of the language signal is not visibly evident. If these children have access to gesture, they develop idiosyncratic gestural systems used with family members, referred to as home sign.

Goldin-Meadow and her colleagues (Goldin-Meadow 1982, Goldin-Meadow and Mylander 1984 and Goldin-Meadow et al. 1994) have investigated the development of home signs. They found that deaf children creatively systematise gestures in a way very similar to linguistic structure. The following system has been recognised in the speech of the children:

1. Consistency in the gesture order,
2. Distinction between semantic roles (transitive verbs followed by a marker for the patient and ditransitive verbs by a marker for the recipient, while the actor in both cases is less frequently indicated),[2]
3. Well-formedness in the gestures. Singleton, Morford and Goldin-Meadow (1983) have shown that there is a consistency in the handshape of the home signs from signers when they are asked to represent a concept. This consistency is not found in the gestures of hearing people who are asked to sign on the spot. They tend to produce a different gesture each time.

---

[2] Hudson (1983) proposes that Kriol has a transitivity marker on the verb.

Goldin-Meadow distinguishes between resilient and fragile features. Resilient features are the ones that children develop. The fragile features are the ones that are not developed, such as productive internal morphology and syntactic movement (such as wh-movement). Genie, Goldin-Meadow argues, acquired only resilient features. A prediction can be extrapolated from this. Resilient features would be easier to acquire and are the earliest in normal language acquisition. Similar views have been presented in the development of concepts by Clark (2001). A look at children acquiring American Sign Language (henceforth ASL) naturally as a native language (5% who have deaf signing parents) provides evidence to some extent for Goldin-Meadow's distinction between resilient and fragile features. These children at first do indeed use some kind of sequential order to mark roles such as actor and patient. The internal spatial morphology system is developed only later.

Goldin-Meadow and Mylander (1984) analysed the syntactic structure in the gestures of deaf children of hearing parents. They found that nine out of ten children produced gestures for the intransitive actor (for instance, the mouse in a sentence describing a mouse running in his hole) as often as they produced gestures for the patient (for instance, the cheese in a sentence describing the mouse eating cheese). This production-probability pattern, Goldin-Meadow and Mylander argued, is similar to the structural case marking patterns of ergative languages, in that the intransitive actor is treated like the patient rather than like the transitive actor. However, it is important to recall that in conventional ergative languages it is the transitive actor that is marked, whereas in the deaf children's gesture system the transitive actor tends to be omitted. This could be regarded as being unmarked (cf. Silverstein 1976, Dixon 1979).

Another interesting point is that all ten children generated complex sentences, defined here as containing at least two propositions. These sentences either described a sequence of events or requested that a sequence of events take place. One child pointed at a tower, produced a 'hit' gesture and then a 'fall' gesture to express that he had hit the tower first, and that the tower had fallen. Another interesting observation is that children also produced complex sentences not ordered in time. One child pointed at Mickey Mouse and produced a 'swing' gesture and then a 'walk' gesture to comment on the fact that Mickey Mouse swings and walks on the trapeze at the same time.

In this study Goldin-Meadow and Mylander showed very clearly that these children did go beyond the input they received. The gestures had structural properties at three levels: (1) lexicon, which consists of pointing gestures referring to objects in the surroundings or absent from the surroundings, and characterising gestures which referred to actions and attributes. (2) syntax, which consists of predicate structure, ordering and production-probability rules and recursion. (3) morphology, which consists of derivational and inflectional morphology.

Pidgin is usually defined as a lingua franca or a simplified language code used by people who speak mutually incomprehensible languages. Pidgins arose in trade situations, and between servants and masters in colonial communities. Pidgins are characterised by sharp reduction in grammatical complexity, including the loss of inflectional morphology, reduced lexicon and restricted order in syntax.

According to Bickerton (1981, 1984), children born into the situation mentioned above did not speak the Pidgin. However, they developed the limited input they experienced into a radically restructured, complex language called Creole. This process is also known as nativisation. In this model, it is assumed that the Creole structures are the results of children's innate capacities to create language (Andersen 1981a,b, 1983a,b, Bickerton 1984).

Bickerton claims that this process, also known as creolisation, occurs abruptly within a single generation of child learners. He proposes that children had to rely on their language bioprogram (a sort of default grammar) and created new languages known today as Creole languages. In this way the bioprogram accounts for the similarities found among Creole languages in the world and for the similarities with children's early stages of acquisition, a view that is accepted within the field of first language acquisition but not in Creole studies.

As compared to the groups of children described so far, there are two new factors here. First, Creole children of Pidgin speakers, it seems, formed some sort of community, generating a language together, and second, they were exposed to more input, even if fragmented and not consistent.

Another very strong case for the innateness of language is provided by the case of blind children. Studies on blind children (Landau and Gleitman 1985) show that there is neither delay nor distortion in their language growth as compared to their sighted peers, despite the fact that they do not have access to contextual information. A particularly surprising aspect of blind children's learning is the acquisition of terms to describe visual experience such as *look* and *see*. These two verbs are among the very first verbs to appear in blind children's spontaneous speech. In experiments, blind children raised their hands when asked to look up. In the absence of a working visual system, this is not surprising. Blind children also distinguish between the perceptual term *look* and the contact term *touch*. This finding shows us that despite the radical differences in input opportunity, children develop a system which fits their own perceptual lives (Landau and Gleitman 1985).

In their study, Landau and Gleitman (1985) review two types of evidence for the claim that there is biological endowment in humans supporting and shaping language acquisition. First, there is uniformity in language learning within and across linguistic communities in spite of the extensive variability of input provided. Second, children acquire linguistic organisation that experience cannot account for. From their study of how blind children acquire language, the authors argue that language acquisition in humans entails a specific type of learning that is severely restricted and biologically predetermined to follow a limited pathway. Their findings lead to the conclusion that language is the outcome of the young human brain, such that the least exposure condition is sufficient to produce it in children (Landau and Gleitman 1985).

Non-native signers sometimes have children who are also deaf. This means that the language model for the children is an incomplete form of ASL. Before we proceed any further, we need some explanations concerning non-native signers at this point.

Newport (1990) conducted a study on people learning ASL as a first language. Around 90 to 95 per cent of the deaf people in the USA come from hearing families and thus start to learn ASL at different ages. Some people are first exposed to ASL when they first go to school at the age of six, while others encounter ASL when they start high school and others when they are already adults. Newport's study showed that age of acquisition plays a very important role in the fluency of signers. Newport classified the signers under investigation as native, early and late signers. The native ones are the ones who started signing from birth. The early ones are the ones who started signing between the ages of four and six. The late signers are the ones who started signing at the age of twelve. She found that the native signers had the best performance, followed by the early and the late signers. Native signers learn the complete morphological system of ASL. Late learners, in comparison, learn part of the system and tend to leave out some of the morphological markers in obligatory contexts. They also learn the so-called 'frozen lexicon' of ASL. This consists of complex signs learned as unanalysed wholes. Another study worth mentioning at this point is the one conducted by Emmorey *et al.* (1995) showing similar results, in that native signers show more sensitivity to grammatical errors than late signers.

Coming back to the parents who are non-native signers, they use signs that contain hand-shapes and movements from the morphological system of ASL, but these are not combined into a productive grammatical system. In contrast, their children perform a morphological analysis on this input and redevelop a complex internal morphology, thus producing a system closer to ASL than that of their parents (Newport 1982). In this situation, children are surpassing their language model in a very similar way to Creole-speaking children. This cycle repeats itself and is very similar to what happens in the Creole-speaking communities.

Evidence from studies of language learning support the notion that children impose morphological structure onto the language system they are developing even if structure of this sort is not present in the language model they are receiving. In spoken languages, children who are exposed to Pidgins that tend not to have morphology have been found to creolise the system and in the process develop a system that has morphological structure.

Singleton and Newport (1987) and Singleton (1989) worked with one deaf child of the second generation called Simon. His parents were deaf and learned ASL in late adolescence, which makes them late learners. As a result of this, they behaved like most late learners in that they produced 'frozen lexicon' and had an inconsistent system of signs. At the age of seven, the ASL used by Simon already surpassed the input he was exposed to. This was witnessed especially in the movement and spatial inflections on verbs of motion and location. His parents produced these inflections inconsistently, as seen in late learners (Simon's father 69% accuracy, mother 75% accuracy, as compared to Simon's 88% accuracy and native children 81%). In his use of hand-shape morphemes, his performance was below the mean of native children (Simon 50%, native children 69%) as compared to his father 45% and mother 42%).

Unlike the home-signing children, Simon did not invent new signs. He learned from the lexicon of his parents. In learning these, he took some morphemes that were used inconsistently in his parents' signing and used them more consistently and systematically in his own signing, producing a form of the language that surpassed theirs. This case is very similar to what Creole-speaking children do in that both Simon and Creole children surpass the language model they are exposed to.

Nicaraguan Sign Language also offers a very interesting case study. According to Senghas (1995a,b), in 1979 after the victory of the Sandinista party, as a result of new literacy and health care and social programmes, deaf people were brought together in schools and children started to sign immediately. Kegl and Iwata (1989) described some of the earliest stages of Nicaraguan signing and compared it to ASL. They came to the conclusion that it had the status of a Creole. According to Senghas (1995a,b), two forms of the sign language emerged, which are independent from Spanish, the spoken language of the region, and unrelated to ASL as used in most of North America.

The oldest members of the community, in their mid-twenties, entered school in 1980, each of them with a different home-signing system. Through contact they developed what Senghas defines as a 'partially crystallised pidgin' called Lenguaje de Signos Nicaraguense (LSN), which they apparently still use today.

Younger deaf children who started school at that time received the Pidgin LSN used by the older children as input. Kegl and Iwata (1989) discussed the nativisation process that took place in Nicaragua and proposed that although LSN was not optimal in terms of natural language, and was variable, it was rich enough to trigger nativisation in the next generation. This new form of signing has been called Idioma de Signos Nicaraguense (ISN).

One difference from Pidgin speakers is that the older Nicaraguan signers who were providing the language model to the younger ones did not bring bits and pieces of a developed nativised language to the community. Instead they came with their 'own different sparse, idiosyncratic home sign system' (Senghas 1995a:41). She showed in her work that children were responsible for developing a system of verb argument agreement from a system of spatial inflection. She argued that the processes by which children nativise a language were the same processes by which children learn existing languages. In this respect, we recall that Bowerman (1982) also argued that language acquisition is characterised by the analysis of previously unstructured forms. However, the difference between normal language acquisition and the Nicaraguan case is that the changes made by children persist because there is no adult target language to follow. Nicaraguan children reanalyse their input and expand it.

Language acquisition with a conventional language model

It is often assumed that any child acquiring an existing language (spoken or signed) is exposed to what is known as 'impoverished' input. This means that children are exposed to only a small number of the possible sentences of their native language and yet they succeed in becoming native speakers of the language in question. They acquire the target grammar, and are able to generate complex structures that they have never heard before, to follow rules and use them properly. Chomsky (1965, 1986) calls this phenomenon 'poverty-of-stimulus' and argues that children's input is not sufficient to lead them to the full grammar of their language. Consequently, their innate language faculty helps them reach their target language, in limiting them in their hypotheses and steering their grammars. This characterisation of language acquisition applies to normal situations such as in the case of English, German or French, where children have a language model. In these cases the language concerned is established, meaning that there is a language model (norm, established rules, written tradition, etc.) that the child has access to.

The cases of acquisition discussed in the previous sections represent different degrees of access to input, starting from zero access to minimal access and finally, normal access. Feral children illustrate zero access to input. Deaf children not exposed to a signing model but to a spoken language model can be regarded as zero access in their language modality. The children exposed to Pidgins, and deaf children exposed to non-native models of ASL represent minimal access to input. Children acquiring established languages such as English, then, represent full access to input.

In the discussion on input there are several views. Some scholars argue that input can be 'impoverished', while others claim that it is 'degenerate'. Impoverished input means that it lacks information that would allow children to acquire certain syntactic principles. Degenerate input, on the other hand, is taken to be input with false starts, incomplete sentences and even some ungrammaticalities (Valian 2009). If we take the case of Morisyen and Seselwa, we can see that the acquisition of these two Creole languages to date can be regarded as language acquisition under normal circumstances, in the sense that children do get input. However, input is variable and ambiguous. The variability and ambiguity of input is due to several factors. From a sociolinguistic perspective, French (on Morisyen) and English (on Seselwa) influence the adult grammars (Adone 2006, Florigny 2010). From a psycholinguistic perspective, we find a lack of corrective response of adults in interaction with children. Third, the predominantly oral character of the language seems to be another factor contributing to the laxness in the language. A concrete example of the variability and ambiguity of input is illustrated in the omission of functional categories (TMA (tense, mood, aspect) markers, determiners, relativisers, etc.). Many of these can be omitted without causing a problem of interpretation as is generally the case in discourse-oriented grammars.

Another important factor here is that children acquiring any established language as their L1 will become literate in that language. In the case of both Morisyen and Seselwa, children do not learn their first language at school, instead they become literate in English and French. Further, there is no prescriptive grammar, a situation which leaves children with a vacuum that they exploit fully. As a result, studies on Morisyen and Seselwa are expected to give us some deeper insights into the role of children in acquisition.

CONCLUDING REMARKS

In this chapter I have discussed some central concepts such as UG and innateness as put forward within the generative framework. I have also established that there are different cases of first language acquisition depending on the amount of input. When children are deprived of language, the outcome is what we see in the case of Genie. Language invention seems to be the best explanation to account for the case of home signers. At this point, the cases of Seselwa and Morisyen are both theoretically cases of language acquisition with a language model, although input is variable and ambiguous in nature.

3   Complex Creole syntax

INTRODUCTION

In this chapter I analyse some aspects of complex syntax in both Morisyen and Seselwa in the light of two seemingly incompatible approaches, generative and typological. It will become clear that the combination of these approaches proves to be tremendously helpful for the description of the structures investigated in this book. In the field of first language acquisition, there has been an abundant amount of research conducted on simple syntax. Studies on the acquisition of complex syntax are, however, rare. A few exceptions are Bowerman (1979), Diessel (2004), Lust *et al.* (2009). The term complex syntax is traditionally taken to refer to sentence types which are not simple. Although the distinction between complex and simple syntax is not always clear, the study of complex syntax gives us insight into some basic aspects of syntax and semantics such as hierarchy, order, locality domains and recursion among others (Lust *et al.* 2009). Constructions with pronouns and reflexives, double objects, passive and serial verbs are the focus of this chapter.

PRONOUNS AND REFLEXIVES

In generative grammar Binding Theory (BT) has been formulated to capture the syntactic conditions for referentiality between anaphoric elements (including pronouns and reflexives) and their antecedents. It is considered to be a core component of the computational knowledge of language. This study takes the Binding Theory presented in Chomsky (1981) as a starting point. In recent decades binding has been discussed in the spirit of the Minimalist Program (Kayne 2002,

Boeckx *et al.* 2007, Hicks 2009, Reuland 2011 among others). It has become clear that there is a considerable amount of cross-linguistic variation (Reuland 2011). Syntactic binding is defined in hierarchical terms (c-command). There are three binding conditions stated as principles:

Principle A: Anaphors (reflexives) must be locally bound. Principle B: Pronouns are locally free. Principle C: Referential expressions are free.

These are illustrated by the English examples in (1a–e):

(1) a. She said that Shanna$_i$ likes herself$_i$.
    b. * She$_i$ said that Shanna likes herself$_i$.
    c. She said that Shanna$_k$ likes her$_i$.
    d. She$_i$ said that Shanna likes her$_i$.
    e. * She$_i$ said that Shanna$_i$ likes her.

According to Principle A, reflexive pronouns must have a local antecedent. This means that in (1a) *Shanna* is the local antecedent of *herself*. *Herself* cannot be bound to *she*, thus (1b) is incorrect. Pronouns are, on the other hand, bound non-locally (Principle B). As such, *Shanna* and *her* cannot be co-indexed as seen in (1c). *Her* can be bound to *she* as *her* is locally free, as seen in (1d). Finally, names and other referential expressions such as *Shanna* may not be bound by a c-commanding antecedent (Principle C). Example (1e) illustrates the point.

Syntactic binding and coreference are two distinct mechanisms. Coreference, in contrast to syntactic binding, involves co-indexing, but does not entail c-command. Sentences with quantified NPs show the difference between coreference and syntactic binding. In the sentence *Every boy$_i$ is here and he$_i$ likes himself.* the quantified NP 'every boy' does not have a definite referent and cannot be coreferential with anaphoric elements. In spite of this difference in coreferentiality, Binding Theory applies to quantified NPs, as shown in the examples below:

(2) a. * Everybody$_i$ said that Shanna likes herself$_i$.
    b. Everybody said that Shanna$_i$ likes herself$_i$.

(3) a. * He said that everybody$_i$ likes him$_i$.
    b. He$_i$ said that everybody likes him$_i$.

(4) a. * Everybody$_i$ said that Shanna$_i$ likes her.
    b. Everybody$_i$ said that Shanna$_k$ likes her$_l$.

Example (2a) is an example of Principle A violation. (3a) represents a case of Principle B violation. (4a) is a case of Principle C violation.

Seselwa, like Morisyen, demonstrates a variable pronoun and reflexive system, which can easily lead to confusion. Here are some examples;

(5) a. Zan$_i$ fin   koz   ar   li$_k$
       John   ASP   talk   with   3SG
       'John talked to him.' MORISYEN/SESELWA

    b. Zan$_i$ pe   koz   ar   li$_i$
       John   PROG   talk   with   3SG
       'John is talking to himself.' MORISYEN/SESELWA

    c. Zan$_i$ pe   koz   ar   li   –mem$_i$
       John   PROG   talk   with   3SG   +REFL
       'John is talking to himself.' MORISYEN/SESELWA

(6) Zan$_i$ fin   pandi   so   lekor$_i$
    John   ASP   hang   3POS   body
    'John hanged himself.' MORISYEN/SESELWA

In example (5a) *li* is a 3SG pronoun (him/her) and refers to someone else. Example (5b) shows that *li* can also be used as a reflexive and can thus be co-indexed with *Zan*. However, this happens only with some verbs. In example (5c) we have *li+mem* used to express reflexivity. In example (6) *so lekor* is the body expression also used to express reflexivity.

I conducted a series of experiments with adults speaking Seselwa and Morisyen as their first language to clarify the situation. The results show the following:

1. Bare pronouns are used as pronouns following Principle B, as seen in example (5a).
2. Bare pronouns are also used to mark reflexivity with a particular group of inherently reflexive and transitive verbs such as *benye* 'bath', *amize*

'amuse'. These results confirm Corne (1988), who suggested that these verbs can be classified as 'inherently' or better 'potentially reflexive' verbs. I prefer the term 'inherently reflexive' and will use it throughout the chapter to refer to verbs such as 'scratch', 'wash' and 'amuse'. However, in these cases, Principle B seems to be violated, as seen in example (5b).

3. Pronoun +*mem* form is used to mark reflexivity, as seen in example (5c). It is preferred to the reflexive expression *so lekor* 'his body' in Morisyen. The use of pronoun +*mem* to mark reflexivity is more common in current Morisyen than in Seselwa.

4. *So lekor*, as in example (6), is used only with action verbs in Morisyen. In contrast, in Seselwa it is used with a wider range of verbs.

Comparing the spoken Creole data I gathered in Mauritius in 1993–94 to earlier texts of Morisyen (cf. Chaudenson 1981), I argued elsewhere (Adone 1994b) that *limem* was competing strongly with *so lekor*, establishing itself as the reflexive form per se, thus overtaking the reflexive function of the bare pronoun. In 2000, I noticed that *so lekor* is still used with the same verbs but it is definitely becoming an archaic expression. *Limem* has taken over and makes *so lekor* almost redundant. This development is not witnessed in Seselwa. In Seselwa, *li* is still used both as a pronoun and a reflexive. *Limem* is also used as a reflexive. *So lekor*, however, is used more productively than in Morisyen. Tables 3.1 and 3.2 provide us with an overview of the pronominal systems of both Morisyen and Seselwa.

As the careful reader will note, Seselwa, as compared to Morisyen, has only one pronoun to mark the second person singular and plural, i.e. *u* 'you'. Both Morisyen and Seselwa make a difference between subject and object pronoun. In Morisyen and Seselwa *mo* 'I' is the nominative case pronoun and *mwa* 'me' represents the objective case (accusative or dative case). This applies to *to* 'you' and *twa* 'you' in Morisyen also. The forms *mwa* and *twa* are derived from the French objective pronouns *moi* and *toi*. In spite of the minor differences between these two Creoles, we see that there is a certain amount of variability in this area of grammar which might affect the input provided to the children.

Table 3.1 *Morisyen pronouns*

Person	Singular	Plural
1st	Mo/mwa	Nu/nu
2nd	To/twa	U/u
3rd	Li/li	Zot/zot

Table 3.2 *Seselwa pronouns*

Person	Singular	Plural
1st	Mo/mwa	Nu/nu
2nd	U/u	U/u
3rd	I/li	Zot/zot

DOUBLE-OBJECT CONSTRUCTIONS

Verbs of transfer and communication (also classified in the literature as ditransitive verbs) are known for taking three semantic arguments: the sender, the recipient and the object/message that is being transferred. There are two automatically licensed positions, one for the subject and the other for the direct object. The canonical thematic roles linked with these positions correspond to sender and object/message transferred. Interestingly, we see two options available for the recipient:

a. Either it is in a syntactically unmarked position, that is, external to the verb and object unit and forms part of the prepositional phrase (or verb phrase in serial verb constructions). Two conditions are necessary for this: the language in question must have an element such as English 'to' and a mechanism of transmitting the recipient thematic role of the verb to another case assigner. Example (7) illustrates this point:

(7) Claude gives the book to Karelina.

b. Or, it is in a syntactically special position, that is, in a construction with the direct object (e.g. in a small clause) and its thematic role is received directly. What is special here is the possibility of an argument (object or message) to behave as a predicate that gives the recipient role together with the verb. Sentence (8) is an example:

(8) Claude gives Karelina the book.

Following Bruyn *et al.* (1999), I view option (a) as the result of a lexico-semantic operation, while option (b) can be seen as the outcome of a syntactic operation. The first option is called the prepositional ditransitive construction or PDC and option (b) is called the double-object construction or DOC. In the next section I will address the role played by the double-object construction in Creole languages as compared to the prepositional ditransitive construction.

Before I discuss the nature of DOC, I would like to address the distribution of DOC and PDC in Creole languages. A look at Creole languages shows that many Creoles with European lexifier languages with double objects have DOC. This is true of Negerhollands with Dutch as the lexifier language and Tok Pisin with English as the lexifier language. Examples (9) and (10) taken from Bruyn *et al.* (1999) illustrate this:

(9) Ham a   gi   di   mam si   gout.
     3SG PAST give DET   man 3POS   gold
     'He gave the man his gold.' NEGERHOLLANDS

(10) Mi   soim yu   banara bilong mi.
     1SG show 2SG bow   PREP   1SG
     'I show you my bow.' TOK PISIN

However, DOC also occurs in Creole languages whose European lexifiers have no DOC, such as Portuguese and French. Examples come from Saramaccan (Bruyn *et al.* 1999) with Portuguese as the lexifier language, and Seselwa and Morisyen with French as the lexifier language, as seen in examples (11) to (13):

(11) Mi   ke   pin   dja   I   wan   soni.
     1SG   want tell 2SG   one   thing
     'I want to tell you something (in secret).' SARAMACCAN

(12) Komela mo   pe   don   u   larzan.
     now   1SG PROG give 2SG/PL   money
     'I am giving you money now.' SESELWA

(13) Asterla mo   pe   don   twa   larzan.
    now   ISG PROG give 2SG money
    'I am giving you money now.' MORISYEN

Table 3.3 *Distribution of DOC, PDC and SDC in Creole languages*

	DOC	PDC	SDC
Sranan	+	+	+
Saramaccan	+	–	+
Jamaican Creole	+	+	–
Tok Pisin	+	+	–
Negerhollands	+	+	–
BerbiceDutch	+	-	+
Afrikaans	+	+	–
Haitian Creole	+	–	+
Guyanais	+	–	–
St Lucian	+	–	–
Louisiana Creole	+	+	–
Seselwa	+	+	–
Papiamentu	+	–	–
Palenquero	+	–	–
Guinea-Bissau Kryol	+	–	–
Fa d'Ambu	+	–	+
Principense	+	–	+
Mayo-Portuguese	–	+	–
Sri Lanka Portuguese	+	+	–
Morisyen	+	+	+
Ngukurr Kriol	+	+	+

Adapted from Bruyn *et al.* (1999).

Table 3.3 by Bruyn *et al.* (1999) shows very clearly that DOC is present in almost all these Creole languages. When we check the distribution of DOC in Creole languages from Table 3.1, we see some complementary relation with other constructions such as PDC and serial ditransitive constructions (also known as SDC). Based on the survey conducted by Bruyn *et al.*, it seems that DOC is available in almost all Creoles, while PDC as well as SDC is more limited. DOC is followed by PDC and SDC occurs only occasionally.

Looking at these options in Morisyen, the ditransitive verb *done* 'give' gives us the following picture as seen in examples (14a–c):

(14) a. Mari   pe   don   so   papa   tabak.
        Mary   PROG   give   3POS   father tobacco
        'Mari gave tobacco to her father.' MORISYEN

     b. Mari   pe   don   tabak   pu   so   papa.
        Mary   PROG   give   tobacco   for   3POS   father
        'Mari gave tobacco for her father.' MORISYEN

     c. Mari   pran   tabak   don   so   papa.
        Mary   take   tobacco give   3POS   father
        'Mari gave tobacco to her father.' MORISYEN

The same constructions are also possible in Seselwa. Example (14a) is a DOC. Example (14b) is a PDC with the preposition *pu* 'for'. Example (14c) is a SDC with *pran/don* 'take/give' (see Bickerton 1989 for Seselwa). The PDC is available for benefactives and depends on the existence of a preposition in the Creole in question, similar to the English 'to'.

Bollée (1977) and Corne (1977) provide us with a detailed analysis of Seselwa DOC. They both observe that DOC occurs with verbs of transaction and communication (see also Levin 1993 for a typology of verbs in English). Note that the criteria and all the Seselwa examples, (15) to (19), are also valid for Morisyen:

(15) Si mo vje dalon torti   pa   ti   donn mwa en buse
     If my old friend turtle NEG   TNS   give me   a   bit
     manze...
     food
     'If my old friend Turtle did not give me a bit to eat...' SESELWA

(16) Rakont u   madam zistwar sa   zako
     tell   2POS   wife   story   that monkey
     'Tell your wife the story of that monkey.' SESELWA

In the case that one of the two objects is a pronoun and the other a full NP, the order is fixed as Pronoun-NP (*li-so papa*):

(17) Mari   don   li   so   papa.
     Mary   give   3SG   3POS   father
     'Mari gave it to her father.' SESELWA

If both objects are pronouns, it is always indirect-direct object order (*mwa-li*):

(18) Don   mwa   li.
     Give   me   it
     'Give it to me.' SESELWA

In the case with both objects being lexical NPs, the order is free. There might be a slight tendency for indirect-direct object order (*Klod-semiz*):

(19) Mo   'n   don   sa   semiz   Klod.
     1SG   ASP   give   this   shirt   Claude
     'I gave this shirt to Claude.' SESELWA

Other verbs (verbs of transaction), such as those classified under 'give', future having, bring and take, carry, throw, transfer of message, are also used with a DOC format. A closer look shows that most verbs of communication have DOC similar to examples (20a) and (20b) with the verb *demande* 'ask':

(20) a. Deman   kas   u   misie
       ask   money   2POS   husband
       'Ask money your husband.' SESELWA
    b. Deman   u   misie   kas
       ask   2POS   husband   money
       'Ask your husband money.' SESELWA

At the same time we note two exceptions with the verbs of communication, *demande avek* 'ask' and *direk* 'say with' in Seselwa. These two verbs also allow PDC, as illustrated by examples (21) and (22) (cf. Bollée 1977):

(21) Mo   ti   deman   avek   Zan   Klod....
     1SG   TNS   ask   with   Jean   Claude
     'I asked Jean Claude.' SESELWA

(22) Mo ti dir avek Gabriel
    ISG TNS say with Gabriel...
    'I said to Gabriel...' SESELWA

Note an important difference between the Seselwa and Morisyen verb lexicon. These two verbs have a different argument structure in Morisyen. They have a DOC format, which I take to be the default format. However, the construction *demande avek/ek* shown in example (23a) is rare but still attested in rural areas in Mauritius. The existence of *demande avek/ek/ar* in Morisyen allows some speculation at this point. It is possible that this form was present in early Morisyen, but is disappearing because of language-internal changes such as the regularisation of the lexicon or/and because of the convergence of French and Morisyen:

(23) a. Mo ti deman ek u talerla si u pu aste
      ISG TNS ask with 2PL before if 2PL MOD buy
      sanala
      this one
      'I asked you before if you wanted to buy this one [fish].' MORISYEN
   b. Mo ti deman Zan Klod....
      ISG TNS ask Jean Claude.
      'I asked Jean Claude...' MORISYEN

Dir avek is used only when it is stressed that something has been said to a particular person (24):

(24) Mo ti dir ek Gabriel, pa avek Zan.
    ISG TNS say with Gabriel, NEG with John
    'I said (it) to Gabriel, not to John.' MORISYEN

Table 3.4 gives us an overview of some high-frequency verbs with a DOC format in both Morisyen and Seselwa.

    Both Seselwa and Morisyen have the two options of DOC and PDC. However, the picture is slightly complicated by the fact that there is only one preposition *pu* to express the benefactive relation, equivalent to English 'for', as seen in example (25c). There is no 'to' equivalent in Morisyen and Seselwa. The DOC is thus used to express the ditransitive alternation seen in English. In this respect,

Table 3.4 *Some ditransitive verb classes and members in Morisyen and Seselwa*

Ditransitive verb classes	Verb members in Morisyen and Seselwa
Give verbs	Done 'give', lue 'rent', prete 'lend', ranburse 'pay back', vande 'sell', peye, 'pay', repeye 'repay'
Future having verbs[1]	Garanti 'guarantee', ofer 'offer', dwa 'owe', promet 'promise', vote 'elect'
Bring and take verbs	Pran 'take', amene 'bring, take'
Send verbs	Avoye 'send', poste 'mail, post'
Verbs of instantaneous causation of ballistic motion	Avoye 'throw', tape 'kick'
Transfer of message verbs	Montre 'show, teach' dir 'say', ekrir 'write', demande 'ask', lir, 'read', site 'cite'
Instrument of communication verbs	Kable 'send a cable', faxe 'fax', signal 'signal', telefone 'phone', emel 'e-mail'

examples (25a) and (25b) show that the double-object frame has two forms here: NP1 V NP3 NP2 that represents the classical DOC and NP1 V NP2 NP3 in both Morisyen and Seselwa:

(25) a. Mari   ti   avoy Zan   Klod   en   koli/parsel.
        Mari   TNS   send Jean   Claude   a   parcel
        'Mari sent Jean Claude a parcel.' MORISYEN/SESELWA
        (NP1 V NP3 NP2)

     b. Mari   ti   avoy en   koli/parsel Zan   Klod.
        Mari   TNS   send   a   parcel   Jean   Claude
        'Mari sent a parcel to Jean Claude.' MORISYEN/SESELWA
        (NP1 V NP2 NP3)

     c. Mari   ti   avoy en   koli/parsel pu   Zan   Klod.
        Mari   TNS   send   a   parcel   for   Jean   Claude
        'Mari sent a parcel for Jean Claude.' MORISYEN/SESELWA
        (NP1 V NP2 *FOR* NP3)

---

[1] In the sense of 'commitments that a person will have something at some later point' (cf. Levin 1993: 46).

In English there is an alternation between the prepositional frame NP1 V NP2 *to* NP3 and the double-object frame NP1 V NP3 NP2. The NP (the object of the preposition *to* in the prepositional frame) becomes the first object in the DOC. The DOC format in both Morisyen and Seselwa is seen as complementary to the structure in (14b). There are several ways to interpret example (14b). One of them is to posit a zero-preposition marking ditransitive, thus making the NP1 V NP2 NP3 pattern a PDC. It could also be interpreted as the result of a rightward scrambling rule (cf. Bruyn *et al.* 1999). A third possibility is that this example is also considered as a DOC. In this chapter, I opt for the third interpretation, namely that it is a DOC. This structure follows the French model NP1 V NP2 PREP NP3 without the preposition *à* 'to'. As with most prepositions, the preposition *à* was lost. Only *pu>pour* 'for' was retained.

Levin (1993) observes two restrictions or constraints on the ditransitive alternation in English. One is called the Latinate restriction because it involves the morphological or phonological shape of the verb undergoing the alternation. It appears that verbs of Latin origin found in the NP1 V NP2 *to* NP3 frame do not have DOC, such as 'ask' and 'forgive'. The second restriction involves the nature of the goal phrase. There is an animacy restriction, as seen in the contrast between the English examples (26a) and (26b):

(26) a. Bill sent a package to Tom/London.
b. Bill sent Tom/*London a package.

However the notion of animacy can be extended. As a result, example (26b) is only possible if London refers to an organisation or corporate body such as the 'London office'. The same holds with the Morisyen and Seselwa data, as seen in examples (27a–c):

(27) a. Bill ti   avoy en koli   Zan/Lond.
Bill TNS send a   parcel Jean/London
'Bill sent a parcel to Jean/London.' MORISYEN/SESELWA

b. Bill ti   avoy Zan/*Lond en koli.
Bill TNS send Jean/London a   parcel
'Bill sent Jean/London a parcel.' MORISYEN/SESELWA

c. Bill   ti   avoy   biro   Lond   en koli.
   Bill   TNS   send   office London a   parcel
   'Bill sent the London office a parcel.' MORISYEN/SESELWA

Example (27c) shows that if the *biro* 'office' is added, the sentence also becomes acceptable.

Let us turn to the group of verbs which take PDC. A closer look at these verbs in both Morisyen and Seselwa shows a large overlap between ditransitive verbs with DOC and PDC patterns. These constructions of the type [*pu* X] are used for the benefactive alternation as already hinted at in the previous paragraph. According to Levin (1993) the benefactive alternation differs from the ditransitive alternation in involving the benefactive preposition *for* rather than the goal preposition *to*. In English the benefactive alternation is found with verbs that can be broadly defined as verbs of obtaining or verbs of creation, such as bake, cook, make, draw, sing, buy, etc. (cf. Levin 1993: 48–49). Some of these verbs in Seselwa have an alternation between the [*pu* X] structure in (28a), (29a) and (30a) and DOC examples (28b), (29b) and (30b):

(28) a.   Zan   ti   aste   en   bul   pu   Mari
          Zan   TNS   buy   a   ball for Mari
          'Zan bought a ball for Mari.' SESELWA

     b.   Zan   ti   aste   Mari   en   bul
          Zan   TNS   buy   Mari   a   ball
          'Zan bought Mari a ball.' SESELWA

(29) a.   Mo   mama   pu   kwi   en   gato   pu   Rachel
          ISG   mum   MOD   cook   a   cake   for   Rachel
          'My mum will bake a cake for Rachel.' SESELWA

     b.   Mo   mama   pu   kwi   Rachel   en   gato
          ISG   mum   MOD   cook   Rachel   a   cake
          'My mum will bake Rachel a cake.' SESELWA

(30) a.   Gabi   pe   desin   en   ziraf   pu   marmai
          Gabi   PROG   draw   a   giraffe   for   kids
          'Gabi is drawing a giraffe for the kids.' SESELWA

     b.   ?Gabi   pe   desin   marmai   en   ziraf
          Gabi   PROG   draw   kids   a   giraffe
          'Gabi is drawing the kids a giraffe.' SESELWA

At this point, we can say that both Morisyen and Seselwa have two types of double-object construction to express the ditransitive alternation seen in English. Further, a PDC accompanied by *avek/ek* 'with' also exists but it seems that it is a marked construction possible with only a few verbs. Verbs have the benefactive alternation with DOC and a fixed [*pu X*] construction. However, this alternation is limited to some verbs. Most verbs of obtaining and creation are allowed with a PDC format with *pu*. These constructions are seen in most of the Creole languages, irrespective of their lexifier languages. PDC and serial verb constructions are both limited in their distribution in Creole languages. DOC, in comparison, is a widespread construction. Examples (31) to (33) illustrate these structures. Examples (31) and (32) are DOCs, example (33) is a PDC:

(31) Mo ti   don mo   mama   en   ba
     1SG TNS give 1POS mother DET kiss
     'I gave my mum a kiss.' MORISYEN

(32) Mo ti   don en   ba   mo   mama.
     1SG TNS give DET kiss 1POS mother
     'I gave a kiss my mum.' MORISYEN

(33) Mo n   demand permisyon ek   minis.
     1SG ASP ask   permission with minister
     'I asked permission to the minister.' MORISYEN

Bruyn *et al.* (1999) propose that example (17) is possibly a zero-preposition marking dative found both in Morisyen and Seselwa. But I analyse sentence (32) as a double-object construction with NP2-NP3 pattern.

A look at other French-based Creoles shows similar patterns of DOC, as in example (34):

(34) Mó   bay mó   mama   un   bó
     1SG   give 1POS mother DET kiss
     'I gave my mother a kiss.' CAYENNE CREOLE[2]

The same holds for St. Lucia French Creole and Louisiana Creole (cf. Bruyn *et al.* 1999). However, according to Neumann (1985),

---

[2] cf. Bruyn *et al.* 1999.

Louisiana Creole shows an interesting alternation which reflects a recent development:

(35) a.
Mo	gẽ	pu	mene	msje	Brusaʳ	ẽ	six-pack
1SG	gave	for	bring	Mr	Broussard	DET	six-pack

'I have to bring Mr Broussard a six-pack.'

   b.
Mo	gẽ	pu	mene	ẽ	six-pack	a	msje	Brusaʳ
1SG	gave	for	bring	DET	six-pack	to	Mr	Broussard

'I have to bring a six-pack to Mr Broussard.' LOUISIANA CREOLE

Both Bollée (1977) and Corne (1977) note that verbs of communication such as *dir* and *demande* have PDC, as already illustrated in example (33). Verbs with PDC are rare and can be regarded as exceptions. We note that the group of verbs with PDC in Morisyen and Seselwa is almost identical. A closer look at the verbs shows that the verb *vande ek/avek/ar* 'sell to/with', as seen in examples (36) to (38) in Morisyen, also displays an exceptional pattern:

(36)
Pyer	ti	pu	van	kamyon	la	ek	so	burzwa
Peter	TNS	MOD	sell	truck	DET	with	3POS	boss

'Peter would have sold the truck to his boss.' MORISYEN

(37)
Pyer	ti	pu	van	so	burzwa	kamyon	la
Peter	TNS	MOD	sell	3POS	boss	truck	DET

'Peter would have sold his boss the truck.' MORISYEN

(38)
Pyer	ti	pu	van	kamyon	la	so	burzwa
Peter	TNS	MOD	sell	truck	DET	3POS	boss

'Peter would have sold the truck to his boss.' MORISYEN

Example (36) illustrates the exceptional construction with the preposition *avek* and its variants. (37) is a DOC example and (38) shows a DOC with the direct-indirect object order. Finally, I note that DOC seems to be a regular kind of construction while PDC is limited to certain types of verbs. A close look at the two DOC patterns in Morisyen and Seselwa shows that the input children get from their environment displays some variation.

PASSIVE CONSTRUCTIONS

Several approaches have been taken to explain passive structures. The lexical approach claims that all properties of passive are derived from the lexical properties of the passive morpheme (hereafter PM) (cf. Baker *et al.* 1989). As a result, there are cross-linguistic variations in the realisation of passive structures. An alternative theory of passive has been proposed by Borer (1996). In her theory, the syntactic properties at the sentential level play a crucial role. Borer proposes that arguments in lexical entries are not specified as external or internal. Instead, the lexical entry for a verb like 'jump' is specified as taking one nominal argument, a verb like 'eat' is specified for two nominal arguments. The ordered arguments of the verbs are licensed in a functional specifier above VP by Case-assignment. The mapping of a verb's arguments onto syntactic positions is reached by arguments being moved to some specifier of a functional projection. Accusative Case is assigned in the SPEC position of a functional phrase immediately dominating VP which is labelled ASP_E. It is optional. Nominative Case is assigned to the specifier position of a phrase co-indexed with Tense (for a thorough analysis see Verrips 1996). Examples (39a) and (b) show an active and a passive sentence in English:

(39) a. John kisses Mary.
      b. Mary is kissed (by John).

Example (39a) is a verbal passive which is regarded as involving a syntactic chain between the subject's and object's surface and underlying positions. Verbal passive participles cannot assign objective case. As such, the internal argument Mary in (39b) cannot receive case in the object position. The internal theta-role and the subcategorised (object) position are preserved in verbal passives. The passive morphology absorbs the external theta-role. Together with the fact that objective case may no longer be assigned in that position, this results in the movement of the internal argument to the external subject position in verbal passives. A trace must thus be left behind after NP movement, which forms a syntactic chain with its antecedent in subject position. This is called A(rgument)-chain. The objective theta-role is assigned to that chain by the participle. This yields the surface representation as seen below in (39c):

(39) c. Mary was kissed [e]$_i$ (by John).

The derivation of verbal passives involves the recovery of movement traces, which is a core component of the computational knowledge of language.

It is common to distinguish three types of passives: verbal, adjectival and get-passives (Levin and Rappaport 1986). Verbal passives have a dynamic reading whereas adjectival passives have a stative reading. A number of properties distinguish verbal passives from adjectival passives. In English, the adjectival passive is formed by a copula combined with an adjective/verb, as in example (40):

(40) The door is closed.

Examples (41) and (42) show the equivalents in Morisyen and Seselwa:

(41) Laport   la   ferme.
      door   DET   close
      'The door is closed.' MORISYEN

(42) Batri   la   plat.
      battery   DET   flat
      'The battery is flat.' SESELWA

The idea here is that in an adjectival passive the copula is combined with an adjective, which predicates over the sentence subject. Note that in contrast to the English example (40), the Creole sentences (41) and (42) do not have a copula. In this respect it is interesting to note that the distinction between verbs and adjectives is not always as clear in Creole languages as one would wish. Adjectival passives must be lexically derived, whereas verbal passives can be syntactically derived (as argued by Borer 1984). In the discussion that follows, I will briefly examine some of these properties distinguishing adjectival from verbal passives. Morisyen and Seselwa will be compared to English.

It has been claimed that verbal passives have an implicit argument. Adjectival passives, in contrast, do not. The distinction between examples (43a) and (43b) below illustrates the argument.

Sentence (43a) describes a state whereas sentence (43b) describes an activity performed by some assumed participant.

(43)   a.   The tyre is repaired.
       b.   The tyre is being repaired.

In both Morisyen and Seselwa we have:

(44)   a.   Laru   la   fin   repare.
             wheel   DET   ASP   repair
             'The wheel is repaired.' MORISYEN/ SESELWA
       b.   Laru   la   ape   repare.
             wheel   DET   PROG repair
             'The wheel is being repaired.' MORISYEN/ SESELWA
       c.   Laru   la   ape   geny   repare.
             wheel   DET   PROG get   repair
             'The wheel is being repaired.' SESELWA

Example (44c) is a Seselwa sentence, marginally accepted in Morisyen. The *geny*-passive is not commonly used in Morisyen.

However, the absence of implicit arguments in the interpretation of adjectival passives is not a clear issue, as it cannot be taken to be an indicator of adjectival passives as argued by Roeper (1988). Take a look at examples (45) and (46):

(45)   The burned book.

(46)   The burnt book.

The minimal contrast between the passive participles (burned/ burnt) illustrates Roeper's point. The passive participle appears in a typically adjectival position. Yet it can be interpreted with implicit argument (as in (45)) or without implicit argument (as in (46)). Another observation concerns the *by*-phrases. Typically, *by*-phrases accompany verbal passives (cf. Levin and Rappaport 1986, Zubizaretta 1987). Roeper (1987a) also points out that the presence of *by*-phrases with verbal passives cannot be taken to be a core property which distinguishes between verbal and adjectival passives. Example (47) illustrates a stative passive with a copula, accompanied by a *by*-phrase.

(47)   The code remained unbroken by the Russians.

It is worth noting that in some languages such as Dutch, the grammaticality of *by*-phrases does not distinguish between the verbal and adjectival passive (Verrips 1996). The preposition *door* 'by' in Dutch is used in a wider range of contexts than the English 'by'. In addition to this, the occurrence of a *by*-phrase in Dutch is not sufficient or necessary for a verbal interpretation of a passive participle. The Dutch *by*-phrase can introduce causation with stative adjectives, as seen in example (48):

(48)   De   auto   is/wordt   helemaal   schoon   door   de   regen.
       the   car   is/becomes   completely   clean   by   the   rain
       'The car is/becomes completely clean through the rain.' DUTCH

The same is true for both Morisyen and Seselwa, as seen in example (49):

(49)   Loto   la   fin   vin   kompletman   prop   ek/par/ar   lapli.
       car   DET   ASP   become   completely   clean   with   rain
       'The car became clean with rain.' MORISYEN/ SESELWA

Note, however, that this sentence, though not common in everyday use, is considered to be grammatically correct by native speakers of both Morisyen and Seselwa. In Morisyen *avek/ek* or *par/ar* introduce the *by/with*-phrase. In Seselwa this is possible only with *avek/ek* and *par*.

In the verbal passive in Morisyen and Seselwa there is an implicit argument. In the discussion about implicit arguments, alternating causative verbs play an important role because they can be transitive and unaccusative. The unaccusative use of these verbs denotes a change of state and the transitive use denotes the causation of that change of state with the external argument functioning as causer. The transitive in (50a) is called the causative verb, the unaccusative in (50b) is called an anti-causative:

(50)   a.   Zan   ape   kas   ver   la.
            John   PROG   break   glass   DET
            'John is breaking the glass.' MORISYEN/SESELWA

b. Ver   la   ape   kase.
Glass DET PROG break
'The glass is breaking.' MORISYEN/SESELWA

The difference between the passive 'break' and the anti-causative 'break' is that in the passive sentence (50a) an agent is involved in causing the change of state. This means that passive sentences have an implicit (external) argument. In the anti-causative sentence (50b), there is no implication of this sort, which means that there is no implicit external argument:

(51) a. Ver   la   fin   kase.
Glass DET ASP break
'The glass is broken.' MORISYEN/SESELWA

b. Ver   la   ti/pe   kase.
Glass DET TNS/PROG break
'The glass broke/is breaking.' MORISYEN/SESELWA

Note that *fin* and *ti* could possibly contribute to differentiating between passive and anti-causative as in (51a) and (51b). This is based on the intuition of some of my Morisyen-speaking informants who accepted (51a) with an *avek/par*-phrase 'by-phrase' and not (51b). The Seselwa informants did not make any difference between *ti* and *fin* in these contexts, as in examples (52a) and (52b):

(52) a. Ver   la   fin   kase.
glass DET ASP break
'The glass is broken.' SESELWA

b. Ver   la   ti   kase.
glass DET TNS break
'The glass broke.' SESELWA

However, this issue remains speculative at this point as we need more data.

Passives of intransitive verbs are normally called impersonal passives. In the linguistic literature they are characterised by their dynamic reading. Adjectival impersonal passives do not exist. German has a set of verbs allowing for impersonal passives as seen in the following example:

(53) Es wird im Garten getanzt.
     it become in+DAT garden danced
     'There is dancing in the garden.' GERMAN

Two types of intransitive verbs are distinguished here: unergatives and unaccusatives. Unergative verbs denote activities with no implied endpoint (as such they are atelic verbs). 'Laugh', 'dance' and 'walk' are typically regarded as unergative verbs because there is control implied by their participants. Unaccusative verbs such as 'die', 'sink' and 'fall' characterise a change of location or state and imply an endpoint. As such they are regarded as telic verbs. Moreover, they are not controlled by their participants (cf. Perlmutter 1978, Burzio 1986). Intransitive verbs in Morisyen and Seselwa cannot undergo passivisation, as seen in examples (54) and (55b):

(54) * Dan lakur ape danse.
      in garden PROG dance
      'There is dancing going on in the garden.' MORISYEN/SESELWA

(55) a. Zot pe riy Zan Klod.
       they PROG laugh Jean Claude
       'They are laughing at Jean Claude.' MORISYEN/SESELWA

     b. Zan Klod ape rye.
       Jean Claude PROG laugh
       'Jean Claude is laughing.' MORISYEN/SESELWA

Example (55b) means that *Zan Klod* is laughing and not is laughed at. This sentence is interpreted as an active sentence rather than a passive in both Creoles. For a passive interpretation Morisyen, similar to Seselwa, can use the *geny/ganny*-passive[3] as in (55c):

     c. Zan Klod ape ganny riye.
       Jean Claude PROG get laugh
       'Jean Claude is being laughed at.' SESELWA

However, the *geny*-passive in Morisyen is marginally accepted.[4]

---

[3] *Geny* is used in Morisyen. *Ganny* is used in Seselwa.

[4] The pressure of standardisation on Morisyen will probably lead to the establishment of *ganny*-passive, and a similar development has been seen in Seselwa (cf. Kriegel 1996).

Other intransitive verbs such as *ule* 'want', *kone* 'know', *vwar* 'see' cannot be passivised easily, as seen in examples (56) to (58):

(56) * Pyer ti   ule
      Peter TNS   want
      'Peter was wanted ...' MORISYEN/SESELWA

(57) * Sa   zistwar ti   kone.
      this story   TNS   know
      'The story was known.' MORISYEN/SESELWA

(58) * Sa   misie fin   vwar.
      this man   ASP   see
      'The man was seen.' MORISYEN/SESELWA

As already pointed out by Verrips (1996), there is an interesting interaction between aspect and passivisation in general, which is also noticed here. Some intransitive verbs can, however, undergo passivisation, as seen in the Seselwa sentence (59):

(59) Sa   bato   ape   gany kule.
     The   boat   PROG   get   sink
     'The boat is being sunk.' SESELWA

This example shows us that some intransitive verbs in Seselwa and not in Morisyen can be passivised if the *geny*-passive is used and combined with the durative aspect marker accompanying it. This observation also applies to other Creoles (cf. for example, Veenstra 2001 for Saramaccan).

At this point I will also present some facts on the *geny*-passive in Morisyen and Seselwa. The *geny*-passive is similar to the English get-passive. Examples (60a) and (60b) illustrate the point:

(60) a. Mari in   bat   Pyer.
        Mari ASP   flog   Pyer
        'Marie flogged Pyer.' MORISYEN/SESELWA
     b. Pyer in   geny   bate   ar/ek Mari.
        Pyer ASP   get   flog   with   Mari
        'Pyer got flogged by Mari.' MORISYEN/SESELWA

A difference between Morisyen and Seselwa is that the *geny*-passive in Morisyen seems to follow an animacy constraint [+animate arguments]. According to Syea (1985) *geny* is used in constructions with verbs subcategorising for animate object NPs and animate subject NPs only. But this is not always the case, as example (61) shows:

(61) Mo   lisyen in   geny   tape   ek   loto
      my   dog   ASP   get   hit   with   car
      'My dog has been hit by a car.' MORISYEN

Although one could argue that it is the car driver who is implied, the fact remains that an instrumental PP [inanimate] is used. Example (62) shows that the animacy constraint does not hold:

(62) Ban   pye   banan   in   geny   bate   ek   syklon.
      PLU   tree banana   ASP   get   flog   with   cyclone
      'The banana trees got hit by the cyclone.' MORISYEN

Up to now *geny*-passive in Morisyen is still used in restricted circumstances. In Seselwa, however, there does not seem to be any constraint, as witnessed in example (63):

(63) En kongre ekstraordiner pou kapab ganny organize par komite santral.
      'An extraordinary congress will get organised by the central committee.'[5]

With respect to the development of the *ganny*-passive in Seselwa, Kriegel (1996) argues that this form became conventional due to the fact that Seselwa became an official language and the need for grammatical apparatus became urgent. In this respect I would like to note that the influence of the English get–passive on Seselwa is probably a contributing factor. As mentioned before, the passive in Creole languages is typically not marked by overt morphology (see Corne 1970, Veronique 1984, Syea 1985, Bruyn and Veenstra 1993, Kriegel 1996), as can be seen in the following sentences:

(64) a. Mari   fin   kup   pye   la.
          Mari   ASP   cut   tree   DET
          'Marie has cut the tree.' MORISYEN

      b. Pye   la   fin   kupe.[6]
          tree   DET   ASP   cut
          'The tree has been cut.' MORISYEN

---

[5] This example is taken from Kriegel (1996: 118). In the literature there are different orthographies for *geny*.

[6] The long form of the verb *kupe* 'cut' is not necessarily related to passive. It seems to be a phonological phenomenon.

(65) a. Mari fin kas so lamen.
       Mari ASP break 3POS hand
       'Marie has broken her hand.' MORISYEN

   b. So lamen fin kase (ek laport).
       her hand ASP break (by/with door)
       'Her hand has been broken (by the door).' MORISYEN

The word order and the implicit argument in (64b) suggest that it is a passive sentence. Sentence (65a) and the passive in (65b) also show that these two forms are not morphologically marked.

At this point the main properties of the verbal passive in Morisyen and Seselwa will be summarised as far as their distribution and their semantic and syntactic properties are concerned:

1. The internal argument of the verb appears in the subject position.
2. The external argument can be unexpressed.
3. Passives can be formed with transitive verbs only, unless the *ganny*-passive is used.
4. Verbal passives have a dynamic reading.
5. The implicit argument is optionally expressed in a *by*-phrase.
6. The implicit argument is not coreferent with the internal argument in the subject position.
7. The passive is formed without morphology.

Interestingly, the lack of morphology, the absence of *by*-phrases and the preference for passives with highly transitive action verbs found in these two Creoles, as well as in numerous other Creoles (cf. Veenstra 2001), seem also to be typical properties of children's passive. Given this close similarity between Creoles and child language, we would thus expect the acquisition of the Creole passive to be relatively easy.

SERIAL VERB CONSTRUCTIONS

A serial verb construction (SVC) is a chain of verbs which functions as a single predicate without coordination, subordination, or syntactic dependency. Although serial verb constructions are attested in languages of various typological profiles, such as the languages of West Africa, Southeast Asia, Amazonia and Oceania, and Creole languages, they seem to be a common feature of isolating languages (Dixon 2006).

In Creole studies, SVCs have been taken as evidence 'par excellence' for the transfer hypothesis, as is the case in Caribbean Creoles. SVCs in these Creoles are attributed to the transfer of substrate influences from West African languages (Alleyne 1980, Boretzky 1983, Holm 1988, McWhorter 1997). Other scholars have challenged this view and argued that the resemblance between the Creole and West African SVCs is accidental (see e.g. Byrne 1987, Bickerton 1988). These constructions in Creoles emerged to compensate for the structures missing in the rudimentary syntax of the earliest stages of Creole development.

Aikhenvald (2006) proposes a series of properties pervasive to SVCs that are briefly described here. For a more detailed discussion see Aikhenvald and Dixon (2006):

- SVC as a single predicate. This means that the verb sequence acts as one single predicate.
- Monoclausal constructions. This implies that they do not allow markers of syntactic dependency.
- Prosodic properties of SVCs are the same as those of a monoverbal clause. There is no intonation break or pause between the components of a SVC.
- Tense, aspect, modality and polarity values are shared. This implies that there cannot be independent choice in any of these categories in a SVC.
- SVC as 'one event'. The sequence of verbs has to match a 'recognizable event-type' (Durie 1997: 322), which is based on cultural parameters.
- Argument sharing. At least one argument is shared. Both core and peripheral arguments belong to the construction. In this respect, SVCs have one argument structure.

Turning to Creole languages, Muysken and Veenstra (1995) proposed to classify Creole languages into three groups with respect to their types of SVCs. One group of Creole languages such as Jamaican Creole, Gullah, Haitian Creole, Kriol and Negerhollands Creole has a wide range of SVCs. A second group of Creole languages consists of languages with a limited range of SVCs. These include languages such as Papiamentu, Tok Pisin, Hawaiian Creole, Seychelles and Mauritian Creole. Finally, a third group of Creole languages including Reunion Creole[7] and Senegal Creole, have no SVCs at all.

Muysken and Veenstra (1995), discussing Creole languages, established two types of language; one with clausal serial verb constructions and the other with phrasal serial verb constructions. The clausal type seems to show more independence between the various sub-events represented by the separate verbs and a free lexical selection. The phrasal type exhibits less independence and a limited set of verbs. Languages with clausal serial verb constructions include Saramaccan and Berbice Dutch. Languages with phrasal serial verb constructions include Haitian, Papiamentu, as well as Saramaccan and Berbice Dutch. Muysken and Veenstra add three observations to this division. First, languages with phrasal serial verb constructions are a subset of the group of languages with clausal serial verb constructions. Thus, Saramaccan-type languages represent the superset (with both phrasal and clausal) types. Haitian-type languages constitute the subset with only a phrasal type of serial verb construction.

Up to now the set of serialising languages with only the clausal type is not found in the literature. Both the terms clausal and phrasal are used here for descriptive purposes only. The two factors distinguishing the different types of SVCs noted above lead to four logically possible types of SVC, as can be seen below:

Type 1 (phrasal)   Less independence between sub-events + lexically restricted

Type 2   More independence between sub-events + lexically restricted

Type 3   Less independence between sub-events + lexically free

Type 4   (clausal) More independence between sub-events + lexically free

(adapted from Veenstra 1996: 92)

---

[7] Reunion Creole is probably still decreolising given the heavy French influence.

Veenstra (1996) defines the notion of 'lexically restricted' as one in which one verb is taken from a certain semantic or aspectual class and occurs in a 'fixed' position. Lexically free refers in contrast to constructions in which verbs do not show such a restriction. The 'more or less independent sub-events' refer to the event composition of the construction. 'Less independent sub-events' involve combinations of modality or state predicates and event predicates and combinations of two state predicates. More independent sub-events involve combinations of event predicates only.

Type 1 (phrasal) consists of four major groups of SVCs: directional, argument-introducing, aspectual and degree-marking ones. Type 2 consists of causative as well as argument-introducing ones such as 'take' verbs. Type 3 consists of resultative serial verbs. Type 4 (clausal) consists of multiple verb constructions.

Directional serials

Verbs *ale/vini* 'come/go' (Type 1) are used in non-initial position to mark direction away or towards a point of reference. They are used with other verbs of movement and can be accompanied by a locative PP as in examples (66) to (72):

(66) Li   galupe <u>ale</u>.
      s/he   run   go
      'He ran away.' MORISYEN

(67) Bann pirog   in   sove n'   <u>ale.</u>
      PL   dinghy ASP   flee ASP go
      'The dinghies took off.' SESELWA
      (Bickerton 1989: 13)

(68) I'   'n   taye   n   <u>ale</u>.
      s/he ASP   run   ASP go
      'He ran away.' SESELWA
      (Michaelis 1994)

(69) Zot   pe   marse <u>vin</u>   kot mwan
      they PROG   walk   come   to   my place
      'They are walking to my place.' SESELWA

(70) Nu   marse   <u>vire</u>   dan   lakur.
     we   walk   go round   in   garden
     'We walk around in the garden.' MORISYEN

(71) Ti   garson   la   in   tonbe   <u>al</u>   dan   turbiyon.
     little boy   DET   ASP   fall   go   LOC   whirlpool
     'The little boy fell into the whirlpool.' MORISYEN

(72) Ena   en   simen   sorti   kot   leglis   <u>al</u>   lor   larutroyal.
     EXIST   a   road   come out   LOC   church   go   LOC   main road
     'There is a road which comes out next to the church and arrives on
     the main road.' MORISYEN

Argument-introducing serials

The verb *don* 'give' (Type 1) can introduce Goal/Recipient (GOAL),
Benefactive (BEN), Experiencer (EXP) and Source (SOURCE) arguments. It appears in a non-initial position and can be combined with
any other verb, as seen from examples (73a) and (73b):

(73) a. Zan   in   <u>tir</u>   kas   dan   labank   in   <u>don</u>   li.
         John   ASP   take   money   in   bank   ASP   give   her/him
         'John withdrew money from the bank for her.' MORISYEN/SESELWA
     b. Zan   in   <u>kas</u>   tu   koko   in   <u>done</u>.
         John   ASP   break   all   coconut   ASP   give
         'John distributed/gave away all the coconuts.'
         MORISYEN/SESELWA

This serial with *dir* exists only in Seselwa and not in Morisyen. The
expression *purdir* (Type 1) follows the verb *dir* to say. *Purdir* functions very much like the subordinator 'that' as seen in the example
below. *Purdir* can be combined with the verb *dir* 'say'. It seems to
be an idiomatic construction and is not productive. It is rare in the
speech of young Seselwa today as compared to the speech of the older
generation (74):

(74) Si   mo   deza   dir   u   <u>pur dir</u>   mo   kontan   Mimi...
     if   I   already   tell   you   that   I   love   Mimi
     'If I have already told you that I love Mimi...' SESELWA
     (Baker and Corne 1982: 119)

Aspectual serials

The verb *fini* 'finish' (Type 1) is the one used in the second part of the construction to express the meaning of an end to something. Such constructions are rare both in Morisyen and Seselwa. When presented with sentence (75), not every informant accepted it:

(75) Zan in kup latet so madam in <u>fini</u> ar li.
     John ASP cut head his wife ASP finish with 3SG
     'John was done with her (by cutting her head).' MORISYEN

Serials of degree

These serials (Type 1), as seen in Saramaccan (examples (76) and (77)) do not seem to have equivalents in Morisyen and Seselwa.

(76) A   bebé daán pása/moó mi.
     3SG drink rum pass/more 1SG
     'He drinks more rum than me.' SARAMACCAN

(77) A   fátu pása/moó mi.
     3SG fat pass/more 1SG
     'She is fatter than me.' SARAMACCAN

Causative serials

The verb *fer* 'make' (Type 2) is seen in causative serials in both Morisyen and Seselwa:

(78) So destin   fin fer li vin   violent
     His destiny ASP make him become violent
     'His destiny has turned him into a violent person.'

Argument-introducing serials ('take' in first position)

Verbs in this serial (Type 2) are in a fixed position. The verb *pran* 'take' is used in the first position and some other verbs can be used in non-initial positions. Two examples, (79) and (80a), one from Saramaccan[8] and the other from Morisyen/Seselwa illustrate the point:

[8] Veenstra (1996).

(79) A <u>téi</u> fáka kóti di beée.
 3SG take knife cut DET bread
 'He took the knife and cut the bread.' SARAMACCAN

(80) a. Li ti <u>pran</u> kuto met dan bwat.
  3SG TNS take knife put in box
  'He put the knife into the box.' MORISYEN/SESELWA

Nowadays in Morisyen we have the following construction which is common and mostly accepted:

 b. Li ti <u>pran</u> kuto pu met dan bwat.
  3SG TNS take knife to put in box
  'He put the knife in the box.' MORISYEN

To get 'he cut the bread with a knife' we would have sentence (81):

(81) Li ti kup dipen ar/ek kuto.
 3SG TNS cut bread with knife
 'He cut the bread with a knife.' MORISYEN/SESELWA

Resultative serials

Resultative serial verb constructions (Type 3) are also seen in both Morisyen and Seselwa. The position of the result-denoting verb is more or less fixed (in a non-initial position). The list of verbs used here is unrestricted. However, there is a restriction on the second verb in that it has to be transitive, as seen in sentences (82) to (84).

(82) Zot fin bat li <u>tuye</u>.
 3PL ASP beat him kill
 'They beat him dead.' MORISYEN

(83) Li fin ris lakord la <u>kase</u>.
 3SG ASP pull rope DET break
 'He broke the rope off.' MORISYEN

(84) Zan fin kup pye la <u>zete</u>.
 John ASP cut tree DET throw
 'John felled the tree.' MORISYEN

Multiple verb constructions

There are no restrictions here on the number or order of verbs (Type 4) as long as the construction is semantically or pragmatically sound. These constructions typically involve three verbs. Corne (1977) did not have any examples of such constructions in his corpora. However, these constructions are witnessed in both Morisyen and Seselwa, as seen in examples (85a) and (85b):[9]

(85) a. Zan in kup ziromo met dan panyer amen lakaz
Zan ASP cut pumpkin put in basket bring home
fer
make
'ladob' ar/avek li.
sauce with 3SG
'John cut the pumpkin, put it in the basket, brought it home to do "ladob" with it.' MORISYEN

b. Zan in kup ziromo met dan pannier amen lakaz fer
'ladob' avek.
'John cut the pumpkin, put it in the basket, brought it home to do 'ladob' with it. SESELWA

Bickerton (1989: 170) gives the following example from Seselwa. Sentence (86) comes from Theophile Rosalie:

(86) Dan lasme pirog i ale i al serse i amene
In week boat 3SG go 3SG go get 3SG bring
'During the week, the fishing boat went and fetched [provisions].'
SESELWA

In a folktale *Napa met ki pa war son met* ('there is no boss without a boss' approximate translation) (Bollée 1977: 108)[10], one finds the following example:

(87) I pran sa ban depuy i met anba son
3SG take the PL feather TNS put under his

---

[9] The crucial difference between Morisyen and Seselwa here is that Seselwa has preposition-stranding.

[10] Note that Bollée considers the second 'i' in the sentence to be a tense marker. There is disagreement about the status of 'i' in Seselwa. One group of researchers regard it as a tense marker. Others see in it a short form for 'li'.

blenket   pu li   -mem.
blanket   for 3SG -REFL.
'He hid the feathers under his own blanket.' SESELWA

In a survey of both Morisyen and Seselwa, I observed that SVCs are used in both languages – however, one will encounter more easily SVCs in rural Creole (coastal variety) in Mauritius. Educated Morisyen speakers (mostly belonging to the middle class) are reluctant to accept these sentences or sometimes categorically reject them. In Seselwa, SVCs seem to be common and are found in the speech of both urban and rural speakers. On the basis of my data I could not make a distinction between urban and rural forms of Seselwa.

So far, I have distinguished the following types of SVCs in Morisyen and Seselwa: directional, ('give', 'take', 'say'), resultative and three serial verb constructions. 'Say' serials exist only in Seselwa.

Another point worth mentioning here is the coexistence of prepositional structures with serial structures (cf. Muysken 1988). Byrne (1987) and Bickerton (1989) see SVCs in Saramaccan as a compensating strategy for the paucity of prepositions. This one-to-one relationship does not seem to be relevant here in Morisyen and Seselwa. Both languages have SVCs as well as prepositional structures with *pu* 'for/to'.

Examples (88) to (91) illustrate three types of SVCs in Seselwa. Chapter 8 gives an overview of the whole range of SVCs in both Morisyen and Seselwa:

(88) Ban rebel fin   pran ban zarm in   <u>tay</u> dan lapay
      PL   rebel ASP take PL   arm   ASP run in remote place
      'The rebels took off with the arms.' SESELWA

(89) Nu ti   pe   <u>marse</u> *vin* kot u   letan...
      1PL TNS PROG walk   come LOC 2SG as...
      'We were walking to your place when ....' SESELWA

(90) Marmai in   <u>pran</u> ti   krapo <u>kasiet</u> dan sak
      kid   ASP take little frog hide   in   bag
      'The child hid the little frog away in the bag'. SESELWA

(91)   Zot   in   <u>bate</u>   <u>pil</u>   li   amor   dan   prison
        they   ASP   beat   beat   3SG   death   in   prison
        'They have beaten him to death in prison.' MORISYEN

Interestingly, SVCs are not used productively in either Morisyen or Seselwa. From the examples discussed above, it seems that only certain verbs can be combined with others in SVCs. This is extremely important to remember because it means that the input children get is restricted.

CONCLUDING REMARKS

To summarise, in this chapter I have outlined some complex aspects of both Morisyen and Seselwa syntax, including pronouns and reflexives, passive, double-object, and serial verb constructions. Although the focus of the study is on Seselwa grammar, I included Morisyen adult data to give the reader a comparative perspective on these two languages, which will be extremely useful when interpreting the acquisition data.

When asked to give judgments on the acceptability of structures, adults gave a straightforward answer most of the time. When presented with variable structures as in serial verb constructions (i.e. novel combination of verbs), or passivised constructions, Seselwa adults showed some degree of insecurity by giving inconclusive judgments, hesitation, or restricted approval such as: 'Yes, you can say it like this, but I would not use it this way.' This insecurity can be partly explained by the fact that these adults are not literate in their L1. In terms of E-language this means that there is no conventional language model. Thus, there are no conventional rules. If there are some exceptions, they are not reinforced. The outcome is that the linguistic system is highly variable. In other words, the fairly high level of variability in language can be partly accounted for by the lack of a conventional language model (see also Adone 2006).

4   Child Creole data

INTRODUCTION

Studies on child language are old. Even Darwin (1877) took notes on his son's early speech. However, most of the earliest work on child language acquisition consisted of longitudinal diary studies, developed by parents who documented the development of their children's grammar and lexicon (e.g. Stern and Stern 1907, Gregoire 1937, 1947). Since then, both the scope and methods used in the field of first language acquisition research have seen enormous expansion. With the emergence of new technology (such as video recording, digital recording, computed tomography (CT) and positron emission topography (PET) scans among others) significant progress has been made in both the quantitative and qualitative nature of material collected as well as the types of research issues to be addressed.

A primary goal of language acquisition research has been to assess the notion of grammatical competence as formulated by Chomsky (1986). It is often more difficult to assess young children's knowledge of language than adults'. However, methodology, which is crucial for the testing of hypotheses, has not been given the attention it deserves. In the field of linguistics, for instance, it has been a tradition to adduce data to test hypotheses, but the methods of data collection were not really considered to be important. In the field of experimental psychology, on the other hand, for a phenomenon to be psychologically real, it has to occur more than once, and individual differences are typically classified as 'noise', a term used to define variability. As we can see the philosophies underlying these two fields are very different. However, the field of child language acquisition has successfully combined these two approaches. This has led to the creation and implementation of various methods that can be regarded as more sophisticated and complex, as well as more appropriate to assess young children's early grammatical abilities.

TYPES OF DATA

Three types of data are normally collected and relied on for the testing of theories in first language acquisition studies: production, comprehension and judgment data. Production data is the oldest type of data used in studying language acquisition. Under production data we normally understand two types of data: either spontaneous speech production (cross-sectional or longitudinal) or elicited data. The latter can take the form of elicited imitation or elicited production (see Demuth 1996 and Stromswold 1996, among many others, for a detailed discussion on the advantages and disadvantages of spontaneous production data). It is widely agreed that when collected carefully, spontaneous production data provides a very rich basis for the investigation of children's grammatical competence and especially for evaluating hypotheses concerning the acquisition of syntax.

Comprehension data, according to some scholars, gives the researcher a more accurate picture of the child's grammar (see Hirsch-Pasek and Golinkoff 1996, among others) and is thus preferred over spontaneous production. I agree with this view to the extent that comprehension assessment, for instance, allows the researcher to investigate (probe for) structures that are not yet produced. However, comprehension data alone is not automatically always sufficient.

Judgment data, on the other hand, has only recently been used to investigate children's grammars. One reason for this is closely linked to the belief that children are not able to give grammaticality judgments. This view was supported by work done on the development of metalinguistic skills. The hypothesis was that before entering the operational stage of cognitive development, children cannot make distinctions between forms and content, which is a necessary condition for reliable well-formed judgments (see Hakes 1980 and

Van Kleeck 1982). In psychology, the operational stage of cognitive development is defined as one in which children have acquired the ability to decentre, and therefore, to conserve. In this respect, it is interesting to note that de Villiers and de Villiers (1974) as well as Schlisselberg (1988) called this belief into question with their results.

In spite of the abundance of research methods to study human cognition, only some of the methods can be used in research on first language acquisition. The limitation on the choice of experimental paradigms is related to two factors, one being the nature of the research questions, and the other being the population chosen. This study is empirical in nature and thus relies heavily on data from first language acquisition research. Therefore, in the next section some of the issues closely relating to the collection of child data in general are addressed and in the final section the rationale for the methods chosen to collect child Creole data is presented.

METHODOLOGICAL ISSUES

Research design

Depending on the research objective, researchers have to make a choice with respect to the kind of studies they are conducting. Are the performance differences between age groups expected to reflect developmental changes, or are the performance differences focused on several individuals? The first goal can be achieved by adopting a between-subjects design that is also known as a cross-sectional design. The second one can be achieved by choosing the within-subjects design, which is also known as longitudinal design. A cross-sectional design is used to compare the performance of different children from various age groups observed at one point in time. A longitudinal design compares the performance of the same children at several points in time (cf. Hsu and Hsu 1996).

The between-subjects design was chosen as the research design for my previous (1994a, 1997) and current work investigating the acquisition of Morisyen, Kriol and Seselwa. Given the time and financial constraints of such research programmes, it was not possible to conduct a longitudinal study.

Taken together, the results of the previous work provide us with a snapshot of the different possible stages Creole-speaking children go through before reaching the adult Creole grammar. The results gathered in my previous study (Adone 1994a) have also provided a solid basis for further experimental studies and hypothesis testing. I reanalysed the results obtained in the cross-sectional data to make some developmental claims, following the technique of implicational scaling as used by Meisel, Clahsen and Pienemann (1981) and used successfully for L2 as well as L1 acquisition (see Hatch and Farhady 1982, Vainikka and Scholten 1994).

The population

The children were all native speakers of Seselwa, on the island of Mahé, in the Seychelles. Most of the children selected came from the St Joseph Preschool, one of the biggest day-care centres in town. Only a few children came from the La Retraite day-care centre. In the experiments the number of children varied between 70 and 84 for reasons relating to health, weather, family, culture or religion. Both boys and girls were included. In the experiments the children were classified into six developmental age groups of six-month periods. The first group included children between 3;0 and 3;5 and the final group included children between 5;6 and 5;11. Parallel to this, I also gathered half-hour recordings of spontaneous speech from nine children between 2;0 and 3;0 which contribute to complete the developmental picture.

Another issue concerning subjects is the inclusion of an adult control group in every experiment. There are two purposes for including adults. One is to test the reliability of the task in reflecting grammatical knowledge. Generally, if the adults do not accept certain sentences, it is probably because the sentences or contexts are not well designed or ambiguous in meaning. In that case, refinement work has to be performed before starting with children. The second reason is that an adult control group allows us to verify the judgments of the community which represents the target grammar for the child. However, this can become a confusing enterprise when dealing with a Creole community in which the Creole is not yet established as a written language, as is the case with Morisyen. I used the same protocol with both the adult and children groups. Further, the adult group consisted of six people. The breakdown of age groups of Seselwa children is shown in Tables 4.1 to 4.6. Spontaneous speech was gathered from the nine children aged 2;0 to 3;0 as shown in Table 4.7. Table 4.8 shows the control adult group aged from 25 to 45 years.

Training and practice sessions

Pre-experimental training, it has been recognised, is a necessary condition for the success of experiments. As with most procedures, it is best to give the subjects some kind of introduction and training before the actual experiment takes place. Given the methods chosen, the training session played an important role. It allowed me to establish language as the topic of interest. Young subjects, most of the time, do not have any experience of conversations on language. Although there are many ways to establish language as a topic, the discussion of using different languages proved to be a very good tool to start with.

Following the practice session, it was very useful to give a pretest to screen out the subjects who did not understand the task. The sentence types used in the practice session were used again as pretest items, but the lexical items were changed. In this regard, it is also recommended to run a vocabulary pretest, to minimise the number of so-called nuisance variables, also known as 'noise', associated with the vocabulary used in the experimental sentences. One typical case is semantic bias. The vocabulary items used in the sentences may steer towards response biases associated with semantic features such as gender and role. Children would, for instance, accept only fathers fishing or washing cars (see Kearney and McElwain 1976

Table 4.1 *Age group 3;0–3;5*

Name	Years	Months
Stephanie	3	0
Tarah	3	0
Kathryn	3	0
Lyn	3	2
Djamila	3	2
Rye	3	3
Nelly	3	4
Aaron	3	4
Natasha	3	4
Anissa	3	5
Leeroy	3	5
Duane	3	5
Mean age	**3**	**3**

Table 4.2 *Age group 3;6–3;11*

Name	Years	Months
Jean Yves	3	6
Jeven	3	6
Jean Luc	3	7
Wilnette	3	7
Anthony	3	8
Laurent	3	8
Aaron	3	8
Larah	3	9
Nissa	3	9
Terryna	3	10
Stephanie	3	10
Angie	3	11
Liam	3	11
Rajan	3	11
Mitch	3	11
Marcus	3	11
Mean age	**3**	**9**

Table 4.3 *Age group 4;0–4;5*

Name	Years	Months
Cytra	4	0
Nafouna	4	0
Emma	4	1
Shemila	4	1
Shafira	4	1
Keisha	4	1
Nightarra	4	1
Yuhan	4	2
Graham	4	2
Fabio	4	2
Edrick	4	2
Aysha	4	2
Anisa	4	2
Shauna	4	3
Farook	4	4
Sheryl	4	4
Tania	4	4
Elmo	4	4
Brandon	4	4
Raphael	4	5
Eilish	4	5
Shanna	4	5
Mean age	**4**	**3**

Table 4.4 *Age group 4;6–4;11*

Name	Years	Months
Aneesa	4	6
Alexander	4	6
Benjamin	4	7
Archille	4	7
Vicky	4	7
Paule	4	7
Marcus	4	8
Christian	4	8
Queeny	4	8

Name	Years	Months
Anielle	4	9
Sherman	4	10
Tim	4	10
Mean age	**4**	**8**

Table 4.5 *Age group 5;0–5;5*

Name	Years	Months
Oneill	5	0
Marius	5	1
Annie	5	1
Darren	5	2
Chloe	5	2
Farah	5	3
Farlayne	5	3
Elaine	5	4
Andrew	5	4
Kenny	5	4
Shawn	5	5
Mean age	**5**	**3**

Table 4.6 *Age group 5;6–5;11*

Name	Years	Months
Warren	5	6
Leffa	5	6
Sophie	5	6
Laurent	5	6
Abigail	5	7
Anthony	5	7
Kevin	5	7
Shannon	5	8
Denis	5	8
Cindy	5	9
Michel	5	9
Mean age	**5**	**7**

Table 4.7 *Nine children between 2;0 and 3;0*

Name	Years	Months
Stefan	2	4
Eloise	2	4
Andre	2	5
Benjamin	2	6
Stefanie	2	9
Ruben	2	9
Julio	2	9
Brigitte	2	11
Emma	2	11
Mean age	2	7

Table 4.8 *Six adults*

Name	Age range
Tracy (F)	20s
Daniella (F)	30s
Pierre (M)	40s
Zan Klod (M)	40s
Mary-Ann (F)	40s
Gabriel (M)	40s

for a discussion on cultural differences[1]). Further, there were two other variables worth checking in the training session, namely the familiarity of vocabulary items and their phonological characteristics. While adult Seselwa has *mesanste/malis* 'mischief/wickedness' *galupe/taye* 'run' and *satuye/tiktike* 'tickle', Seselwa-speaking children are more familiar with *malis, taye* and *tiktike*. During the training session, the subjects' incorrect responses were corrected and the training material was repeated as many times as required.

---

[1] For cultural differences in child-rearing practices, see O'Toole (1990), Vincent *et al.* (1990), Pomerleau *et al.* (1991) and Roggoff *et al.* (1991). Essack (personal communication) gave me an overview on Seselwa child-rearing practices.

Thus, pre-experimental training proved necessary to ensure that children understood the procedures as well as to help the researcher overcome the tension between rigorous experimental structures and the reality of working with children.

Materials

Special care was taken with respect to the number and complexity of the experimental sentences. Although in terms of reliability it helps to include a high number of tokens of each construction type, fatigue and limited attention spans do constrain the length of the testing session. As a result of this important limitation, I worked with twenty sentences as the upper limit. The test sentences in each battery were randomised and the inclusion of fillers/distractors helped in controlling fatigue or attention effects. In the next section a detailed picture of the material sentences will be presented. A complete list of the experimental materials and the order of presentation is given in Appendices (A to D). No correction of incorrect responses was allowed in the test session; positive reinforcement was used (e.g. *byen bon, u'n byen fer/u byen kone!* equivalent to 'Well done, you've done a good job, very good!').

Rationale for the research methods

In order to cover the three data types used here, production, comprehension and judgment, I focused on different methods designed to test specific hypotheses regarding the children's syntactic and lexical knowledge. Due to time limitation on the project and time limits on the experiment sessions, it was not feasible to use all the methods listed in Table 4.9 for the four constructions. In the case of pronouns and reflexives I replicated the experiment conducted by Chien and Wexler. For passive constructions I used the experiments designed by van der Lely and Verrips. In the case of double-object constructions I tested the judgment of children and was interested to find out whether children would favour double-object constructions at the expense of other alternative constructions such as prepositional

Table 4.9 *Overview of experiments*

Area of grammar	Number of experiment and method
Pronouns and reflexives	1, 2, 3: Act-out task
	4: Truth value judgment task
Double-object construction	1: Grammaticality task
Passive	1: Picture-selection task
	2: Sentence-completion task
Serial verb construction	1: Elicited production task

ditransitive constructions. Together, I expected the findings would converge with those from other studies on the acquisition of syntax and lexicon (cf. McDaniel *et al.* 1996).

The reason for choosing pronouns and reflexives, double-object, passive and serial verb constructions is because these form part of complex syntax. While there has been abundant research on how young children acquire simple syntax, there has been far less work done on the acquisition of complex sentences (e.g. Bowerman 1979, Diessel 2004, Lust *et al.* 2009). As accurately noted by Lust *et al.* (2009) the study of complex sentences can provide us with deeper insights into the basics of syntactic and semantic knowledge on, for instance, hierarchical structure, locality domains, recursion and structure dependence. In each chapter concerned with these areas, I discuss the significance of these areas for the working hypothesis of this study. Table 4.9 shows an overview of the experiments. Both scoring and data analysis are discussed separately for each experiment in the relevant chapters.

EXPERIMENTS ON COMPREHENSION, PRODUCTION AND JUDGMENT

Comprehension data

Picture selection task
An adapted version of the passive test as developed by van der Lely (1996) was used here in Passive Experiment 1. It consists of

forty-eight sentences. Four pictures were presented to the child at a time and the child was asked to match the sentence s/he heard with the most appropriate picture. The subject was also advised that sometimes two possible pictures could match with the sentence. The test took between 15 and 20 minutes to be administered, depending on the age of the children. This test was chosen for several reasons: for one, because it is well designed to test the comprehension level of children, especially with very young children of three years of age (cf. van der Lely 1996); for another, because it allows me to compare the data of Creole-speaking children to children with other languages.

There were four conditions as already mentioned in Chapter 3: verbal passives, adjectival passives, short verbal passives and short adjectival passives.

Act-out task
Following Chien and Wexler (1990) I used this task to test binding experiments 1, 2 and 3. In these experiments, a version of the act-out task called the Simon-Says game was used. The experimenter held two puppets (Mari and Zan) and read a sentence. The child was asked to perform an action when s/he heard *'Zan dir'* or *'Mari dir'*. These tests took around five minutes each to be completed.

Production data

Sentence completion task
Passive Experiment 2 is an adapted version of Verrips' experiment on the passive (1996). The aim of the experiment was twofold. First, it included young children, and second, its design allowed the effects of contextual inference to be teased apart from syntactic representation. The child was given a picture to look at which depicted an activity. The experimenter described the picture to the child, and the child was asked to complete the experimenter's description. Each picture description ended with the preposition *ek/avek* 'with'. Each picture depicted both an accompaniment and

an instrument for the activity. I assumed that if a child completes the with-phrase as an instrument phrase, the child's representation of the description sentence includes an agent. When the picture description is a short passive, the instrument-response indicates the presence of an implicit agent. Example (1) is an example for clarification:

(1) Ala   en karusel   pe   turne ek   (en lisyen
     look a   merry-go-round   PROG   turn   with   (a dog
       lorli/en lapel)
       on it/a   spade)
     'Here, the merry-go-round is turned with (a dog on it / a spade).'
     MORISYEN/SESELWA

There were fifteen sentences and three test conditions: anti-causative verbs, the passive of transitive verbs and the passive of alternating verbs. In the anti-causative condition, both readings are grammatical in the adult system. The same applies for the two passives.

Elicited production task

Elicited production tasks sometimes have to be modified to accomplish the goals of a particular experiment. Many variations of the task have incorporated the strategy of involving children in a game in which they interact with a puppet. In the task used here in Experiment 1 of Serial Verb Construction, I used a combination of two techniques: the puppet technique (in which the child helps the puppet learn to speak Seselwa correctly) and the elicitation of certain structures that have already been given. The puppet and the child were sitting next to each other and were presented pictures showing, for instance, a dog stealing the shoe of a girl and running away with it. The puppet would say a non-matching sentence to the picture such as *gete, li pe monte desan* 'look, it is going up and down'. The child was asked to say whether the puppet said the right thing or not. If not, as was often the case, the child had to correct the puppet in saying *'non, li pe pran sulyer tay avek'* 'no, it has taken the shoe is running away with it' [approx.]. This method was preferred to others because it allowed children to use the structures they are familiar with. Thus, some children also used *li pe koken sulyer pe taye* 'it is stealing the shoe running away', *li pe pran sulyer pe taye* 'it is taking the shoe is running away', or *li pe pran sulyer pe taye ale* 'it is taking the shoe, is running away is going away'. There were twenty sentences and it took around twenty minutes to complete. A colleague took care of the recording while I played the role of the puppet. She assisted me in general with all the experiments.

Judgment data

Truth-value judgment task

The truth-value judgment (TVJ) has proved to be one of the most effective methods used to assess children's linguistic competence. The core property of this task is that it steers the child in making a bipolar judgment about whether a statement accurately describes a particular situation in a specific context. This task is particularly successful because it relies on the simplicity of the child's response and the amount of information about the child's understanding of complex constructions. As Gordon (1996) points out, this test allows for evaluation of the child's understanding of complex structures which were considered to be non-testable until recently. There are two types of TVJ tasks: yes/no tasks and reward/punishment tasks, in which the child is asked to reward a puppet for making a true statement or to punish the puppet for making a false statement. The yes/no task presented in binding experiment 4 was chosen to determine the knowledge of children regarding quantifiers, names and pronouns, as in Chien and Wexler's binding experiment 4 (1990).

In the pretest I used this task with a puppet for the double-object construction. However, it is interesting to note that I encountered similar problems to those encountered by Gordon and Sandalo with Kadiweu children in southern Brazil. These children had not encountered puppets before, and as a result, some children reacted with extreme fear and curiosity which delayed the experiment. This problem was overcome by having the teachers including the puppet in everyday classes for two weeks.

Grammaticality task

As the grammaticality judgment task has proved adaptable for children of almost any age, I chose it for the investigation of the double-object construction. It was presented in Double-Object Construction Experiment 1. Children were asked to describe to their parents a particular event which took place at school. They were presented with two sentences and had to choose one of them as what they would use during their conversation, such as 'John gave Paul a book' or 'John gave a book to Paul'. Props were used to make the context clear.

CONCLUDING REMARKS

As we can see from the above, there are basically three types of data; production, comprehension and judgment data. For the purpose of this study I have chosen various techniques appropriate for data collection within a Creole-speaking population. Some degree of modification has been necessary to meet the requirements of each specific study. Furthermore, clear lines among methods were not always drawn, as a combination of different methods seemed to be more appropriate to maximise the quality of the output data.

5 Pronouns and reflexives

INTRODUCTION

The study of pronouns plays a major part in understanding the mental representations of language. The cross-linguistic diversity and richness of pronominal systems have shown that these systems follow constraints. These are of great importance for theoretical issues such as functional categories, types of licensing mechanisms and locality constraints. Thus, much attention has been devoted to this topic (see Kayne 1975, Rizzi 1986, Brandi and Cordin 1989 among others). To define the nature of pronouns is not an uncontroversial task. In the current literature, pronouns are most commonly classified as either clitics or full pronouns, because of their different syntactic behaviour (see Brandi and Cordin 1989).

In this chapter I present the pronominal systems of both Morisyen and Seselwa couched in the Government and Binding framework (GB) (Chomsky 1986) and explore the data gathered on four binding experiments conducted with Seselwa-speaking children. I argue that Creole-speaking children confirm the Principle B violation attested in other studies. I will show that children oblivious to the input use the pronoun *li* reflexively before acquiring the target grammar. In spite of its evolution, Seselwa has retained a pronoun that can be used reflexively, a feature of the early unmarked Creole grammar. These findings suggest strongly that children might start with a default grammar in which pronouns are also used reflexively.

PRONOUNS AND REFLEXIVES IN FIRST
LANGUAGE ACQUISITION

Within the generative field, Binding Theory (BT) is considered to be a major component of the computational system of adult syntax. A widespread view concerning the acquisition of binding is that young children do not have knowledge of Principle B of the BT (see Lust 1986 for a review). Several theories have been proposed to account for the type of knowledge children acquire before they reach the target system in their respective language. Chien and Wexler's influential paper (1990) revealed that children have a good understanding of variable-binding as compared to their understanding of coreference. This finding of Chien and Wexler has been shared by a series of cross-linguistic studies (English, Korean, Japanese, Dutch, Icelandic, Italian and Portuguese) since then.[1] Children's knowledge of Principle B remains undeniably a central area of investigation in language acquisition research (Gibson and Pearlmutter 2011).

I present evidence here for the view that children do not reliably obey Principle B. However, the results presented here do not reveal that children do not know Principle B, as we will see later in this chapter. A large number of acquisition studies have concluded, on the basis of spontaneous and experimental data, that children violate Principle B. There are basically three proposals that have been developed to account for the data. One group of researchers proposes that children have not found out which expression is used for which principle. As a result, children bind both pronouns and reflexives locally (Jakubowicz 1984, Solan 1987). A second group of researchers claims that Principle B matures, as suggested by Borer and Wexler (1987). A third view is that BT has to be reformulated to allow children to conform to it from an early age (Chien and Wexler 1988, 1990). These researchers rely on the work of Reinhart (1983a,

---

[1] Solan (1983), Jakubowicz (1984), Deutsch *et al.* (1986), Lust (1986), Cairns and McDaniel (1987), Chien and Wexler (1987a,b, 1988, 1990), Crain and McKee (1987), Grimshaw and Rosen (1990), Hyams and Sigurjónsdóttir (1990).

b), who adopts the position that Principle B constrains pronouns only when they are bound variables.

I discuss a series of experimental studies regarding the knowledge of pronouns and anaphora and their antecedents of Morisyen-speaking children and argue that Morisyen-speaking children have knowledge of c-command and locality aspects of Principle A for reflexives. I propose the following: whenever children allow a pronoun to be coreferential with a local c-commanding antecedent (which means violation of Principle B), they are falling back on options not allowed in their target grammar but possible in early Creole grammar. In Morisyen as well as in many other Creole languages, the bare pronoun can be non-locally as well as locally bound. This has consequences for the acquisition of binding for Morisyen-speaking children, which will be discussed together with other findings on Seselwa in the following sections.

SPONTANEOUS DATA

A look at the spontaneous Seselwa data shows that all nine children have both *li* and *limem*, although *limem* is less frequent. *So lekor* is also used occasionally.

(1) Daniel i   bat li   lor   so   koko
    Daniel ASP hit him on   his   head
    'Daniel hit him (Benjamin) on his head.' (Andre 2;5)

(2) Benjamin i   mord zorey Ruben
    Benjamin ASP bite   ear   Ruben
    'Benjamin bit Ruben's ear.' (Stefanie 2;9)

(3) Stefan pe   zwe   ek   telefon   limem
    Stefan ASP play   with   telefone   himself
    'Stefan himself is playing with the phone.' (Julio 2;9)

(4) Marmay i   kasiet so   lekor anba   latab
    Child   ASP hide   his   body   under   table
    'The child has hidden himself under the table.' (Brigitte 2;11)

(5) Teddybear   in   manz   gato   limem
    Teddy bear   ASP   eat   cake   himself
    'The teddy bear has eaten cake/sweet himself.' (Emma 2;11)

The Morisyen data also shows that *li* is well attested in the corpora of children around 2;4. Similar to the Seselwa data, the reflexive *limem* is not as common as *li*. In contrast to the Seselwa data, *so lekor* is absent. Here are some examples (6–9):

(6) li   zoli
     3SG   nice
     'It is nice.'   (Laura 1;9)

(7) Ø   pa   kone.   Ø   bat   li
     Ø   NEG   know.   Ø   beat   3SG
     'I don't know. I am beating her (the doll).' (Ludovic 2;4)

(8) a. Kisana   ti   kondwir   loto?
         who   TNS   drive   car?
         'Who drove the car?' (Mother of child)
     b. mo-   mem
         1SG   REFL
         'Myself.'   (Rodney 2;4)

(9) li   travay   dan   lizin
     3SG   work   in   factory
     'He (his father) works in the factory.' (Benito 2;7)

Given that the data is based on spontaneous speech, we cannot be sure whether children master the pronoun–reflexive distinction. In order to clarify this, I conducted a binding experiment with children of the ages of four and five, which is presented in the following section.

EXPERIMENTS

Previous work on binding with Morisyen-speaking children

The study was based on methods developed by Crain and McKee (1985) and used in studies such as Kaufman (1984), Chien and Wexler

(1988), McDaniel *et al.* (1990) and Grimshaw and Rosen (1990). Its focus was on the truth-value judgments of four- and five-year-old children on sentences with Principle B violation and their judgments on otherwise identical sentences without violation. This design was chosen because it allowed us to compare acceptances of BT-grammatical and BT-ungrammatical sentences. Ten children between four and five years of age were investigated.

The sentences below (10–15) illustrate the test sentences with one verb *grate* 'scratch'. The test sentences were classified into six basic types, two with each of the three pronouns and reflexives *li*, *limem* and *so lekor*. These sentences included violations of Principle B. Each BT-ungrammatical sentence was paired with a grammatical counterpart.

Sentences with *li*:

a.   BT-grammatical. Scenario 1 shows that the monkey is scratching the bear. Krapo says:

(10) Mo   fin   truv   Ti   Zako   pe   fer   kitsoz
      ISG   ASP   see   little   monkey   PROG   do   something
      ek   Lurs.
      with   bear
      Ti   Zako$_i$ fin   grat   **li$_k$**.
      little monkey   ASP   scratch   3SG
      'I saw the monkey doing something to the bear. The monkey scratched him.'

b.   BT-ungrammatical. Scenario 2 shows that the monkey is scratching himself. Krapo says:

(11) Mo   fin   truv   Ti   Zako   pe   dibut   kot   Lurs.
      ISG   ASP   see   little   monkey   PROG   stand   next   bear
      Ti   Zako$_i$ fin   grat   **li$_k$**
      little   monkey   ASP   scratch   3SG
      'I saw the monkey standing next to the bear. The monkey scratched him.'

Sentences with *limem*:

a. BT-grammatical. Scenario 3 shows that the monkey is scratching himself. Krapo says:

(12) Mo fin truv Ti Zako pe dibut kot Lurs.
ISG ASP see little monkey PROG stand next bear
Ti Zako fin grat **li -mem**.
little monkey ASP scratch 3SG -REFL
'I saw the monkey standing next to the bear. The monkey scratched himself.'

b. BT-ungrammatical. Scenario 4 shows that the monkey is scratching himself. Krapo says:

(13) Mo fin truv Ti Zako pe fer kitsoz ek
ISG ASP see little monkey PROG do something with
Lurs.
bear
Ti Zako$_i$ fin grat **li -mem**$_i$.
little monkey ASP scratch 3SG -REFL
'I saw the monkey doing something to the bear. The monkey scratched himself.'

Sentences with *so lekor*

a. BT-grammatical. Scenario 5 shows that the monkey is scratching his body. Krapo says:

(14) Mo fin truv Ti Zako pe dibut kot Lurs.
ISG ASP see little monkey PROG stand next bear
Ti Zako fin grat **so lekor**.
little monkey ASP scratch 3POS body
'I saw the monkey standing next to the bear. The monkey scratched his body.'

b. BT-ungrammatical. Scenario 6 shows that the monkey is scratching his body.
Krapo says:

(15) Mo fin truv Ti Zako pe fer kitsoz
    ISG ASP see little monkey PROG do something
    ek Lurs.
    with bear
    Ti Zako$_i$ fin grat **so lekor$_k$.**
    little monkey ASP scratch 3POS body
    'I saw the monkey doing something to the bear. The monkey scratched his body.'

I used a modified version of the Grimshaw and Rosen experiment (1990, see also Appendix A). Instead of a scenario on TV, two adults represented two figures *Ti Zako* 'a monkey' and *Lurs* 'a bear'. The experimenter had a hand puppet *Krapo* 'Froggie'.

Three verbs, *grate* 'scratch', *benye* 'wash' and *penye* 'comb' were used. In total, there were eighteen sentences. Each target sentence was preceded by a context sentence so that an antecedent for the pronoun could be provided. The context sentence introduced the two participants: *Ti Zako* and *Lurs*. The children were told that *Krapo* 'the frog' was learning to speak Morisyen. Their task was to help teach the frog the difference between *li* and *limem*. After the child watched the scenario, the experimenter talked with the child *gete kisana ki la; Ti Zako fin fek grat lours.* 'Look who is there; the monkey just hit the bear.' After the second repetition of the scenario, Froggie quickly repeated the scenario and target sentence. After the frog had spoken, the child who thought that the frog had spoken correctly patted the frog. If the child thought that the frog was wrong, s/he gave it a smack.

As can be seen from Table 5.1, the data shows that children know well how to respond to the BT-grammatical sentences. But the performance on the BT-ungrammatical sentences looked as if children performed at chance. These results replicate the results already obtained in other studies, with non-Creole children. Children violate Principle B. At this point it is worth mentioning that the supposed ungrammatical sentences were not entirely ungrammatical in Morisyen, given that the adult grammar allows for a bare pronoun to

Table 5.1 *Correct and incorrect BT responses*

	BT-Grammatical	BT-Ungrammatical
Principle B	75%	25%

have a local binder. We will come back to this issue in the following sections.

Binding with Seselwa children

Four experiments based on Chien and Wexler's study (1990) were used to test Seselwa-speaking children's knowledge of the locality condition in Binding Theory.

Binding experiment 1

Experiment 1 was designed to test children's knowledge of the locality part of Principle A (reflexives). The sentences contained two potential antecedents for the reflexive. Both antecedents c-commanded the reflexive, but only one was local. Adults were expected to choose the local antecedents as correct for the reflexive. The experiment aimed at checking whether children did the same as adults. Knowledge of Principle B was also tested in that the pronouns alternated with reflexives, the aim being to find out what children do with pronouns. Adults were expected to choose the non-local antecedents for the pronouns. In this experiment I tested fifty children and six adults. The mean age of the child subjects was 4;6.

Two sentence types were chosen as the design of the test constructions: reflexive sentences as in (16) and (17) and pronouns sentences as in (18) and (19). I modified the experiment in two ways. Given that Seselwa does not have gender-specific pronoun or reflexives, I did not use the pronoun gender control sentences to control gender. However, the use of an asexual name for the puppet (Daniel/le) helped to detect what choice the child made. As there is no difference in the pronunciation of the word 'Daniel' to make clear whether it is a male or female puppet, it remains open to the child and s/he can interpret it the way s/he wants. Sentence (16) is said to a girl and *limem* refers to 'herself', which should be interpreted as Anielle in the target grammar. However, the child could interpret it as referring to either Anielle or Danielle. Sentence (17) is used with a boy. *Limem* refers here to 'himself' which should be interpreted as Raphael in the target grammar, but again the child could interpret it as either Raphael or Daniel. Sentence (18) is presented to a girl and *li* refers to 'her' which can be interpreted as either Anielle or Danielle in the target grammar. Sentence (19) is used with a boy with *li* referring to 'him', again with the interpretation of either Raphael or Daniel being acceptable in the target grammar. Interestingly, *li* can be bound either to the matrix or to the embedded subject, thus illustrating variability in the adult grammar:

(16) Danielle dir Anielle pu bizen montre li -mem.
     Danielle say Anielle MOD need show 3SG -REFL
     'Danielle says that Anielle should point to herself.'

(17) Daniel dir Raphael pu bizen montre li -mem.
     Daniel say Raphael MOD need show 3SG -REFL
     'Daniel says that Raphael should point to himself.'

(18) Danielle dir Anielle pu bizen montre li.
     Danielle say Anielle MOD need show 3SG
     'Danielle says that Anielle should point to her.'

(19) Daniel dir Raphael pu bizen montre li.
     Daniel say Raphael MOD need show 3SG
     'Daniel says that Raphael should point to him.'

Each test sentence involved a matrix verb *dir* 'say' and a tensed complement. There were eight sentences in total, with two items for each verb (*li* vs. *limem* 'him/her' vs. 'himself/herself') and four different verbs (*tuse* 'touch', *montre* 'point to', *grate* 'scratch' and *tiktike* 'tickle'). This experiment used an adaptation of the Simon-Says game, in which the child was asked to carry out an action whenever

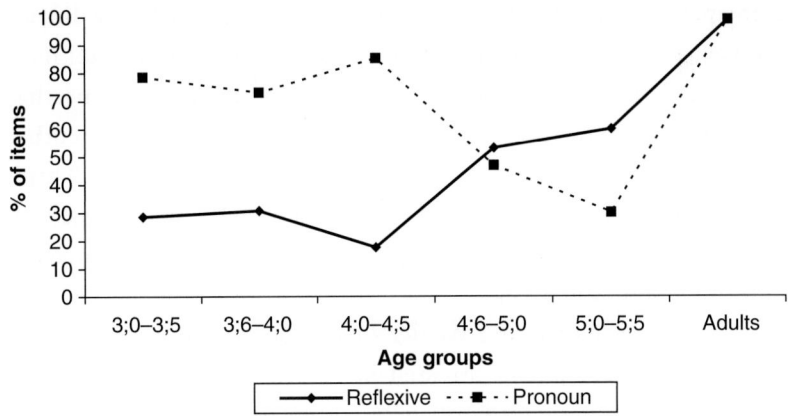

FIGURE 5.1 Reflexives and pronouns in binding experiment 1

s/he heard a sentence such as *Danielle/Daniel dir*. The results are shown in Figure 5.1.

In Figure 5.1 we find the ages in six-month intervals, starting with children in the age group of 3;0–3;5 and going up to 5;0–5;5 on the x-axis. On the y-axis we find the percentage of items (*li* (pronoun) vs. *limem* (reflexive)). The major findings of this experiment can be summarised as follows: The line marked with diamonds illustrates the correct answers to the reflexive sentences. This means that children took *limem* to be local. As indicated by the line marked with diamonds, children in the age group 5;0–5;5 knew the main property of reflexives, that is that the antecedent must be local. This age group reached a correct percentage of 60%. This line also indicates that the children's performance on the locality property of reflexives increases continuously from about the 30% level at age 3;0–3;5 to 60% at age 5;0–5;5.

The results for the pronoun, however, look more complex. The line marked with squares illustrates the correct answers for the pronouns, meaning that children correctly chose *li* to refer to the puppet. It starts at around the 80% level and falls to the 30% level with the 5;0–5;5 age group. As indicated by this line, children of the age group 5;0–5;5 still do not show the stable behaviour predicted by

Principle B grammaticality judgments. This means that they did not always obey the Principle B constraint that a pronoun may not have a local c-commanding antecedent. There are three questions that come to mind here: first, is this development also witnessed in other languages? Second, if not, then is it an artefact of the data? Third, what provokes such a U-shaped development here? With respect to the first question, the answer is yes. The results here are reminiscent of those found in English.

A look at Chien and Wexler's data shows some similarity to the type of development attested here. Their children of the age group 6;0–6;6 (G8) showed only 64% correct answers with pronouns (see Appendix A for translated sentences). Their Figure 1 also shows a rapid fall with this age group. It seems that Chien and Wexler were right that children of that age still violate Principle B, thus allowing a pronoun to be coreferential with an antecedent that locally c-commands it. A tentative explanation for the U-shaped development will be given later in this chapter when discussing the overall results. However, it is crucial to note that when comparing results, the distance between the development of pronouns and reflexives reduces by the age of 4;6–5;0. At 3;0–3;5 the distance is 50%. It reaches its peak in the 4;0–4;5 age group, at 67% and reduces in the 5;0–5;5 age group to 30%. This narrowing of the margins could be interpreted as a signal that children are actually learning to use both. The main findings of this experiment are that children of age 5;0–5;5 demonstrate knowledge of Principle A but appear to allow violation of Principle B. The developmental results of Principle A are predicted from the structure-building and lexical learning hypotheses as formulated by Radford (2006). However, the developmental results of Principle B are not. In order to clarify the issues above, I conducted two further experiments.

The rationale for Experiments 2 and 3 was threefold. I replicated and investigated in depth the results from Experiment 1, especially those involving the responses of the younger children with regard to reflexives and the older children's responses with regard to pronouns. The violation of Principle B looked serious enough to be investigated again in case it held up with other types of experiments and with different linguistic materials. Since Experiment 1 used tensed complements, I used sentences with the matrix verb *ule* 'want' and an infinitival complement and applied the same methodology, i.e. the Simon-Says game in Experiment 2. In Experiment 3 I used the party game.

Binding experiment 2

As mentioned above, Experiment 2 was designed to test infinitivals and gender control for reflexives and pronouns in Chien and Wexler's experiment. In contrast to English, Seselwa does not have a gender distinction in the pronoun/reflexive forms. Despite this fact, I included the gender-control pronoun and the gender-control reflexive sentences, to double-check that the gender of the matrix subject did not strongly influence the children's responses. The raw data shows negligible variation so the results are merged. Eighty children and six adults were tested here. The design of the test constructions was as follows: four sentence types were included: reflexive sentences such as in (20), (24), and (26) with *li-mem* being bound by the children (here Annie or Fabio) only. Pronoun sentences as in (21), (25) and (27) with *li* are bound by the children's name (here Annie or Fabio) or the puppet's (Mari/Zan).

Girl scenario:

(20)   Mari   **ule**   Annie   montre   **li**   **-mem**   ek   so   ledwa.
        Mari   want   Annie   show   3SG   -REFL   with   3POS   finger
        'Mari wants Annie to show herself with her finger.'

(21)   Mari   **ule**   Annie   montre   **li**   ek   so   ledwa.
        Mari   want   Annie   show   3SG   with   3POS   finger
        'Mari wants Annie to show her with her finger.'

(22)   Zan   **ule**   Annie   montre   **li**   **-mem**   ek   so   ledwa.
        Zan   want   Annie   show   3SG   -REFL   with   3POS   finger
        'John wants Annie to show herself with her finger.'

(23) Zan **ule** Annie montre **li** ek so ledwa.
     Zan want Annie show 3SG with 3POS finger
     'John wants Annie to show him/her with her finger.'

Boy scenario:

(24) Zan **ule** Fabio montre **li** **-mem** ek so ledwa.
     Zan want Fabio show 3SG -REFL with 3POS finger
     'John wants Fabio to show himself with his finger.'

(25) Zan **ule** Fabio montre **li** ek so ledwa.
     Zan want Fabio show 3SG with 3POS finger
     'John wants Fabio to show him with his finger.'

(26) Mari **ule** Fabio montre **li** **-mem** ek so ledwa.
     Mari want Fabio show 3SG -REFL with 3POS finger
     'Mari wants Fabio to show himself with his finger.'

(27) Mari **ule** Fabio montre **li** ek so ledwa.
     Mari want Fabio show 3SG with 3POS finger
     'Mari wants Fabio to show her/him with his finger.'

All sentences had a matrix verb *ule* 'want' and an infinitival complement. There were two potential antecedents (that is the matrix subject NP *Zan* or *Mari* and the embedded subject NP that is the child's name) for the reflexive or the pronoun. The reflexive and the pronoun sentences were designed so that the reflexive or pronoun would refer to either the embedded subject or the matrix subject. Four different action verbs were used (*tuse* 'touch', *montre ar ledwa* 'point to', *grate* 'scratch' and *tiktike* 'tickle'. There were two items for each verb (*li* and *limem*), yielding ten sentences for each sentence type. In this experiment I used the Simon-Says game and the procedures were the same as in binding experiment 1. However, the verb *dir* 'say' was replaced by the verb *ule* 'want'.

    The results of this experiment are illustrated in Figure 5.2. In general, these results replicated the results indicated in Experiment 1. Two points become clear here: the first is that children have knowledge of the reflexive and pronouns as early as 3;0–3;5. It seems that most children prefer the pronoun *li*. The second point is that the

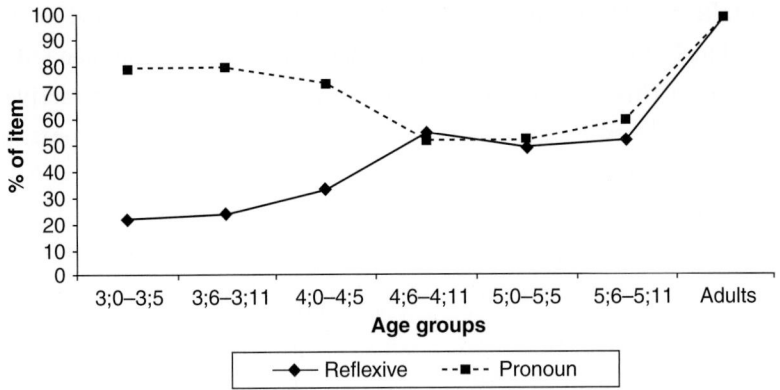

FIGURE 5.2 Reflexives and pronouns in binding experiment 2

children's performance on the locality property of reflexives continuously increases from about 21% at the age of 3;0–3;5 to 50% at
the age of 5;6–5;11. The development of the pronoun is different. The
U-shaped development is not as drastic as witnessed in Experiment
1, but the line indicates that children in the age range 5;0–5;5 still
do not show adult-like behaviour in accordance with Principle B.
Their performance on the requirement that pronouns may not have
a local c-commanding antecedent does not change too much; in the
oldest age group, it remains at about 60%.

Binding experiment 3
Given the previous results from Experiments 1 and 2, that children
tend to select a non-local antecedent for both pronouns and reflexives, it was necessary to check if children had determined that *limem* 'him/herself' was a reflexive or were using some pragmatic
strategy to answer the questions. Experiment 3 was thus designed
to test whether young children see reflexives and pronouns as need-
ing non-local antecedents. In contrast to the two previous experiments, another situation, the party game, was presented to the
children. The experimenter set up a female and male puppet sitting
in front of the child. There was a plate with several small toys or
props between the child and the puppet. The child was expected

to take a toy from the plate and put it either in her/his bowl or in the bowl of the one of the puppets, depending on the sentence s/he heard. In this situation I made the local response more attractive to the children by decreasing the response bias. In other words, I expected children would prefer to give a toy to themselves rather than the puppet. The design of the test constructions is as follows: reflexive sentences (28) to (31) and pronoun sentences (32) to (35) for the girls; reflexive sentences (36) to (39) and pronoun sentences (40) to (43) for the boys.

Girl scenario, reflexive sentences:

(28) Mari **dir** Anissa **pu** **bizen** don li **-mem** en loto.
Mari say Anissa MOD need give 3SG -REFL a car
'Mari says Anissa should give herself a car.'

(29) Mari **dir** Anissa **pu** **bizen** don en loto li **-mem**.
Mari say Anissa MOD need give a car 3SG -REFL
'Mari says Anissa should give a car to herself.'

(30) Mari **ule** Anissa don li **-mem** en bul.
Mari want Anissa give 3SG -REFL a ball
'Mari wants Anissa give herself a ball.'

(31) Mari **ule** Anissa don en bul li **-mem**
Mari want Anissa give a ball 3SG -REFL
'Mari wants Anissa give a ball to herself.'

Pronoun sentences:

(32) Mari **dir** Anissa **pu** **bizen** don li en draze.
Mari say Anissa MOD need give 3SG a lolly
'Mari says Anissa should give her a lolly.'

(33) *Mari **dir** Anissa **pu** **bizen** don en draze li
Mari say Anissa MOD need give a lolly 3SG
'Mari says Anissa should give a lolly to her.'

(34) *Mari **ule** Anissa don en serviet li
Mari want Anissa give a napkin 3SG
'Mari wants Anissa to give a napkin to her.'

(35) Mari **ule**   Anissa don **li**   en   serviet
      Mari   want   Anissa give 3SG a   napkin
      'Mari wants Anissa give her a napkin.'

Boy scenario, reflexive sentences:

(36) Zan **dir** Leeroy **pu**   **bizen** don   li   **-mem** en loto.
      Zan   say   Leeroy MOD   need   give   3SG   -REFL   a   car
      'Zan says Leeroy should give himself a car.'

(37) Zan **dir** Leeroy **pu**   **bizen** don   en loto li   **-mem**.
      Zan   say   Leeroy MOD   need   give   a   car   3SG   -REFL
      'John says Leeroy should give a car to himself.'

(38) Zan **ule**   Leeroy don **li**   **-mem** en bul.
      Zan   want   Leeroy give 3SG -REFL   a   ball
      'John wants Leeroy to give himself a ball.'

(39) Zan **ule**   Leeroy don en bul **li**   **-mem**.
      Zan   want   Leeroy give a   ball 3SG   -REFL
      'John wants Leeroy to give a ball to himself.'

Pronoun sentences:

(40) Zan **dir** Leeroy **pu**   **bizen** don li   en   draze.
      Zan   say   Leeroy MOD   need   give   3SG   a   lolly
      'John says Leeroy should give him a lolly.'

(41) *Zan **dir** Leeroy **pu**   **bizen** don   en draze **li**.
      Zan   say   Leeroy MOD   need   give   a   lolly   3SG
      'John says Leeroy should give a lolly to him.'

(42) Zan **ule**   Leeroy don **li**   en   serviet.
      Zan   want   Leeroy give 3SG a   napkin
      'John wants Leeroy to give him a napkin.'

(43) *Zan **ule**   Leeroy don en serviet **li**.
      Zan   want   Leeroy give a   napkin 3SG
      'John wants Leeroy to give a napkin to him.'

Half of the sentences in each type involved the matrix verb *dir* 'say' that subcategorises for a tensed complement. The other half involved the matrix verb *ule* 'want', which subcategorises for an infinitival

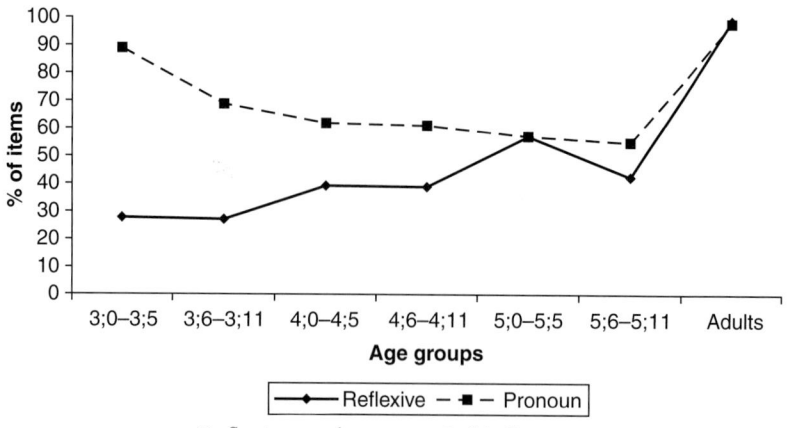

FIGURE 5.3 Reflexives and pronouns in binding experiment 3

complement. Here, I used two ditransitive constructions (*Mari don li en zuzu* 'Mary gives her/him a toy' and **Mari don en zuzu li* 'Mary gives a toy him/her'). The second ditransitive construction is not grammatical in adult Seselwa. I included these ungrammatical constructions here to test whether the deviant word order in the second type of construction would in any way affect the response of children in terms of binding. The results show that it did not. There were four items per condition (two for each of the two dative constructions), and one set (*Mari* and *Zan*) was used, adding up to a total of sixteen sentences per subject. The experimenter used the party game as already mentioned earlier in the chapter. The results show the following picture.

Figure 5.3 illustrates the results reached in binding experiment 3. As far as reflexives are concerned, we note a strong within-task (the party game) and between-complement-type consistency (*ule*-infinitive vs. *dir*-tensed). For all groups the children's performance on the locality property of reflexives increases continuously from 30% (chance level) at the age 3;0–3;5 to nearly 60% at 5;0–5;5 and decreases at 5;6–5;11 to around 42%. Similar to the previous results, the age groups 5;0–5;5 and 5;6–5;11 seem to be the most problematic.

In the age group 5;0–5;5 pronouns and reflexives meet at around 60%, thus showing that children have knowledge of both principles A and B. However, children of 5;6–5;11 do not perform as well as the 5;0–5;5 age group.

A preliminary conclusion with regard to the three experiments is as follows: Experiments 2 and 3 seem to replicate the results of Experiment 1. When asked to make coreference judgments between reflexives and pronouns and the two sentence-internal antecedents, older children differentiated reflexive sentences from pronoun sentences. This applied regardless of the complement types used in the test sentences and the tasks applied in the experiments (Simon-Says game versus the party game). All three experiments have one development in common: there is a U-shaped curve in the development of pronouns. Children in the age groups 5;0–5;5 and 5;6–5;11 have still not yet learned the non-locality condition for pronouns. Note that similar results have been also observed in other studies with different languages including English, Chinese, Korean, Japanese, Dutch, Icelandic, Italian and Portuguese (cf. Otsu 1981, Deutsch and Koster 1982, Solan 1983, 1987, Jakubowicz 1984, Deutsch et al. 1986, Lust 1986, 1987, Chien and Wexler 1987a, b, 1988, Crain and McKee 1987, McDaniel and Cairns 1987, McKee 1988, Sigurjónsdóttir et al. 1988, Hyams and Sigurjónsdóttir 1990, Thornton and Wexler 1999).

The general findings are first, that children have knowledge of both the c-command and locality aspects of Principle A for reflexives by about age 5;6, and second, that the performance of the children on Principle B for pronouns appears to be 'greatly' delayed when compared to Principle A. The results in this study agree with the general findings to a certain extent. Seselwa-speaking children show that they start at chance level with reflexives; however, the correct judgment continuously increases until age 5;6–5;11. I follow Chien and Wexler (1990), who argue that the delay of Principle B is due to problems with pragmatics pertaining to reference (Wexler 2011).

Binding experiment 4

Experiment 4 was designed to test the hypothesis that children will accept a pronoun as coreferential with a local antecedent, but they will not allow a pronoun to be a bound variable when it has a local antecedent. Following Chien and Wexler (1990), I repeated the examples with coreference, to make sure that the method did not have any influence on the data. I did not rely on the earlier experiments to show children accepting a pronoun as being coreferential with a local c-commanding antecedent. Explicit quantifiers (such as 'every') were used as bound variables. Simple sentences were used because of the complexity of the task. So, children were presented with one situation and one sentence at a time and they had to say 'yes' or 'no' according to whether the sentence matched the situation. The subjects were the same as in the previous experiments. A Yes/No judgment (Y/NJ) task was used here to check the children's grammaticality judgment of sentences such as those in (44) to (50). The child was presented with a cartoon picture, an introductory sentence and a question related to the picture. After careful inspection of the picture, the child was expected to answer 'yes' or 'no'. An example would be: I first presented a picture and said *Anielle, vwar sa portre. Sa Mari, sa Mama tediber. Eski Mama tediber pe tus limem?* 'Anielle, look at this picture. This is Mari and this is Mama Bear. Is Mama Bear touching herself?' Anielle might answer *wi* 'yes' or *non* 'no' depending on her current grammar development.

The design of the test constructions included four types of questions. These questions were similar in their syntactic structures but they were different with regard to the types of NPs occurring in their subject or object position. Half of the experimental questions included proper names such as *Mama tediber* as their subject, as seen in examples (44) and (45). The other half included quantified NPs such as *sak tediber* 'every bear', *tu ban tediber* 'all bears' as their subject, as seen in examples (46) and (47). The object-NPs were pronouns *li* or reflexives *limem*. According to the NPs occurring in their subject and object positions, there were four types of experimental

questions: name-reflexive questions, name-pronoun questions, quantifier-reflexive questions and quantifier-pronoun questions. The picture presented to the child, paired with each question type, matched
the question in only half of the cases (for instance, (44) to (47)). In the
other half there was a mismatch between the sentences and the pictures. Together this match and mismatch factor to each of the four
question types gave us eight different experimental conditions.

Added to the four types of experimental questions, there were
three types of control questions included. These were designed to
check whether children know the concept of quantified NP, such as
'every bear' and the corresponding pictures. The control questions
were similar in syntactic structure to the experimental questions.
They differed with regard to the types of NPs occurring in the subject position. These subject NPs were proper names such as *Mama
tediber*, or quantified NPs such as *sak tediber* 'each teddy bear' or *tu
ban tediber* 'all teddy bears'. The NPs occurring in the object position were all of the same type: proper names such as *Mari*. These
three types of control question were named the name-name questions, quantifier every-name questions and quantifier all-name questions. Similarly to the previous set of experimental sentences, there
were both match and mismatch cases. This gave us a total of six
control conditions. However, due to time limitation, I used only one
verb, *tuse* 'touch' in each condition. Sentences (44) to (47) illustrate
the examples.

Experimental questions

The match cases
Name-reflexive:

(44)   Sa Mari; sa Mama Tediber. Eski Mama Tediber pe tus **limem**?
       'This is Mary; this is Mama Bear. Is Mama Bear touching herself?'

Name-pronoun:

(45)   Sa Mama Tediber; sa Mari. Eski Mama Tediber pe tus **li**?
       'This is Mama Bear; this is Mary. Is Mama Bear touching her?'

Quantifier-reflexive:

(46) Sa Mari; sa ban tediber. Eski sak tediber pe tus **limem**?
    'This is Mary; these are the bears. Is every bear touching herself?'

Quantifier-pronoun:

(47) Sa ban tediber; sa Mari. Eski sak tediber pe tus **li**?
    'These are the bears; this is Mary. Is every bear touching her?'

For the mismatch cases the sentences did not match the pictures.

Control questions

The match cases
Name-name:

(48) Sa Mama Tediber; sa Mari. Eski Mama Tediber pe tus Mari?
    'This is Mama Bear; this is Mary. Is Mama Bear touching Mary?'

Quantifier 'every'-name:

(49) Sa ban tediber; sa Mari. Eski sak tediber pe tus Mari?
    'These are the bears; this is Mary. Is every bear touching Mary?

Quantifier 'all'-name:

(50) Sa ban tediber; sa Mari. Eski tu ban tediber pe tus Mari?
    'These are the bears; this is Mary. Are all the bears touching Mary?'

As above, in the mismatch cases the sentences did not match the pictures.

The results for the six control conditions are illustrated by the lines in Figures 5.4 and 5.5. The line marked with diamonds shows the results of the name-name condition. The line marked with squares shows the results of the quantifier-name condition involving 'every N' as the subject. The line marked with triangles shows the results of the quantifier-name condition involving *tu ban Ns*, 'all Ns' as the subject.

As seen in Figure 5.4, the response patterns of the children to the three types of control questions were the same when the question matched the picture, with a minor difference for the age group 4;0–4;5.

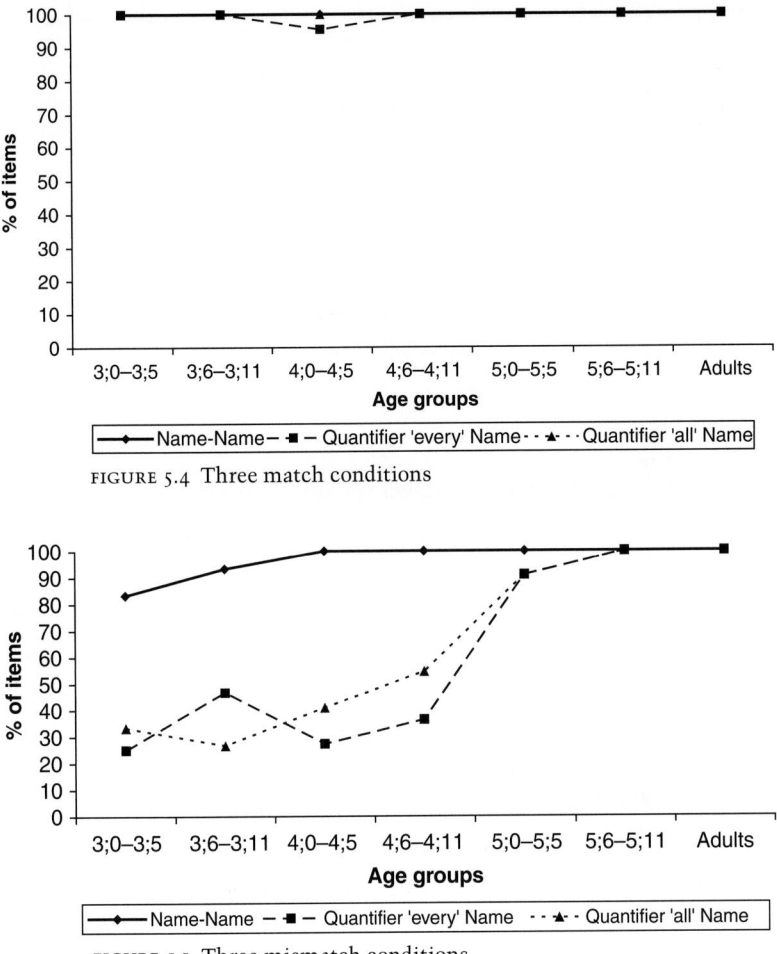

FIGURE 5.4 Three match conditions

FIGURE 5.5 Three mismatch conditions

The children's response patterns to the three types of control questions show that children made correct judgments almost all the time.

Figure 5.5 illustrates that when there was a mismatch between question and picture, this had an effect on the responses. The correct response was 'No'. In the name-name condition the children answered correctly with 'No' most of the time. However, many children of all ages had problems with the 'mismatch cases' *sak* 'each' and *tu ban* 'all'. Similar to English-speaking children (from Chien

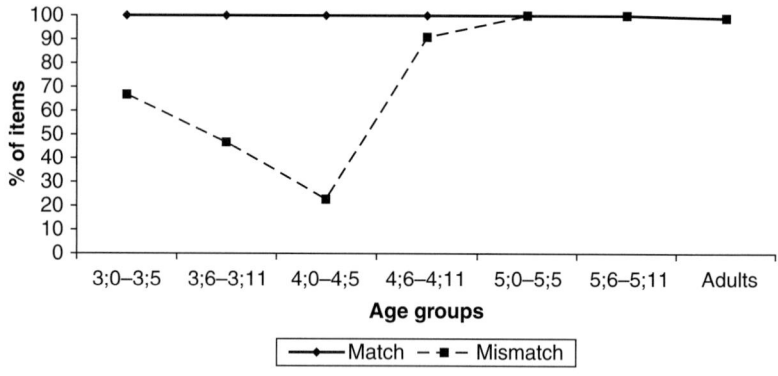

FIGURE 5.6 Name-reflexive

and Wexler's study 1990), Seselwa-speaking children of around five years old seemed to have a concept of quantified NPs such as 'every N' and 'all Ns'. The percentage of correct answers (that is, a 'No') is around 90%. Around 4;6–4;11 it is still around 30% and 50% respectively. This means that the children were saying 'Yes' to the mismatch cases. As this had already happened in a pilot study, I decided to ask the children to explain what they saw and what they chose immediately after their answers. It is particularly interesting to note that when these children were asked for an explanation of the situation, they did say correctly that two teddy bears were touching *Mari* and that the third one was not. This shows that these children did indeed recognise the situation correctly, and it supports the idea that children of this age do have a concept of quantified NPs. However, they may have problems with the lexical items corresponding to these concepts. This disparity will be the subject of deeper investigation in future studies.

The results of the four types of experimental questions are illustrated by Figures 5.6 to 5.9.

Figure 5.6 shows the results of the name-reflexive questions. The line marked with diamonds shows the results of the match cases. The line marked with squares shows the results of the mismatch cases. Children at age five and older demonstrate

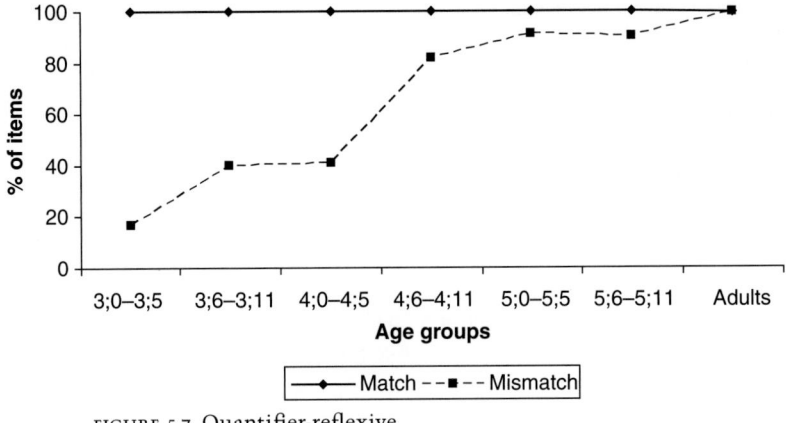

FIGURE 5.7 Quantifier-reflexive

clear knowledge of Principle A. They know that reflexives must be bound locally. They identified local binding for reflexives and also correctly rejected non-local binding for reflexives. The age group 4;0–4;5 shows around 25% of correct responses. This means that these children know that it was correct to co-index a reflexive to refer to the local antecedent but they also allowed the reflexive to refer to the non-locally bound antecedent. Children younger than five years of age did not show clearly the behaviour predicted by Principle A. The younger children (3;0–3;11) seemed to do better than the four-year-olds. This result replicated the results found in the previous studies.

Figure 5.7 shows the results of the quantifier-reflexive questions. The line with diamonds shows the results of the match cases. The line with squares shows the results of the mismatch cases. Children younger than five similarly did not show a solid knowledge of reflexives and quantified antecedents. Here the development of the mismatch line is very similar to the English results. Similar to the responses to the name-reflexive questions, the children allowed a reflexive to be coreferential with an external referent.

Figure 5.8 illustrates the results of the name-pronoun questions. The line with diamonds indicates cases where young children

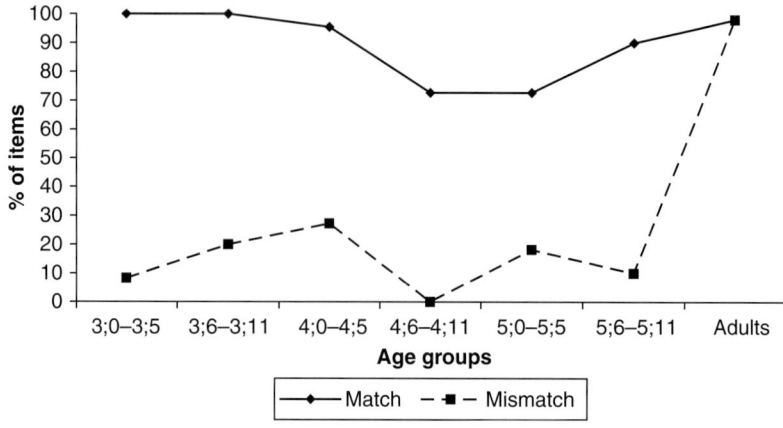

FIGURE 5.8 Name-pronoun

gave nearly always perfect responses when pictures and sentences matched. Even three-year-old children seemed to know that a non-reflexive pronoun could refer to a sentence-external definite NP. The line marked with squares indicates that when there was a mismatch between the question and the picture, this mismatch did indeed have an effect on the response of the children. It reduced the correct responses. In many of the name-pronoun cases, children allowed a non-reflexive pronoun to be coreferential with its local c-commanding antecedent. For instance, when presented with picture (45) and asked the question *eski Mama tediber pe tus li?* (is Mama Bear touching her?) children younger than 4;6–4;11 answered 'yes' more often than those of 4;6–4;11 and 5;0–5;5. The plateau at these two age groups (4;6–4;11 and 5;0–5;5) is nothing new. However, it shows that children between 4;6 and 4;11 did not know that a pronoun must not refer to the local-c-commanding antecedent. These results replicated the results in Experiments 1 to 3. It seems that when children demonstrate knowledge of Principle A, they do not demonstrate knowledge of Principle B for pronouns that are not bound variables. So, there is a difference between children's development of Principle A and Principle B.

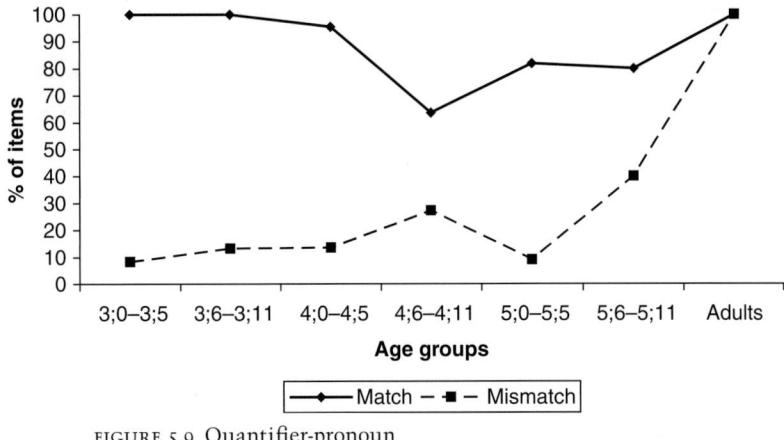

FIGURE 5.9 Quantifier-pronoun

Figure 5.9 shows the results related to the children's knowledge of Principle B as applied to the bound-variable cases. The line marked with diamonds shows the results of the match cases and the line marked with squares shows the results of the mismatch cases. When the question matched the picture, five- to six-year-old children gave correct answers about 80% of the time. When there was a mismatch, they answered correctly between 10 and 40% of the time.

To summarise, children between 5 and 6 did not demonstrate clear knowledge of the concept of quantified NPs such as 'every bear'. In fact, there was a discrepancy between the children's answers and the explanation they gave afterwards. The answers were wrong, but when asked to explain, they gave the right information, that is, they said that not all bears were involved in touching Mama Bear. This result is interesting because it poses a problem for the lexical learning hypothesis. The LLH predicts that by the time children have learnt the concept of 'every N' and that *limem* 'her/himself' is a reflexive and *li* 'him' a pronoun, s/he should be able to link these lexical items to the corresponding Principles A and B. But this is not the case here. The other intriguing result is that children still allow *li* to be locally bound sometimes, although they show knowledge of Principles A and B.

CONCLUDING REMARKS

The results obtained in this study with Seselwa-speaking children (binding experiments 1 to 4 based on Chien and Wexler's experiments (1990) and the results with the Morisyen-speaking children (Experiment 1, as used in Grimshaw and Rosen (1990)), complement each other and point towards one direction, namely that Creole-speaking children behave in a similar way when compared with children who speak other languages. They bind the reflexives locally, and with respect to pronouns, the Seselwa-speaking children also seem to violate Principle B in that they co-index the pronoun with a local antecedent. However, this violation is, strictly speaking, not a violation, because the current adult target system still allows pronouns to be locally bound, which was an option in the early stages of Seselwa. If reconsidered from this perspective, it means that the 4;0 and 5;0 children do not make mistakes. The presence of *limem* strongly competing with *li* in marking local antecedents is a typical example of variable input that gives the children a hard time. The dip in the two groups (4;6–4;11) and (5;0–5;5) replicated in all the experiments can be accounted for by the variable nature of the input and also because at school these children get a conventional language model in French and English but not in Seselwa. Thus, this inconsistent behaviour of children is not surprising.

This development is indeed interesting for several reasons. The results on Seselwa support the view that cross-linguistically children seem to violate Principle B during acquisition. The use of *li* to mark non-local and local antecedents, as Seselwa-acquiring children do, is reminiscent of the early stages of creolisation (as discussed by Carden and Stewart 1989). It seems that these Seselwa-acquiring children, in the face of variable input and in the absence of a conventional language model, re-creolise their grammars. In other words, it could be that in the absence of a conventional language model, children fall back on a default option available in UG. Briscoe (2002a, b) has also proposed that Creole learners (in creolisation) keep their default option as a result of being exposed to inconclusive primary linguistic data. He explains that this learning behaviour is a direct result of the Bayesian parameter-setting procedure, commonly assumed in a computational simulation and mathematical modelling of the language development framework.

6   Double-object constructions

INTRODUCTION

Many studies have confirmed that the syntactic behaviour of verbs is closely tied to their meaning (Hale and Keyser 1987, Levin 1993). This means that knowing the meaning of a verb is crucial in determining its behaviour. Further, verbs fall into classes according to shared behaviour that shows common meaning components. The close links between verb behaviour and meaning on the one hand, and the classification of verbs of the same semantic type on the other, are manifested across languages of the world. Although interesting individual differences between languages have been demonstrated, there are great similarities between languages with respect to meaning components and classes of verbs, and the expression of their arguments. Studies of diathesis alternations reveal clearly that verbs fall into classes on the grounds of common meaning components. The members of a class have a range of properties that they share with each other including the expression and interpretation of their arguments, related morphological forms, etc.

In this chapter, the case of verbs of transfer and communication will be discussed. It will be argued that the double-object construction (hereafter DOC) is the default structure associated with ditransitive verbs available to children by Universal Grammar. If we assume this, children are then expected to acquire and produce this structure more easily than the prepositional ditransitive construction (hereafter PDC). Both English and Dutch acquisition studies seem to point in this direction. Here we will take a look at two Creole languages, Morisyen and Seselwa, which use both constructions, DOC and PDC. Creole children, however, I argue, exploit DOC from the beginning and use it productively. This, together with other acquisition factors, suggests strongly that DOC might very well be a default option of marking ditransitive constructions that children exploit when no language model is available.

DITRANSITIVE VERBS IN FIRST LANGUAGE ACQUISITION

In the preceding chapters we have seen that most Creole languages have DOC associated with ditransitive verbs. Bruyn *et al.* (1999), analysing early data on Sranan and Negerhollands, come to the conclusion that DOC had already appeared in the early stages of creolisation. Two reasons account for my conclusion that DOC is an unmarked option of UG. First, it is widespread in Creole languages, and second, its early appearance in the genesis of Creole languages as shown by Bruyn *et al.* (1999) for Saramaccan.

In the field of language acquisition, DOC has received a lot of attention ever since Baker's influential paper (1979) on the logical problem of language acquisition, showing how some argument-structure alternations (such as the ditransitive alternation) in English are limited in their productivity. Initially Baker assumed that children never make errors as seen in example (1):

(1) *John donated the library a book.

He also showed that children do not get negative evidence that would make them realise that (1) is ungrammatical. He thus hypothesised that children can acquire such rules by conservative learning, that is, on a verb-to-verb basis. Since then the overgeneralisation of DOC by children has been put forward as counter-evidence for those claiming the role of UG in language development (see Bowerman 1987). Many studies also showed that children do make errors with double-object constructions, as they use these for verbs that do not allow it. Mazurkewich and White (1984) gave examples of children's utterances such as 'I'll brush him his hair' (cf. also Gropen *et al.* 1989). Pinker (1989) showed that children do retreat from overgeneralised argument-structure alternations (including the ditransitive alternation) in English. Ting Ting and Gordon's (1998) study of the acquisition of DOC and PDC in Chinese interestingly confirms the surprising 'ease' with which Chinese children acquire DOC with verbs of obtaining (e.g. 'steal', 'buy') which involve deprivation rather than transfer as in English. Chinese violates a universal linking rule with these verbs as it assigns to the first object the source/loser role rather than the goal/beneficiary role.

Snyder and Stromswold (1997) observe that there is a widespread belief that children acquire prepositional ditransitives before double-object constructions. As pointed out by Bruyn et al. (1999), such a misconception has been maintained for a long time due to the fact that grammatical theories treated DOC as a marked phenomenon based on English data. Pinker (1984), however, pointed out that DOC is not acquired later than PDC. Instead, the two constructions are acquired more or less simultaneously. Early studies of children's ditransitive constructions showed that children had more difficulty in DOC imitation and comprehension tests than in PDC tests. This result is not surprising since children were confronted with two full NPs in the DOC sentences, as seen below (2):

(2) The teacher showed the girl the boy.

White (1987) showed that children between three and five years succeeded in imitating and acting PDC and DOC successfully. Gropen et al. (1989), analysing the CHILDES corpora of English spontaneous speech, came to the conclusion that there is no time lag between the appearance of DOC and PDC. Snyder and Stromswold (1997) also analysed the spontaneous speech as found in the CHILDES database of twelve native monolingual English children. Their findings can be summarised as: the acquisition of DOC and PDC were correlated. Almost all the children, except for one, acquired the DOC before the 'to'-ditransitives (that is PDC). The reverse development was not found. In addition, this finding could not be attributed to the frequency with which the children or parents used these constructions.

Snyder and Stromswold formulated an interesting theory of parametric learning that explains the attested developmental order. However, as Bruyn *et al.* (1999) pointed out, there is a severe empirical weakness in this analysis, namely it cannot account for the existence of languages such as French that do not have DOC.

SPONTANEOUS DATA

Before we turn to experimental data, let's look at some spontaneous data on Seselwa. The data illustrates the early stages in the acquisition of Seselwa. There are more DOCs than PDCs. Only three verbs, *done* 'to give', *aste* 'to buy' and *dir* 'to tell', are attested in examples (3–6): Examples of DOC:

(3) Ø in   don   mwen en doll
     Ø ASP   give   me   a   doll
     'She gave me a doll.' (Eloise 2;4)

(4) Mami i   don   Miss Tracy   gato
     Mum   ASP   give Miss Tracy   cake
     'Mum gave me cake.' (Benjamin 2;6)

Examples of PDC:

(5) Miss Tracy i   al   aste   biskwi   pu mwen
     Miss Tracy ASP   go   buy   biscuits   for me
     'Miss Tracy went to buy biscuits for me.' (Brigitte 2;11)

(6) Stefanie i   move, i   dir   en kekzoz   ek   Julio
     Stefanie ASP   bad   ASP   tell a   something   to   Julio
     'Stefanie is bad, she told something to Julio.' (Brigitte 2;11)

The following examples illustrate DOC and PDC in the Morisyen data:

(7) Mo   ti   don   twa gato
     ISG TNS   give   you sweet
     'I gave you sweets.' (Terry 2;4)

(8) Bougol ti   don   mwa dipen.
     Bougol TNS   give me   bread
     'Bougol gave me bread.' (Rodney 2;4)

(9) Lerla   li   don mwa kas   mo   aste bis   mwa.
    When 3SG give me   money 1SG buy bus   me
    'When he gives me money I buy a bus for me.' (Benito 2;7)

(10) Ø   al   aste gato   pu   mo   papa.
     Ø   go   buy   sweet for 1SG father
     'I go buy sweet for my father.' (Janick 2;11)

Examples of PDC:

(11) Mo   pu   aste   en pasti   pu   mwa
     1SG   MOD   buy   a lolly   for me
     'I will buy sweets for me.' (Terry 2;4)

(12) To   pu   dan   lalo   pu   mwa.
     2SG   MOD   give ladies fingers for me
     'You will give ladies fingers for me.' (Janick 2;11)

(13) Don mwa dite   mami   pu   Lurd.
     Give me   tea   mum   for Lourde
     'Give me tea Mum for Lourde.' (Janick 2;11)

(14) Ma   don   en   lot   pu   mwa.
     Mum   give one another   for me.
     'Mum, give another one for me.' (Terry 2;4)

Rodney (2;4), however, also uses the verbs *montre* 'to show' and *dir* 'tell' in DOCs:

(15) Mo   montre papi   sa.
     1SG   show   dad   this
     'I show dad this.' (Rodney 2;4)

(16) Dir mwa en lot.
     tell me   another
     'Tell me another [story].' (Rodney 2;4)

The fact that the data is cross-sectional in nature means that it is not possible to determine when these children first used a DOC and a PDC. The first conclusion from the data here is that in both child Seselwa and child Morisyen, DOC appears to be more common than PDC, similar to English and Dutch data. Second, there is a similarity in the choice of verbs that appear as first verbs in ditransitive constructions. In all corpora, the verb 'give' seems to be the first candidate in the DOC pattern (cf. Snyder and Stromswold 1997, Bruyn *et al.* 1999, among others).

Bryun *et al.* (1999) also analysed the French CHILDES data collected by Suppes *et al.* (1973). Although they could not find any evidence for the productive use of DOC in native French children, they did find the fixed formulae: '*donne moi X*' in Philippe's corpus. The first productive use of *donner* appears around 2;06.27,[1] followed by the first examples of PDC at 2;07.18. All indirect objects in Philippe's utterances with the verb *donner* are expressed as clitics on the verb (17) and (18), or as objects of the preposition à as seen in (19):

(17) Tu   m'   as   donne   un   grand   bout
     2SG   ISG CLI have   give   a   big   punch
     'You have given me a big punch.' (Philippe 2;06.27)   FRENCH

(18) C' est   papa   me   l'   a   donné   les   sous
     It is   dad   ISG CLI   2SG CLI   have   give   the   money
     'it was dad (who) gave me the money.' (Philippe 2;07.11) FRENCH

(19) Je   vais   lui   donner   une   fessée   à   Michel
     I   FUT   3SG CLI   give   a   spanking   to   Michel
     'I'll give Michel a good spanking.' (Philippe 2;08.15) FRENCH

(20) Je   te   le   donne   pour   que   tu   enlèves
     I   2SG CLI   3SG CLI   give   so   that   you   take away
     'I give it to you to take away.' (Philippe 2;11.00) FRENCH

Example (20) shows the correct order of the clitics [NP CLI (IO) CLI (DO) V...] by the age of 2;11. The previous examples show that this French child uses the [CLI V] format quite early. So, the French data could be interpreted as: if clitics are present, the DOC will be absent. It looks as if in the case of the French child Philippe, he does not receive any DOC in the input and thus does not produce any DOC.[2] However, even the fixed formulaic structures such as '*donne moi X*'

---

[1] The child's age is denoted using the format (years;months.days).

[2] As noted by Bruyn *et al.* (1999), a more thorough analysis of more French children might show different results. As such, the absence of DOC should not be taken for granted.

in early French could be cautiously interpreted as support for DOC as an unmarked value of UG for the realisation of ditransitive verbs that children are equipped with. On the other hand, data from early child grammars from three different languages, Dutch, English and Morisyen, show that when children receive DOC in their input, they use it quite productively too. The move from this type of grammar [+DOC] to the more adult-like grammar (that is retreating from this option), as it would be in the case of French, may be accounted for by the availability of clitics in the target grammar. In the case of English, Dutch and Creole children, they do not have to retreat from this option [+DOC] as the DOC format is part of the target grammar. So, children can carry on with the DOC pattern.

With respect to the Creole spontaneous data, I conclude at this stage that the Creole acquisition findings confirm the general tendency that has already been seen in English and Dutch acquisition studies: that is, DOC is obviously acquired easily. From the cross-linguistic data there seems to be no stage in which children use PDC without DOC. However, there is a stage in which both are absent. The first uses of ditransitive constructions involve the verb 'give'. Given that DOC is widespread in Creoles, I assume the ease of acquisition in Dutch, English and Morisyen suggests strongly that DOC is an unmarked value of UG and can therefore be regarded as a component in the computation of the mental grammar.

EXPERIMENTS

In this section, I evaluate the claim made in the previous section by looking at some experimental data with Seselwa-speaking children. As already mentioned in Chapter 4, the grammaticality judgment task has also proved adaptable for very young children. This is the reason I chose it for the investigation of the double-object constructions in children's grammar. The experiment was preceded by a pilot study to check the suitability of children for this experiment. Seventy-one children participated in the experiment with six adults as a control group.

Table 6.1 *DOC and PDC verbs in the ditransitive alternation with Seselwa children*

Semantic class	Ditransitive alternation		
Communication	DOC1*	DOC2†	PDC (ek)
Demande 'ask'	+	+	+
Rakonte 'tell'	+	+	−
Dir 'say'	+	+	+
Ekrir 'write'	+	+	−
Sante 'sing'	+	?+	−
Explike 'explain'	+	+	−

* DOC1 has the pattern NP3-NP2.
† DOC2 has the pattern NP2-NP3.

To recapitulate, children were presented a context referring to an event that took place at school, followed by two sentences for grammaticality judgments. The children were asked to choose one of these two sentences, 'John gave Paul a book' or 'John gave a book to Paul', or to say another sentence if they thought both sentences presented to them were not suitable. This means that there were thirty-two sentences in all, with sixteen verbs, as seen in Tables 6.1 and 6.2 (for further details see Appendix B). Eight verbs belonging to the group of verbs allowing a DOC and eight verbs allowing a PDC were tested. Of the eight DOC verbs there were three typically DOC verbs. This means that these three verbs were correct only if used with a DOC.

Props were used to make the context clear. The rationale for the experiment is twofold. I was investigating which types of structure children choose with which verb. Do they treat all verbs as having a DOC format or do they distinguish between verbs? If they do distinguish, then which verbs are used with a DOC and which with a PDC? I also aimed at finding out more about the nature of the PDC. The results of this experiment are illustrated in Figures 6.1 to 6.4.

Table 6.2 *DOC and PDC verbs in the benefactive Alternation with Seselwa children*

Semantic class	Benefactive alternation	
Transaction	DOC	PDC (pu)
Aste 'buy'	−	+
Kwi 'cook/bake'	−	+
Amene 'bring'	−	+
Rande 'return'	−	+
Montre 'show'	+	+
Peye 'pay'	−	+
Done 'give'	+	+
Desine 'draw'	−	+
Fer 'make'	−	+
Avoye 'send'	+	+

Figure 6.1 shows the percentage of correct and incorrect responses across all age groups for both sentences with a DOC and PDC context. In the DOC context column we have the percentage of ditransitive verbs with a DOC format that were answered with a DOC response, thus these are marked as correct. Examples (21) and (22) illustrate the answers:

(21) Warren ti   don   Kevin en draze
     Warren TNS give Kevin a   sweet
     'Warren gave Kevin a sweet.' (Warren 5;6)

(22) Cindy ti   avoy Annie en kado
     Cindy TNS send Annie a   present
     'Cindy sent Annie a present.' (Cindy 5;9)

Note, however, that this column does not include correct PDC responses to DOC verbs, i.e. if the verb has a DOC structure and the child chooses a PDC with it, it is not counted here. The percentage starts at around 64% in the youngest age group (3;0–3;5) and gradually climbs to 99% in the oldest group (5;6–5;11). These

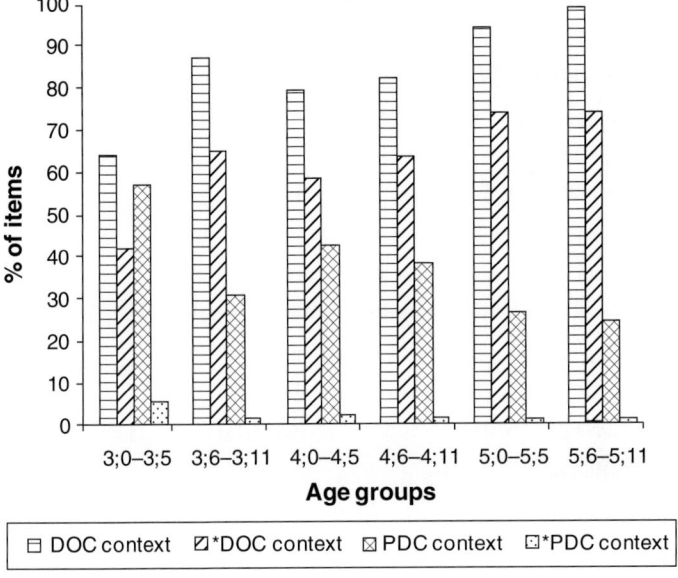

FIGURE 6.1 DOC versus PDC contexts

results reveal an increase of 35% across the groups that can be interpreted as evidence for the stabilising knowledge of DOC in child grammar.

The *DOC column shows the percentage of the eight verbs with a PDC format (either with *ek* or with *pu*) that were 'incorrectly' answered with a DOC response. Here we see a rough type of development with increasing tendency, starting with 42% in the first age group (3;0–3;5) and reaching 74% in the two last age groups (5;0–5;5 and 5;6–5;11). The verbs affected here are *aste* 'buy', *kwi* 'cook', *sante* 'sing', *rande* 'give back', *desine* 'draw', *fer* 'build', *done* 'give' and *amene* 'bring', which are accompanied by a preposition *pu* 'for'. Examples (23) to (28) illustrate the point. The star indicates that these sentences are not correct in the adult grammar.

(23) * Chloe   ti   aste   en bul Annie
         Chloe   TNS   buy   a   ball Annie
         'Chloe bought Annie a ball.' (Chloe 5;2)

(24) * Tania   ti   fer   en   sankarsel Edrick
        Tania   TNS   make   a   sandcastle Edrick
        'Tania made Edrick a sandcastle.' (Tania 4;4)

(25) * Raphael ti   sant Elmo en   sanson
        Raphael TNS   sing Elmo a   song
        'Raphael sang Elmo a song.' (Raphael 4;5)

(26) * Aysha   ti   rand   Nightarra en   liv
        Aysha   TNS   give back   Nightarra a   book
        Aysha gave a book back to Nightarra.' (Aysha 4;2)

(27) * Nissa   ti   pey   Mitch dis Rupi
        Nissa   TNS   pay   Mitch 10   rupees
        'Nissa paid Mitch 10 rupees.' (Nissa 3;11)

(28) * Wilnette ti   desin Zan   en   lakaz
        Wilnette TNS   draw   John a   house
        'Wilnette drew John a house.' (Wilnette 3;7)

The PDC column indicates the percentage of correct PDC responses
for the eight verbs with a PDC format, as illustrated by example (29):

(29) Aaron   ti   aste   en   bul   pu   Zan
       Aaron   TNS   buy   a   ball for John
       'Aaron bought a ball for John.' (Aaron 3;8)

In this case we have a decrease from 57% in the youngest group to
24% in the last age group. This decrease correlates with the increase
of DOC answers. Finally, there are only three DOC verbs that can
be answered with a PDC response. This value is a percentage of the
*PDC responses out of the total number of verbs (16). This column is
very low, almost insignificant, as it starts with 5% and disappears in
the last age group. This result makes clear that children may potentially classify these three DOC verbs as PDC verbs; however, they
retreat from this option later. The overall finding of Figure 6.1 highlights two major developments: one is that children across all age
groups incorrectly use the DOC structure with verbs with a PDC
format. The other is that there is a gradual increase in the percentage
of DOC responses to verbs with a PDC format as the children age,
thus indicating that overregularisation of the DOC pattern is taking

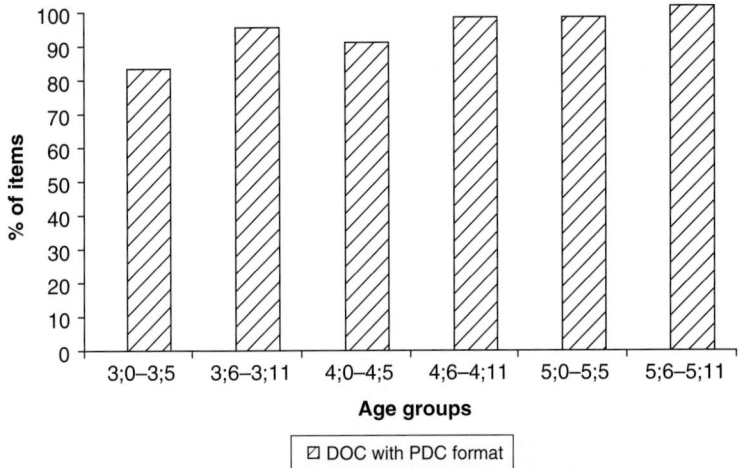

FIGURE 6.2 DOC verbs potentially having PDC format

place. Therefore, this confirms the view that DOC is acquired with little effort. Examples of PDC verbs used with a DOC are seen in (23) to (28). Note that the DOC pattern with PDC verbs, as seen in examples (30) and (31), is marginally accepted in Morisyen[3] but is considered the default construction in Seselwa.

The results of Figure 6.2 give us an overview of the correct percentage of verbs which normally have a DOC format, but which can potentially be used in a PDC format, with the values ranging from 81% for the youngest group (3;0–3;5) to almost 100% for the three oldest groups from 4;6 to 5;11. The verbs *demande*, *dir* and *montre* have been classified as DOC, as adult native speakers accept them in DOC constructions, but they are occasionally used in a PDC format with *ek* constructions. Furthermore, these verbs cannot be used with the preposition *pu* to express the benefactive alternation. The incorrect answers in the first three age groups refer to cases in which these verbs have been used with a *pu* construction. Only four children (from 3;6 onwards) used two of the three DOC verbs with a

---

[3] Officially, this is an ungrammatical structure. However, when individually asked, adults said that this structure was not of good quality but possible. Here it is obvious that the official decision influences the individual speaker's grammar.

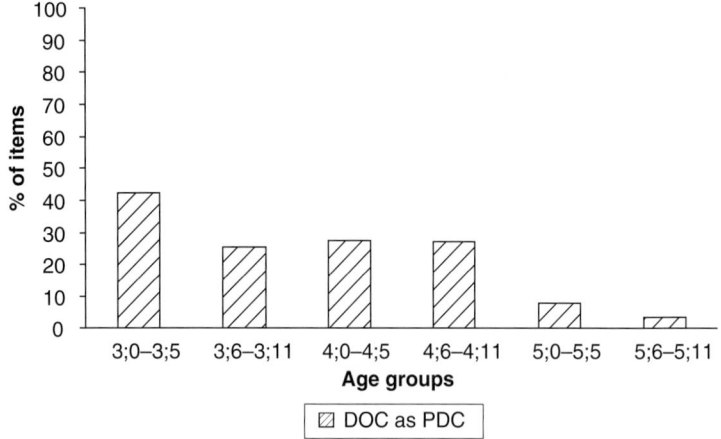

FIGURE 6.3 Verbs with DOC format used in PDC format

PDC *ek* construction. None of the 3;0-year-old children used *ek* at any point. Here are two examples of the two verbs (*dir* and *rakonte*) expressed with *ek* by older children:

(30) Raphael ti dir keksoz ek Shaun
     Raphael TNS say thing with Shaun
     'Raphael said something to Shaun.' (Raphael 4;5)

(31) Sherman ti rakont en zistwar ek Tim
     Sherman TNS tell a story with Tim
     'Sherman told a story to Tim.' (Sherman 4;10)

These results replicate clearly the results achieved in the previous figure in that they show the overwhelming use of the DOC pattern, regardless of the format associated with the verb in the adult grammar.

Out of the eight DOC verbs, five of them could be answered with a PDC and be counted as correct, as they allow a *pu* construction for the benefactive alternation. Figure 6.3 illustrates the percentage of these five DOC verbs that were answered with a PDC. The youngest age group starts with 42%, showing that young children were more inclined to use a DOC verb with a PDC. The percentage of DOC with a PDC gradually declines to 3% in the oldest

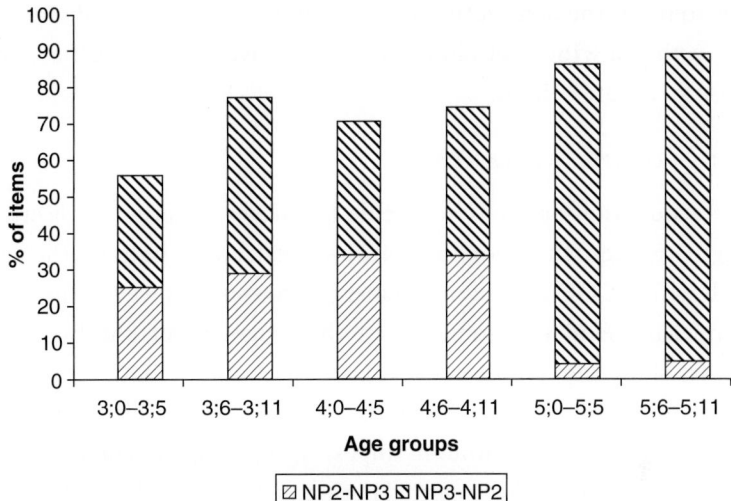

FIGURE 6.4 NP2-NP3 versus NP3-NP2

age group. This observation is compatible with the results shown in Figure 6.1.

Now a close look at Figure 6.4 shows an interesting development. The NP structures were counted when a child gave a DOC response to any of the sixteen sentences, including incorrect DOC responses to PDC contexts. Given that there were PDC responses to some of the sixteen sentences, the sum of the values for the NP2-NP3 and NP3-NP2 results may not always accumulate to 100%. The first age group (3;0–3;5) shows a result of 31% with the NP3-NP2 pattern ('*Zan don Pol en bul*' John gives Paul a ball) increasing to 48% in the next age group but falling to 37% and 41% in the next two groups, with a dramatic leap to 82% and 84% in the final two groups.

This result, together with the results of the incorrect PDC, makes it obvious that children overgeneralise the DOC structure to verbs with a PDC format. In doing so, they choose the NP3-NP2 structure, as seen in examples (23) to (28), that represents the syntactic frame of the classical double-object construction. Note that this type of error has also been observed with English-speaking children. The most common PDC structure is used with the preposition *pu* 'for' to mark the benefactive alternation, which is easily adjoined to any verb, showing that children did not have any difficulties with these structures either.

CONCLUDING REMARKS

The acquisition data of two Creole languages, together with cross-linguistic acquisition studies, throws considerable light on the ease with which DOC is used in an emerging system. However, the more compelling evidence comes from the judgment of children. The results show that children use a DOC with many PDC verbs, thus overregularising the DOC pattern. This finding can be interpreted as strong evidence for children imposing regularisation on the input. The use of DOC as the preferred option by Creole children, together with other acquisition findings, including bilingual language acquisition of Chinese and English (Yip and Matthews 2007), seem to support the view articulated earlier in this chapter, namely that DOC might be a default option in child grammar. Further support for this view comes from cross-linguistic studies showing that it is universally preferred. Children use PDCs with some regularity, too, as the default structure is always accompanied by the preposition *pu*. Both overgeneralisation and regularisation here seem to be mechanisms in first language acquisition in the absence of a conventional language model.

7   Passive constructions

INTRODUCTION

Passive is a widespread construction in languages, but it is not a universal one. Typological investigation has shown that there are languages with passive, languages without passive and languages with passive but without passive morphology. German, Dutch and French belong to the first group of languages, Yidin, and Enga (Papuan language) to the second group. Creole languages, as well as Chinese, belong to the third group of languages.

In the first part of this chapter I review the main theoretical approaches available in the literature on the acquisition of passive. I then take a closer look at the acquisition of passive constructions in Seselwa, supported by data on Morisyen. After a brief presentation of child spontaneous data, I analyse findings from two experiments conducted with Seselwa-speaking children bearing on central issues in the field, such as the emergence of passive constructions, their nature and the mechanisms children employ to acquire them. Finally, the implications of such findings are discussed with respect to the field of language acquisition.

PASSIVE IN FIRST LANGUAGE ACQUISITION

The acquisition of passive constructions is an area of argument structure that has been extensively studied in the field of first language acquisition. A look at the literature shows a vast number of studies based on spontaneous and experimental data showing differences on passives used by children, as compared to adults (cf. Bever 1970, de Villiers and de Villiers 1973, Maratsos 1974, Mills 1985, Pinker *et al.* 1987, among others).

One major finding on the acquisition of passive is that children show some sensitivity to semantic classes of verbs that affects the acquisition of passive. Sudhalter and Braine (1985) showed that a large group of children (40 per cent) perform better with action verbs than with mental verbs. Similar results were reported in Maratsos *et al.* (1985), Pinker *et al.* (1987) and Gordon and Chafetz (1990). Pinker *et al.* (1987) also studied the productivity of passive in spontaneous speech and in four experiments with three- to eight-year-old children. They found that in spontaneous speech children produced passives that did not exist in the input, such as *'is it all needled? She's scribbed.'* In the experiments children produced passives of novel verbs that they had been taught in the active. The researchers concluded that children are not conservative, especially not the ones below 5;5, although they have a tendency to passivise action verbs more readily than spatial verbs.

Another finding is that passives appear relatively late, around 4;0 years of age in English spontaneous data. In further experiments it became obvious that children's performance on reversible passives was not errorless both at the production and comprehension levels, although these children did distinguish active from passive constructions (de Villiers and de Villiers 1973, Horgan 1978, Mills 1985).

It has also been argued that the acquisition of passive seems to be affected by the frequency of passive in the input. Allen and Crago (1996), among others, have shown that children overgeneralise passive constructions to verbs that do not passivise. They argue that this could not have been encountered in the input. Brooks and Tomasello (1999) taught children two novel verbs in either the active transitive or passive structure. The results suggest that children have some verb representation of the active structure and a weaker representation of the passive structure. Bencini and Valian (2008) used a priming study to argue that children around the age of three have abstract knowledge of full passives.

Fox, Grodzinsky and Crain (1995), investigating the comprehension of long and short passives of mental verbs and physical action verbs with children aged 3;6–5;5, report that eight out of thirteen children have comprehension problems only with the long passives of mental verbs. The long and short passives of action verbs are comprehended 100 per cent correctly, as are the short passives of mental verbs. The results indicate that the problem the children had with passives of mental verbs may be partly associated with the *by-phrase*. The authors suggest that children have problems with the by-phrases of passives of mental verbs because they do not get access to the mechanism linking the interpretation of the by-phrase to the thematic information of the implicit argument.

Borer and Wexler (1987), one of the early studies on passive, argued that children are not capable of comprehending and producing non-actional passives because they are unable to form A-chains. Actional passives, on the other hand, are understood successfully because children interpret these sentences as adjectival passives. According to these two scholars, the ability to form A-chains is determined biologically. More recently Israel, Johnson and Brooks (2000) argued that the earliest passive structures are adjectival.

To recapitulate, we find a substantial body of research done on the acquisition of passive structures. However, there has been no research done on the acquisition of Creole passive, which promises to be an interesting enterprise, given that Creole passive has no morphology.

SPONTANEOUS DATA

The first passive sentences are produced between the ages of 2;5 and 3;0. This Seselwa data shows that these children produce a few passive-like sentences, especially the short and *geny/ganny* 'get' passive construction, around this time. While *geny* passives were attested in all of the nine children's corpora, short passives were rare. Some examples are:

(1) Mo frer   in   ganny lafiev
    My brother ASP   get   fever
    'My brother has got fever.' (Eloise 2;4)

(2) So   sulyer in   trempe
    his   shoe   ASP   wet
    'His shoe got wet.' (Andre 2;5)

(3) Vwar marmay in   ganny   dimal
    Look child   ASP   get   hurt
    'Look at the child, he has got hurt.' (Stefanie 2;9)

(4) Benjamin in   geny bate   ek   Miss Tracy
    Benjamin ASP   get   smack   with Miss Tracy
    'Benjamin has been smacked by Miss Tracy.' (Brigitte 2;11)

A look at the Morisyen data confirms the observation that children produce a few passives. There is no example of long passive in the corpora. The following examples (5–11) illustrate the sentences that could be interpreted as passive types in children's data:

(5) Get   bondye so   liku   in   kase.
    look god   his   neck   ASP   break
    'Look, god's neck is broken.' (Terry 2;4)

(6) Furmi la   fin   mor.
    ant   DET   ASP   dead
    'The ant is dead.' (Benito 2;7)[1]

(7) Garaz kase.
    garage break
    'The garage is broken.'
    (Benito 2;7, pointing at the broken box)

(8) Mo   lakaz kase   sa.
    my   house break   there
    'My house is broken.' (Janick 2;11, pointing at the broken house)

(9) Mo   lakaz [...] ar   li   sa   bebet.
    my   house [...] by   him/her   this animal
    'My house is broken by him, this animal.' (Janick 2;11)[2]

---

[1] He says this after he killed the ant on the table with his fingers.
[2] Janick is talking to her godmother and is telling her that Yanick broke her house. *Sa bebet* is an insult.

(10) Mo   zano   in   perdi.
     my   earring   ASP   lose
     'My earrings are lost.' (Janick 2;11)[3]

(11) Mo   'n   geny   bate   akoz   mo   'n   sali   mo   savat.
     I   ASP   get   flog   because   I   ASP   dirt   my   shoe
     'I got a flogging because I made my shoes dirty.' (Bertrand 3;3)

Some of these examples (5–8) are adjectival passives. Example (11) is a *geny*-passive. The data is interesting because it offers a similar picture to the one already seen in the development of passive in other languages. First, passive constructions are rare in spontaneous speech. Second, examples of by-phrases are rare. Example 9 illustrates the point. Third, it is difficult to distinguish verbal from adjectival passives, given the fact that there is no overt passive morphology. However, although scarce, there are examples of passive constructions in early Creole grammars (around the age of 2;7). This is consistent with the findings in the acquisition literature.

EXPERIMENTS

Two types of experiment were administered: one comprehension and one production. A picture-pointing paradigm was chosen for the comprehension experiment. In this experiment, the focus is on the investigation of the comprehension of passive sentences. For the elicited production experiment I chose the sentence completion task.

Comprehension experiment

As already mentioned, this experiment was designed to test Seselwa-children's knowledge of verbal and adjectival passive interpretation in short passive sentences. The experiment aimed at showing whether children made a difference in the interpretation of these passives. I tested eighty-two children from 3;0 to 6;0 years. There were six adults as a control group.

---

[3] This is the answer Janick gives when her mum asks for her earrings.

Table 7.1 *Transitive active sentences used in the experiment*

Test sentences	English equivalents
Sa tifi pe beny sa garson	The girl washes the boy
Sa garson la pe beny sa tifi	The boy washes the girl
Sa tediber pe kud sa tifi	The teddy bear mends the girl
Sa tifi pe kud sa tediber	The girl mends the teddy
Sa madam pe penn sa misie	The woman paints the man
Sa misie pe penn sa madam	The man paints the woman
Sa misie pe manz sa pwason	The man eats the fish
Sa pwason pe manz sa misie	The fish eats the man
Sa lelefan pe kup sa ti garson	The elephant cuts the boy
Sa ti garson pe kup sa lelefan	The boy cuts the elephant
Sa loto pe bit ek sa kamyion	The car hits the lorry
Sa kamyion pe bit ek sa loto	The lorry hits the car

A set of transitive active sentences was constructed and can be found in Table 7.1. Six verbs were selected (*benye* 'wash', *kud* 'mend', *penn* 'paint' *manze* 'eat', *bite* 'hit' and *kupe* 'cut') and each verb was presented twice in each of the four sentence types listed below (12 to 15), yielding a total of forty-eight sentences per child.

In a trial run, sentences in the present tense *sa tifi beny sa garson* did not work. Thus I marked the Seselwa verbs with the aspect marker *pe* (progressive), which drastically improved the child's comprehension of the sentences. The same pair of noun phrases is used for both presentations of a particular verb. The word order and hence the thematic roles are reversed in the second sentence (the full verbal passive). For each active sentence there is a corresponding full passive, a short passive and a short ambiguous passive (potentially adjectival) sentence. For each verb there are four pictures drawn on an A4 sheet of paper. The pictures correspond to (1) a transitive response, (2) a reversal response, (3) adjectival-stative response and (4) a semantic distracter.

The four pictures for the verb *kud* 'mend' are (1) a girl mending a teddy, (2) a teddy mending a girl, (3) a mended teddy (sitting down) and (4) a mended girl (a rag doll). The agent is not depicted in the latter two pictures. This means that the sentence presented with the pictures determines which picture corresponds to a transitive or reversal response. Here are some examples of the sentences presented:

Simple active sentence:

(12) Sa   tifi   pe   kud   sa   tediber.
     DET   girl   PROG   mend   DET   teddy bear
     'The girl mends (is mending) the teddy.'

Full verbal passive sentence:

(13) Sa   tediber   fin   kud   par/ek   sa   tifi.
     DET   teddy bear ASP   mend   by   DET   girl
     'The teddy bear is mended by the girl.'

Short passive sentence:

(14) Sa   tediber   pe   kud.
     DET   teddy bear PROG   mend
     'The teddy bear is being mended.'

Short ambiguous passive sentence:

(15) Sa   tediber   fin   kud.
     DET   teddy bear ASP   mend
     'The teddy bear is mended.'

Sentences (13) and (15) differ in that sentence (13) has an *ek/par*-phrase (by-phrase). Sentence (13) has both argument and adjunct, while sentence (15) does not. Sentence (15) is considered to be ambiguous by adult native speakers. Sentence (14) is a short passive. There is ambiguity in the two short passive forms as sentence (14) is formed with *pe*, while sentence (15) is formed with *fin*. Both sentences allow for two interpretations, one as a verbal (action) passive and one as an adjectival (stative) passive.

Active sentence (a picture shows a man putting a fish on a fork into his mouth):

(16) Sa   misie   pe   manz   sa   pwason
DET   man   ASP   eat   DET   fish
'The man eats the fish.'

Active sentence (a picture shows a shark eating a man in the sea):

(17) Sa   pwason   pe   manz   sa   misie
DET   fish   ASP   eat   DET   man
'The fish eats the man.'

Full verbal passive sentence (a picture shows a man putting a fish on a fork into his mouth):

(18) Sa   pwason   fin   manze   par/ek   sa   misie
DET   fish   ASP   eat   by   DET   man
'The fish is eaten by the man.'

Full verbal passive sentence (a picture shows a shark eating a man in the sea):

(19) Sa   misie   fin   manze   par   sa   pwason
DET   man   ASP   eat   by   DET   fish
'The man is eaten by the fish.'

Short progressive passive sentence (a picture shows a man putting a fish on a fork into his mouth):

(20) Sa   pwason   pe   manze
DET   fish   PROG   eat
'The fish is being eaten.'

Short progressive passive sentence (a picture shows a shark eating a man in the sea):

(21) Sa   misie   pe   manze
DET   man   PROG   eat
'The man is being eaten.'

Ambiguous passive sentence (a picture shows a man putting a fish on a fork into his mouth):

(22) Sa   pwason   fin   manze
     DET   fish   ASP   eat
     'The fish is eaten.'

Ambiguous passive sentence (a picture shows a shark eating a man in the sea):

(23) Sa   misie   fin   manze
     DET   man   ASP   eat
     'The man is eaten.'

The task is to get the child to look at four pictures and to listen carefully to a spoken sentence, before pointing to the one picture that s/he thinks best described the sentence. The children are told that more than one picture might be correct, but they should limit themselves to one picture. However, many children still make two choices, so only the first choice is considered in the results. All for-ty-eight sentences are presented in one session and the experiment takes approximately twenty minutes to administer. The responses are coded into the following four categories: (1) *A Transitive (actional) response* is a correct response for all the sentence types in which both the agent and patient thematic roles were correctly depicted. For the ambiguous sentences an adjectival response is also correct. The transitive responses to the three passive sentences correspond to a verbal passive interpretation. (2) *A Reversal response* is a response in which the correct thematic roles assigned to the subject and object are reversed. For the short progressive passive and the ambiguous passive a reversal response is taken to be the one in which the subject is assigned an agent role. (3) *An Adjectival (stative) response* is one in which a stative interpretation of the sentence is given. This means that the subject NP is in the state described by the verb. For the active sentences an adjectival response is taken to

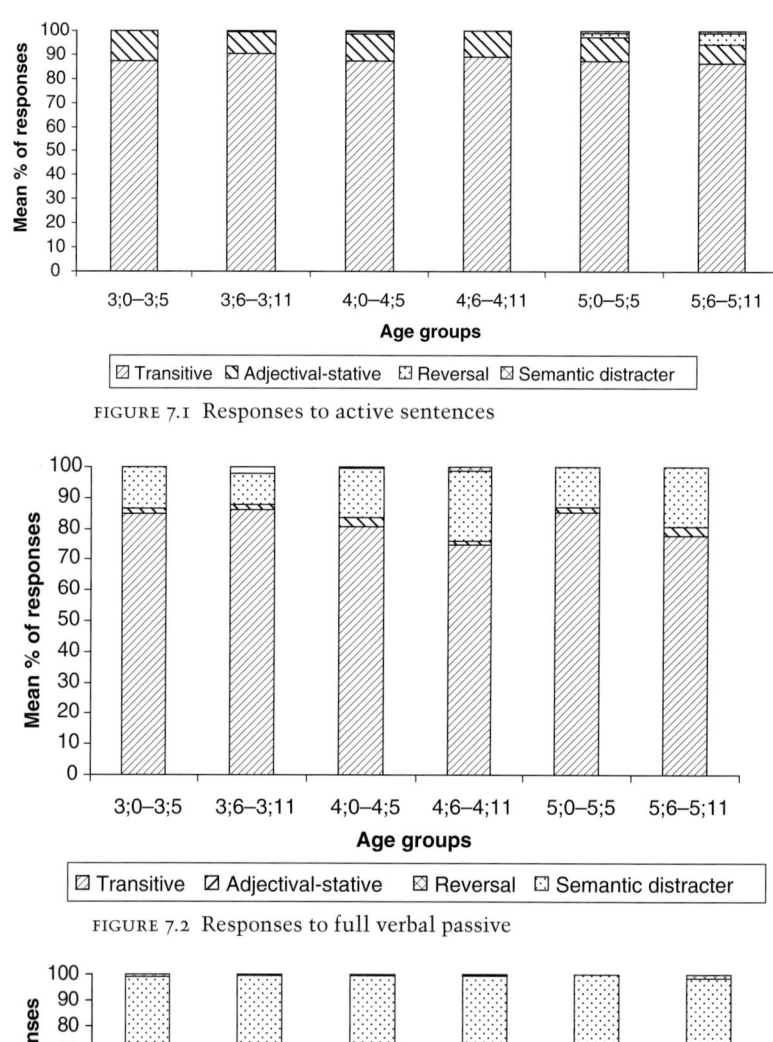

FIGURE 7.1 Responses to active sentences

FIGURE 7.2 Responses to full verbal passive

FIGURE 7.3 Responses to ambiguous passive sentences

be the one in which the object NP is in the state described by the verb. (4) *A Semantic distracter response* is one in which the subject in the active sentences, or the oblique object NP in full passive sentences, or an unmentioned NP in the short passives is described by the verb. The test sentences are all listed in Appendix C. Figures 7.1 to 7.3 illustrate the results of the experiment.

The results show the following picture: the majority of the responses fall into transitive or adjectival responses. This can be seen in Figures 7.1 to 7.3. The transitive response for the three types of sentence shows that the majority of transitive responses is made for active and full verbal passive sentences. A comparison of Figures 7.1 and 7.3 reveals that generally children make significantly fewer transitive responses for the ambiguous passive sentences than the other types of sentence (active sentences and full verbal passives). The group's performance on the active sentences is better than on the ambiguous passives.

The adjectival response for the active and full verbal passive sentences is quite low, as seen in Figure 7.1 and Figure 7.2. Figure 7.3 shows that the percentages of adjectival responses to ambiguous passive sentences range from 33% to 53%. Children in the youngest age group (3;0–3;5) seem to have more reversal answers to ambiguous passives (44%) than the other groups. This is explained given that children at this age also have null subjects in their grammars. This contributes to making the ambiguous passive sentences difficult. From the second-youngest age group (3;6–3;11) upwards the percentage for reversals varies between 24% and 28%.

As can be seen from all three figures, generally there is a very low level of reversal responses for the active sentences. In Figure 7.2 for the full verbal passive sentences, the level of reversal responses is relatively low for most of the age groups. But there is an exception to this pattern in two of the age groups, 4;6–4;11 and 5;6–5;11. These data reveal that children at a certain age may be having problems with assigning thematic roles in full passives because they are more sensitive to pragmatic factors. Although at this stage I do not have

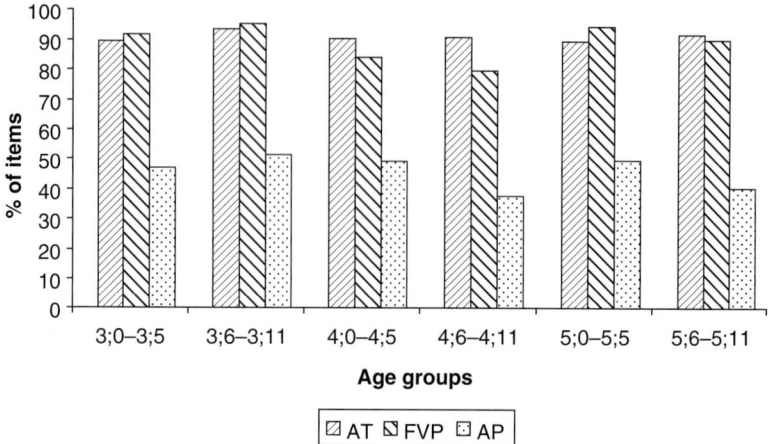

FIGURE 7.4 Transitive responses to the three types of sentences

a coherent explanation for this behaviour, it is worth noting that these two age groups are also known for their troublesome behaviour in the binding experiments. I will come back to this issue later. As can be seen in Figure 7.3 for the ambiguous passive sentences, a high percentage of reversal responses across all groups is seen. It could be that children interpret the patients in these sentences as subjects, and thus these sentences as short active sentences.

There are very few semantic distracter responses for all the three types of sentence (active sentences, full verbal passives and ambiguous passives) across all age groups. Figures 7.4 to 7.7 show the proportion of active transitive (AT), full verbal passives (FVP) and ambiguous passives (AP) for the six age groups.

In Figure 7.4 we have the percentages of responses for active transitive, full verbal passive and ambiguous passive. Both the active transitive responses and full verbal passive responses are high as compared to the adjectival passive responses, and they are both steady across all groups, that is between 80 and 90 per cent. This response pattern is different to that of the English children tested by van der Lely (1996). These Creole-speaking children here do not make significantly more transitive (correct) responses to the active

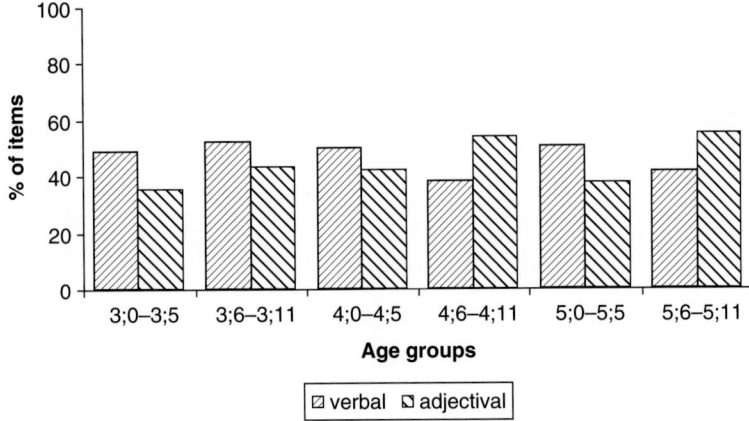

FIGURE 7.5 Verbal and adjectival responses to ambiguous passives

sentences than to the full verbal passive. The ambiguous passive responses (which include both the English short progressive passive and the adjectival passive) range between 30 and 50 per cent. This stands in contrast to the results of the active sentences and full verbal passives.

Figure 7.5 compares the verbal and adjectival responses when children are presented with an ambiguous passive only. It shows clearly that a verbal response is preferred most of the time. However, there is a slight increase in adjectival responses in two older groups (4;6–4;11) and (5;6–5;11).

Figure 7.6 shows the verbal, adjectival and both responses of the children. It is interesting to see that across all groups there are children who gave both a verbal and adjectival response to ambiguous passives, although the percentage is low. When presented with an ambiguous passive, children pick a picture that matches with the verbal response. For example, if, when presented with sentence (15) (the teddy bear is mended), the child picks picture (3) (which shows the girl mending the teddy), then the child has a verbal response, as one child called Nelly does. If the child picks picture (1) (which shows the mended teddy sitting), then it is considered to be an adjectival

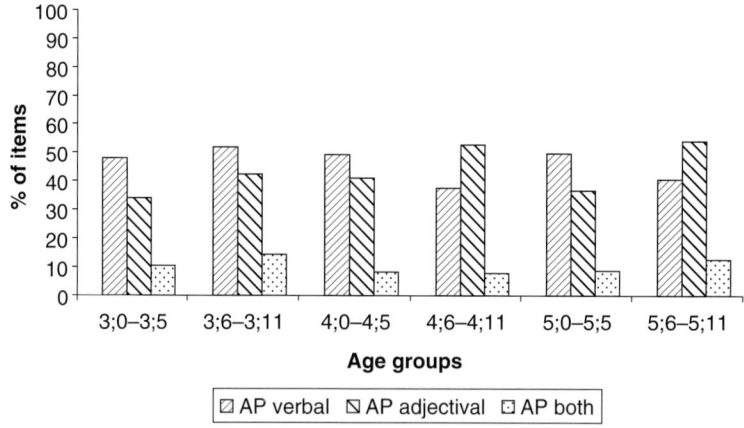

FIGURE 7.6 AP responses

response, as Benjamin T. does. This result is interesting because it shows that Creole-speaking children have more (actional) verbal responses than adjectival (stative) responses for ambiguous passive. This finding in turn strongly supports the claim that children from an early age have a verbal representation of passive.

Figure 7.7 shows the responses to the full verbal passives. The adjectival-stative interpretation of the full passive sentences is quite low in general across all groups, between 12 and 25 per cent. The verbal response ranges between 80 and 95 per cent across all the groups. This means that children give a verbal interpretation of full verbal passive in more than 80 per cent of the cases.

This experiment has investigated Creole-speaking children's syntactic abilities by analysing the pattern of responses in a sentence comprehension task. The comprehension of four types of sentences (active, full passive, short passive and ambiguous passive) has been investigated. The experiment focused on the ability of the children to form a transitive actional verbal passive interpretation versus an adjectival (stative) passive interpretation. To be able to consider the different responses, I used the picture-pointing paradigm designed by van der Lely (1996). The study reveals that Creole-speaking children interpret transitive verbal passive sentences at an early age

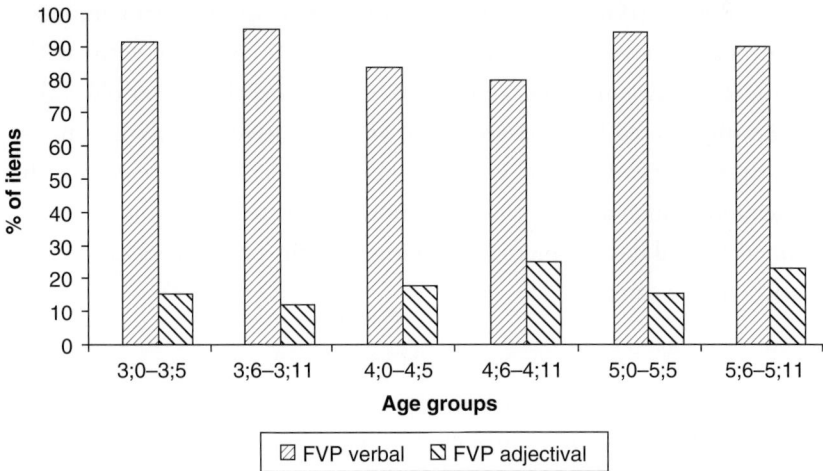

FIGURE 7.7 Verbal and adjectival responses to full verb passives

(youngest children 3;0). The children show a strong preference for the verbal interpretation of ambiguous passive sentences. The data indicate that Creole children do have problems deriving the syntactic representation underlying an adjectival passive sentence, but have fewer problems with the full verbal passive. The findings from this study give us some insight into the acquisition of passive in a language without passive morphology. At the same time they also provide new empirical evidence for the view that children have an understanding of verbal passive from an early age.

Production experiment

Whether children's short passives have implicit arguments is an issue that has been studied in a few studies only. The ones I have included for discussion here all involve the passives of alternating causative verbs. These verbs were chosen because inferred participants and verbal arguments have to be distinguished. By considering only verbs that allow a reading without an external causer, and by comparing passives of causative verbs with their anti-causative counterparts, these studies focus on the presence/absence of implicit arguments.

Roeper (1987b) uses various comprehension experiments and contrasts passives of causative verbs with anti-causative verbs with children between three and seven years. The three-year-old children interpreted both passives and anti-causatives as having implicit arguments. When they were asked to select a picture to match a sentence such as (24), children chose a picture including an agent 'breaker' and not the picture showing only the breaking of the glass, without the causer:

(24)   The glass broke

Roeper thus argues that this causative interpretation of anti-causatives is due to the preference children give to pictures with agents. Roeper interprets this high frequency of the causative interpretation with passives as evidence that children's passives have an implicit argument.

Another study, conducted by Teng (1989), also uses a picture-selection task in which the sentences have an instrumental prepositional phrase. She shows that four-year-old children can link the instrumental phrase to the implicit argument in a passive.

Verrips (1992, 1993) conducts two experiments with Dutch children between 4;2 and 6;9. A story is told to the children followed by a question. For each story-answer there are at least two possible answers, one with and the other without reference to the agent. The appropriate answer depends on the verb used (passive or anti-causative). In the story, one of the rabbits is frying eggs in a frying pan and the children are getting ready in the meantime. The rabbit has put butter in a pan on the stove. The question in (25) is asked:

(25)   'Why was the butter melted?'

Adults answered with reference to the agent, explaining why the rabbit wanted to melt the butter. This answer (26) is possible, because the implicit agent (the rabbit) is represented in an adult's representation of a passive. The answer (27) is not appropriate because it does not refer to the implicit agent:

(26)   'Because the rabbit wanted to fry an egg.' (purpose)

(27)   'Because it was lying in the sun.' (cause)

Verrips conducted this experiment with 'why' and 'how' as the question words. From the results Verrips concludes that passives are represented with implicit arguments for four-year-old children. However, Verrips could not decide for sure whether the findings really reflect the presence of a syntactic argument or the inference from context of an implied participant. If the results reflect children's inference of an agent from the context, then this explanation applies to both passive and anti-causatives. But if the results reflect the presence of a syntactic argument, it has to be assumed that children represent anti-causatives as if they were passive without overt morphology. This is the reason why she designed another experiment to tease apart the effects of contextual interference and syntactic representation.

The experiment involved a sentence-completion task. This experiment will be presented in detail later in this section. The results from Verrips (1996) clearly show that the majority of the children have a syntactic representation of an implicit argument in passives. These results are particularly interesting, as they are relevant for the youngest age groups.

Roeper (1987b), Teng (1989) and Verrips (1996) adduce both empirical and theoretical arguments for the claim that early child passives contain implicit arguments. Verrips' study is especially relevant to my study because her results show that children produce anti-causatives as passives without morphology, which is reminiscent of Creole passives. The absence of morphological marking, the lack of *by-phrases* and the preference for highly transitive action verbs are common to both children's passives and Creole passives. The similarities are striking. Here it is important to investigate whether there is evidence that Seselwa-speaking children's interpretation of passive involves implicit arguments.

Two hypotheses were tested here: the first one tested the problem children have with *by-phrase* passives. The second hypothesis tested whether Seselwa-speaking children's passives (possibly Creole-speaking children) – like adult passives – have implicit arguments.

The experiment involves a sentence-completion task as designed by Verrips (1996). Children look at a picture depicting an activity. The picture is then described to the child by the experimenter. The child is asked to complete the experimenter's sentence. Each picture description ends with the preposition 'with'. Each picture shows both an accompaniment and an instrument for the activity. The experiment makes use of the distribution of instrumental phrases to check whether implicit arguments are represented in children's passives. Note the contrast between the following examples:

(28) Get   en sat ape   rule ek   en baton.
     look a   cat PROG   roll with a   stick
     'Here a cat is rolling over with a stick.'

(29) Get   en sat fin ganny rule ek   en baton.
     look a   cat ASP get   roll with a   stick
     'Here a cat is rolled over with a stick.'

In (28) the phrase introduced by *ek* has an object reading. The cat is rolling the stick. In (29) an accompaniment reading is also possible, the cat is rolling around with a stick. Further, it allows an instrumental reading. The stick is the instrument with an implicit agent. The instrumental reading with *ek*-sentences can be regarded as a signal for implicit arguments.

It is assumed that if children complete the with-phrase as an instrument phrase, then the child's representation of the sentence includes an agent. When the picture description contains a short passive, the instrument response is an indication for the presence of an implicit agent. Example (30) is an illustration:

(30) Get   en karusel   ape   vire ek ...
     look a   merry-go-round   PROG turn with ...
     'Here a merry-go-round is turned with ...'

It is the description of a merry-go-round with a dog standing on it. A boy is pushing it with a spade, making it turn. The *ek*-phrase can refer to an *accompaniment* (a dog standing on the merry-go-round) or an *instrument* (a spade which the boy pushes the merry-go-round with). The picture illustrates the two possibilities. If the child completes the sentence with the sentence *ek en lapel* 'with a spade', this response is scored as an instrument response. This type of response is taken to be an indication of the child's representation of the sentence with an implicit agent.

There are three test conditions: anti-causative verbs, passives of transitive verbs and passives of alternating verbs. Transitive verbs are different from alternating verbs in that they have no counterpart. Furthermore it is possible that they are not conceivable without an agent-argument. Take the verb 'eat' that automatically implies an implicit argument. In the anti-causative condition, the accompaniment reading is grammatical. In the passive condition both readings are grammatical. As this experiment was originally designed for Dutch, some changes were made to suit Seselwa, which does not have the copula equivalent to 'be' in English. After careful discussion and in agreement with adult Seselwa speakers, I used zero-copula sentences. However, the condition was kept that a creative activity was described. The activity was performed with an instrument (a paintbrush) and the result (the picture) consisted of two parts (a woman with a dog). The picture contained the same contrast as the pictures for the other activity, but the description was different.

Control sentences were included to check children's knowledge of instrument-phrases. They were designed to help differentiate between children who have instrument-responses from those who do not. However, all the children investigated were well acquainted with instrument-responses. Overall, there were four test-conditions and one control, listed here for illustration (31–34).

Transitive verb, passive:

(31) Gete, en pom ape ganny manze ek ...
     look an apple PROG get eat with...
     'Here an apple is eaten with...'
     (zoranz, furset)(orange, fork)

Alternating verb, passive:

(32) Gete, en ros fin rule ek ...
      look a   rock ASP roll with ...
      'Here a rock is rolled with...'
      (en zwazo lor li, en lapel)(a bird on top, a spade)

Alternating verb, anti-causative:

(33) Gete, en lisyen ape rule ek ...
      Look a   dog PROG roll with ...
      'Here a dog is rolling with...'
      (bul, balye) (ball, broom)

Zero-copula:

(34) Pyer pe penn. Sa pu en madam ek ...
      Peter ASP paint. This MOD a woman with ...
      'Peter is painting. This will be a woman with ... '
      (lisyen, peinso) (dog, paintbrush)

Control transitive verb, active:

(35) Pyer pe penn latab ek ...
      Peter ASP paint table with ...
      'Peter is painting the table with ... '
      (sez, peinso) (chair, paintbrush)

A total of twenty-six children between 2;6 and 3;11 and six adults as a control group participated in the experiment. Each participant was presented with fifteen items, all in the same order. A full list of all the items is provided in Appendix C. The number of instrument and accompaniment responses per age group per condition is given in Tables 7.2 and 7.3.

Following Verrips (1996), two goals were set in this experiment: to check if the results favour the pragmatic inference theory or the syntactic theory and to test whether implicit arguments are represented in children's passives. The pragmatic inference theory predicts that children will give as many or as few instrument responses in the copula condition as in the other conditions. The syntactic

Table 7.2 *Instrumental and accompaniment responses*

Age groups	Responses	TRP	ALP (Caus. Pass.)	ALE (Anti- Caus.)	Copula	Control TRA
2;6–2;11	Instrument	8	8	5	13	7
(8 children)	Accompaniment	24	16	19	11	9
3;0–3;5	Instrument	19	20	17	27	14
(11 children)	Accompaniment	25	13	16	6	8
3;6–3;11	Instrument	22	15	14	17	12
(7 children)	Accompaniment	6	6	7	4	2

Table 7.3 *Instrumental responses for transitive and alternating passives*

Age groups	Transitive passive (TRP)	Alternating passive (ALP)
2;6–2;11	8	8
3;0–3;5	19	20
3;6–3;11	22	15

theory predicts that the instrumental responses will be less in the copula condition when compared to the other conditions. A look at the data shows that the response pattern in the copula condition is not clearly different from the other conditions. The accompaniment reading in all the three groups is relatively low as compared to the others. However, this is not the case with instrumental responses. In the youngest group, the instrumental response is higher than the instrumental responses of the other conditions. The same applies for the second group. In these cases I assume that children are applying some sort of non-syntactic strategy; that is they are paying more attention to the picture than to the syntactic structure of the sentence. However, in the oldest group the response for the copula condition is similar to the others. Although the frequency of instrument responses is not very low, it is important to note that there is no increase in the number with age. Based on these results, it is possible to interpret an instrument response to a passive or anti-causative as reflecting the syntactic property of the sentence and not as a strategy based on inference from the context or picture.

The next issue addressed here is whether children's interpretation of passive involves an implicit argument. The results do not show us a clear development at this point. In the youngest group, children give both instrumental and accompaniment responses to both transitive and alternating passive conditions. However, the accompaniment responses are slightly higher than the instrumental responses. This observation confirms to some extent that the children's representation of the experimental sentences involves an implicit agent. In the second group (children between 3;0 and 3;5), the instrumental and accompaniment responses are very similar to each other, as shown in Table 7.2, while the majority of the 3;6–3;11-year-old group give an instrumental response.

When transitive verbs (TRP) are compared to their counterparts, i.e. alternating verbs (ALP), there is no quantitative difference in the first two groups, as seen in Table 7.3. But there is a quantitative difference in the oldest group, with more instrumental responses with transitive verbs. The majority of the children give an instrumental response. This is an indication that passives of alternating verbs are represented differently from passives of transitive verbs. The syntactic theory predicts that passives of transitive verbs would yield more instrumental responses. This is confirmed here to some extent.

These results do not provide a sharp picture, but they suggest that there is no developmental stage in which implicit arguments are completely absent from children's representation of passives, since the youngest group has instrumental responses with transitive passives as well as transitive alternating passives. There is no significant quantitative difference between transitive and alternating verbs with respect to instrumental responses in the first two groups. But the 3;6–3;11 group shows a difference. What causes the lack of quantitative difference in the data is not clear at the moment. But it should be kept in mind that the experiment was designed to allow for both an instrumental and a non-instrumental, i.e. accompaniment response. As a result, it is not surprising that children opt for one or the other. Further, more refined follow-up experiments are planned to clarify the situation.

CONCLUDING REMARKS

In this chapter I have discussed the acquisition of passive by Morisyen and Seselwa children. Two experiments, one on comprehension and the other on production, have been administered to get an insight into the acquisition of passive in Creole languages. Combined, these two experiments lead me to conclude the following: first, it seems that Creole children have a syntactic representation of passives from an early age, second, their passives seem to have implicit arguments, and third, more importantly, the passive has no morphology.

Van der Lely's experiment has not been used on children as young as three years old, thus the results in this study are new. They show that children from a very early age have knowledge of verbal passive as well as of adjectival passive.

Further, the findings with Seselwa children based on Verrips' experiment confirm the claim that early child passive is a passive without morphology. Importantly in this context, the experiments show clearly that children comprehend passive constructions despite the paucity of passive constructions in the target grammar. This development is difficult to explain within usage-based theories as these predict that children will use passive constructions because these constructions are in the input. This is definitely not the case here. On the contrary, these findings seem to provide support for the nativist theory which assumes innate knowledge guiding acquisition.

8   Serial verb constructions

INTRODUCTION

Serial verb constructions are regarded as complex predicates containing at least two verbs within a single clause. These constructions are seen in many language families such as in Kwa languages in West Africa, Creole languages of the Atlantic, Pacific and Indian Ocean areas, the Sino-Tibetan language family, Austronesian languages of New Guinea and Malagasy among others.

Serial verb constructions (hereafter SVC) are interesting for grammatical theory mainly because of the interaction of their lexical and syntactic properties. They seem to be lexically restricted since only verbs of movement, for instance, can be combined with other verbs to express direction from or towards the point of reference. They also seem to undergo thematic restructuring to form complex predicates. However, they are clearly separate verbs assigning case and thematic roles to arguments in between. In other words, SVCs are at the interface between syntax and lexicon, which can provide some in-depth insights into the available mechanisms in languages.

In this chapter I will argue that SVCs as expressions of recursion are produced by children as early as 3;0 years of age. Although Seselwa, and Morisyen to a certain extent, show mostly restricted and lexicalised patterns of SVC, young children use SVCs quite productively. This fact suggests that they do not acquire the structure by simply following a model from the input.

SERIAL VERB CONSTRUCTIONS IN FIRST LANGUAGE ACQUISITION

Verb serialisation is a topic that has not been extensively investigated in first language acquisition. This is partly explained by the fact that most of the studies have focused on European languages that do not have SVCs.

Interestingly, a look at studies on the acquisition of English, for instance, confirms the N1 V1 (N2) V2 pattern, although this pattern seems to be short-lived. The SVCs found in English are of the causative type with the following verbs (fall, drop, go, come and bring, come and take, come and pull) (cf. Bowerman 1982). Lebeaux (1989) has already shown similar structures with sentence-initial infinitives, based on adjunction principles (1–5, cf. also Bickerton 1990, 1995, Radford 1997, personal communication):

(1) Mommy push me fall.
    (N1 V2 N2 V2)
    (one child from Bowerman 1982).

(2) Go open door.
    (V1 V2 N2)
    (Seth 23 months, Bickerton 1995).

(3) I did go in the kitchen throw it, dad.
    (N1 AUX V1 PP V2 N2)
    (Seth 27 months, Bickerton 1990).

(4) Didja sit down tray a give me little pudding?
    (N1 V1 N2 V2 N3 N4)
    (Seth 27 months, Bickerton 1990).

(5) Want go in the car.
    (V1 V2 PP)
    (Iris 30 months, Radford 1997).

This phenomenon will be further explored in the following section.

A language with SVCs worth mentioning here is Mandarin Chinese (Erbaugh 1982), mentioned by McWhorter (1997). According to McWhorter, serials are acquired relatively late (after 2;10). It is only the benefactive *gei* that is common at that stage (around 3;0). Others such as *gen* 'with' and *cong* 'from' are used only later, after 3;7. McWhorter (1997) claims that children do not seem to use serials in spite of the heavy serialising input. Although I have not seen the data myself, the only remark I can make at this point is that the discrepancy between acquisition data and input is nothing surprising. It seems that children for some time disregard input. This has been observed for instance in the development of null subjects in non-null-subject languages. A further remark is that the lack of serials does not automatically mean that children do not have knowledge of serials. Interestingly, a more recent study on Cantonese Chinese and English bilinguals by Yip and Matthews (2007) shows that these bilinguals produce serial verb constructions around 2;5. These constructions involve three verbs closely following each other ('buy, give eat'). Although further data is required here, Yip and Matthews (2007) convincingly demonstrate that SVCs are part of the early bilingual grammar.

SPONTANEOUS DATA

A look at the spontaneous Seselwa data shows the following picture: around 2;4 children use the *al* + V ('go' + V) pattern quite often. However, compared to other complex constructions, SVCs are rarely produced. Examples (6) to (8) illustrate the types of SVC-like constructions:

(6) Miss Maryanne pe <u>al</u> aste gato
    Miss Maryanne ASP go buy cake
    'Miss Maryanne is going to buy cake.' (Stefan 2;4)

(7) Yer   mo lisyen kot mwen in zape mord Rubin
    Yesterday my dog at me ASP bark bit Rubin
    'My dog at home bark and bit Rubin before.' (Benjamin 2;6)

(8) Abigail in   pran loto Benjamin kasiet anba   pye   dibwa
    Abigail ASP   take car   Benjamin hide   under tree wood
    'Abigail took Benjamins's car and hid it under the tree.' (Brigitte 2;11)

The Morisyen corpus shows the following picture: around (2;4), Morisyen-speaking children show productive use of *al* + V, *vin* + V patterns in serial-like constructions. Examples (9) to (14) clearly demonstrate that *al* and *vin* 'go' and 'come' are used as first verbs and not as second verbs and this is also seen in adult directional serials. Although these structures are also witnessed in adult language, they are regarded as rare. Their frequent appearance in the children's grammars confirms their productive use in early child grammar.

(9) Ø   in   al   sers   kamyon.
     Ø   ASP   go   fetch   truck/lorry
     '(He) has fetched the truck/lorry.' (Terry 2;4)

(10) Li   pu   al   rod ...
     3SG   MOD   go   look   for
     'He will look for...' (Rodney 2;4)

(11) Mo   al zet   dan   lamer.
     1SG   go throw   in   sea
     'I throw (it) into the sea.' (Benito 2;7)

(12) Mo   ti   al   get   bondye.
     1SG   TNS   go   see   god
     'I visited God.' (Terry 2;4)

(13) Loto   vire   li   vin   ar   loto.
     car   turn   3SG come   with   car
     'The car comes/moves towards the other car.' (Rodney 2;4)

(14) Li   pu   vini   rule.
     3SG   MOD   come   drive
     'He will drive.' (Rodney 2;4)

In example (14) the order of the verbs is reversed and in adult grammar it should be *rule vini*. Examples (15) to (17) are take-serials. There are no resultative serials witnessed at this stage:

(15) Mo   pran   foto   dan [...] mo   met   dan mo   pos.[1]
     1SG   take   picture   in   [...] 1SG put   in   1POS   pocket
     'I put the picture into my pocket.' (Rodney 2;4)

(16) Apre   mo   sarye   disab   mo   al   zet   dan   lamer.
     after 1SG carry   sand   1SG   go   throw   in   sea
     'I put the sand into the sea.' (Benito 2;7)

(17) Pran   tu   gard   ek   twa.
     take   all   keep   with   2SG
     'Take all and look after everything.' (Rodney 2;4)

Examples (13), (15) and (16) are particularly interesting as they can be considered direct evidence for the use of complementation. Children insert an overt subject (*li/mo*) which is not expected in the adult SVCs. Further examples of take-serials are attested in the grammars of children around 3;4, as seen in examples (18) to (20):

(18) Lerla   li   trap   sa   lapolis   la   zet   dan   lamer.
     then   3SG   catch   this   policeman   DET   throw   in   sea
     'Then he threw the policeman into the sea.' (Shirley 3;4)

(19) Ø   in   pran   van   la   ale.
     Ø   ASP   take   bus   DET   go
     'He went away with the bus.' (Cathy 3;7)

(20) Mo   pu   met   li   dan   mo   sak   amen   li   lakaz.
     1SG   MOD   put   3SG   in   1POS   bag   bring   3SG   home
     'I will take it home in my bag.' [approx.] (Cathy 3;7)

As compared to the previous stage, directionals in older children from 3;10 to 5;4 are illustrated in examples (21) to (23):

(21) Ø   ale   poze   kondire   poze.
     Ø   go   land   drive   land
     'I fly the plane and land it.' [approx.] (Guillaume 3;10)

(22) Kot   mo   granmer   mo   returne   ale   vini   kum   sa   mwa!
     at   1POS   grandma   1SG   go back   go   come   like   that   me
     'I come and go like that at my grandmother's place.' (Christine 5;4)

---

[1] In the CHAT format manual (1988) the symbol [...] is used for incomplete but not interrupted utterances.

(23) Mo   ale   vini.
      1SG   go   come
      'I come and go.' (Christine 5;4)

Resultatives are first witnessed in the grammars of four- and five-year-old children, as seen in examples (24) to (26).

(24) Mo   'n   pus   li   fer   li   ale.
      1SG ASP   push   3SG   make   3SG   go
      'I pushed it away.' (Guillaume 3;10)

(25) Ø   met   dilo   diri   bwi   la.
      Ø   put   water   rice   cook/boil   there
      'I boil the water for the rice.' [approx.] (Christine 5;4)

(26) Li   krye   mwa   la   dir   mwa   vin   zwe.
      3SG   shout   me   now   tell   me   come   play
      'She shouts to me to come and play.' (Christine 5;4)

So far, we have a small corpus of SVCs in Morisyen-speaking children. A quantification of SVCs in early child Morisyen grammar would have proved unreliable because SVCs belong to complex syntax and are scant in spontaneous speech, compared to other syntactic phenomena. At this stage it should be noted that despite the paucity of SVCs in spontaneous speech, the data strongly suggests that potentially any verb can subcategorise for serialisation, with a preference for a V+V adjacency pattern. This leads to the assumption that children's SVCs are different in nature from adult SVCs. In order to gain a deeper insight into the nature of SVCs in Creole children's grammar, and especially into Seselwa where SVCs are more common, a set of experiments was administered.

EXPERIMENTS

After careful inspection of the broad range of experiments commonly used with children, I used an elicitation method. The experiment material and procedure were chosen because of their methodological reliability in assessing syntax with children. Elicited production is an experimental technique designed to reveal children's grammar by having them produce sentence structures. The syntactic structures of interest are elicited in the broader context of a game, frequently one in which the child interacts with a puppet.

Children were presented with pictures and a puppet. In introducing the puppet, I explained that the puppet was learning to speak Seselwa. Consequently, it would make mistakes when speaking and the children were asked to help it. They would have to correct the puppet when it made mistakes in describing the pictures. For example, a picture was presented showing two children taking balloons and putting them on the wall. The puppet would say something like 'the children are crying running away.' The children were asked if the puppet produced a correct sentence in response to the picture. If it did not, the children were asked to assist the puppet by giving the right sentence.

All responses were recorded on a portable Panasonic minidisc recorder SJ-MR100. The task was administered with sixty-eight children in six different age groups from 3;6 to 6;0. It was not possible to elicit SVCs with children around 2;5 years old as they proved to be too young. There were twenty-one contexts in which serial verb constructions were used, with all the types of serial found in both Morisyen and Seselwa adult grammars. These include resultative, directional benefactive, finish, say-serials as well as three-verb serials. Sentences (27) to (34) illustrate the SVC types which the children were expected to produce in the test (see Appendix D):

(27) Marmay pe pran balon met lor miray.
children PROG take balloon put on wall
'The children are hanging the balloons onto the wall.'

(28) Pyero i pe taye atrap balon.
Pyero 3SG PROG run catch balloon
'Pyero is running after the balloon.'

(29) Mari i pe ris tediber kas li.
Mari 3SG PROG pull teddy bear break 3SG
'Mari is tearing the teddy bear.'

(30) Ti   lisyen   i   n   pran   sulyer   in   taye.
     little   dog   3SG   PROG   take   shoe   ASP   run
     'The little dog ran away with the shoe.'

(31) Lisyen   i   pe   marse   vire   fer   letur   pye   dibwa.
     dog   3SG   PROG   walk   turn   go   around   tree   wood
     'The dog is going around and around the tree.'

(32) Ti   garson   i   'n   penn   en   bwat   in   fini.
     little   boy   3SG   ASP   paint   a   box   ASP   finish
     'The little boy finished painting the box.'

(33) Ti   garson   i   pe   tap   bul   al   dan   lakaz.
     little   boy   3SG   PROG   kick   ball   go   in   house
     'The little boy kicked the ball into the house.'

(34) Ti   Zan   i   'n   dir   papa   pur   dir   so   sulyer   in
     little   Zan   3SG   PROG   say   dad   that   say   his   shoe   ASP
     kase.
     break
     'Little Zan told his dad that his shoe is broken.'

However, after running a pilot study, I noticed that none of the children used *purdir* (say-serial). Given that this serial was completely absent in the spontaneous data, together with the fact that there was no say-serial response in the pilot study, I excluded *purdir* contexts from the tests, leaving us with nineteen instead of twenty-one contexts. With respect to the responses, children were 'free' to give any type of response matching with the pictures. If a child gave a non-serial sentence as a response to the pictures, this response was also counted as a response but marked as a non-serial response such as the ones seen in *pu*-constructions. This means that there were no correct or incorrect responses as such. If there was an SVC, then two-SVCs and three-SVCs were distinguished. Here are two examples of three-SVCs and *pu* structure:

(35) Mama   pe   tjombo   lamen   sa   ti   garson
     mother   PROG   take/grab   hand   this   little   boy

pe	amen	labutik	pe	rod	sulyer	pu	don
PROG	bring	shop	PROG	look	shoes	COMP	give

marmai
boy

'Mother is taking the hand of this little boy, she is bringing him to the shop and is looking for shoes to give to the boy.' [approx.] (Rajan 3;9)

(36)
Ti	lisyen	pe	taye	pe	swiv	zot	pu	rod
little	dog	PROG	run	PROG	follow	them	COMP	look

balon	pa	war.
balloon	NEG	see

'The little dog is running following them to look for the ball and it can't find it.' (Fabio 4;2)

These sentences were produced without intonation contour or pause. No intervening coordination or subordination was found and one overt subject was given, as witnessed in the adult model. The results are illustrated in Figures 8.1 to 8.7:

From Figure 8.1 we see that all groups of children demonstrated the ability to produce SVCs in their grammars. Even the youngest group of 3;0–3;5 children produced SVCs. It is astonishing that children produce SVCs, especially given that the existence of SVCs in Seselwa, and Morisyen has been called into question (cf. Bollée 1977, Corne 1977, Kriegel 1996). Most of the SVC types reported by Bickerton (1989) for the adult system were found in the children's grammar, except for the *purdir* construction, as mentioned before.

When children use a different verb combination from the ones seen in the adult language, I classify this structure as new. Instead of the adult verb combinations (such as the ones seen in Table 8.1), children have a wide range of 'new' verb combinations.

I also counted all the cases of three- and four-SVCs as new, as the list of these two types of SVC is open-ended in adult grammar. It is interesting to note that children seem to combine verbs easily to form SVCs, as seen in examples (37) to (43). Examples (42) and (43), especially, show how easily children adjoin sentences.

Table 8.1 *Adult as compared to child verb combinations*

Adult	Child
Puse-zete (push-throw)	Puse-tonbe (push-fall)
Tape-ferrantre (kick into)	Tape-rule (kick-roll)
Taye-swiv (run-follow)	Taye-zwen (run-join)
Netoye-met lord (clean-tidy up)	Netoye-zwe (clean-play)
Sorti-tonb/al deor (get out-go/fall)	Sot-tomb (jump-fall)
Pran-mete (take-put)	Pran-fuye (take-search)

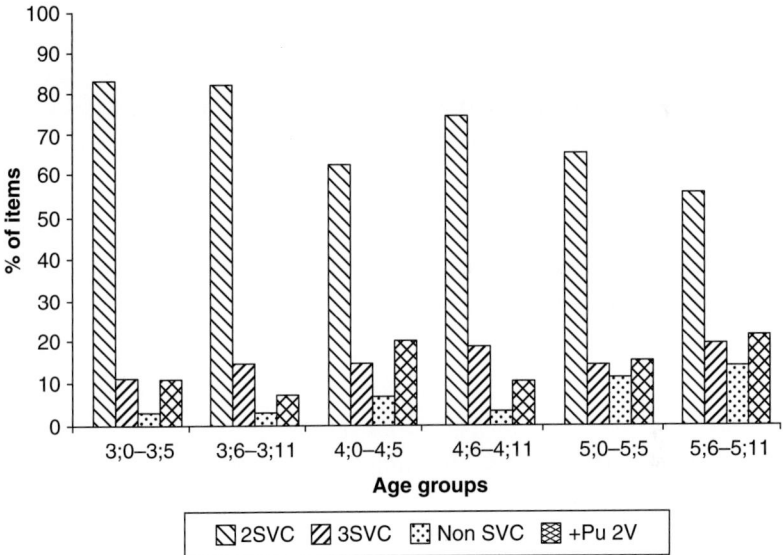

FIGURE 8.1 SVCs, non-SVCs and sentences with *pu*

(37) Papa pe **rod** balon pe **don** marmai
dad PROG look balloon PROG give children
'Dad is looking for the balloon is giving it to the children.' (Fabio 4;2)

(38) Ti lisyen pe **tay** pe **rod** balon
little dog PROG run PROG look balloon
pe **swiv** zot pu **rod** balon pa war.
PROG follow they MOD look balloon NEG see
'The little dog is running looking for the balloon, is following
the children to look for the balloon but does not see it.' (Fabio 4;2)

(39) Lisyen fer   etur   pye dibwa zap ek   balon
     dog   make   around tree wood bark with balloon
     'The dog goes around the tree barking at the balloon.' (Laurent 5;6)

(40) Ti   Zan pe   bat   bul   al   dan lakur.
     little John PROG beat ball go   in   garden
     'Little John is hitting the ball into the garden.' (Oneill 5;0)

(41) Ti   Zan pe   **taye** pe   **pran** bul
     little John PROG run   PROG take ball
     'Little John is running is catching the ball.' (Lyn 3;2)

(42) Sa   lisyen pe   fer   letur   pye   dibwa pe   gete
     this dog   PROG   make   around tree wood   PROG   look
       kot   bul   in   tonbe
       where   ball ASP   fall
     'This dog is going around the tree checking where the ball fell.'
     (Leffa 5;6)

(43) Sa   lisyen pe   taye turne dan pye   dibwa pu   li
     this dog   PROG   run   turn   in   tree wood   COMP   3SG
       pran   sa   balon
       take   this ball
     'This dog is running in circles around the tree to get the ball.'
     (Abigail 5;7)

These verb combinations, although not attested in the adult grammar for the contexts given, are not considered to be ungrammatical
by adult Seselwa speakers. When presented to adult native speakers, they were accepted. The adults made clear that they understood
the meaning of the sentences, although they would not use these
combinations. Most of the adult speakers used *e* 'and', *present* 'now'
or *komela* 'now', thus producing no SVCs. However, adult speakers
accepted sentences (42) and (43).

   The fact that 'standard' SVCs are used by the children means
that they conform to the adult model in two ways: structure-wise
and verb-combination-wise (i.e. the two-SVCs). Overall, we see that
there are more standard SVCs than new ones (see Figure 8.2). In other

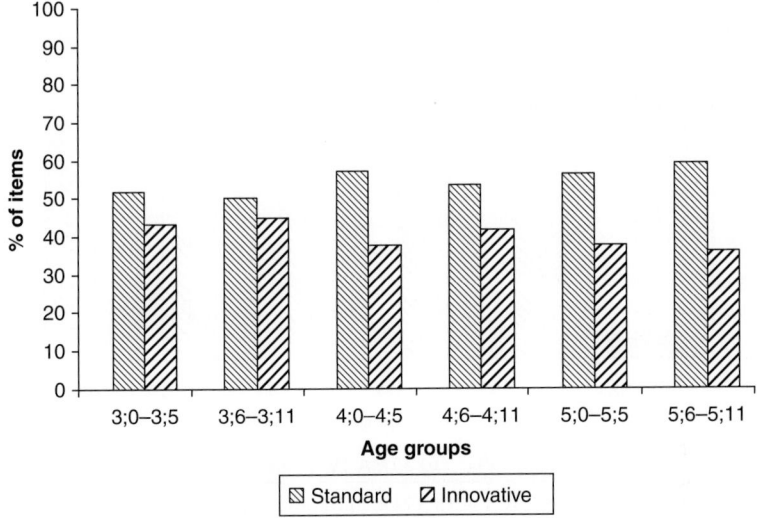

FIGURE 8.2 Standard and new SVCs

words, this means that there are more two-SVCs than three-SVCs and more standard verb combinations than 'new' verb combinations such as the ones given above. As expected, the percentage of the new combinations gradually decreases to around 38 per cent towards the end. This result is expected as these children learn the adult verb combinations and realise that three-SVCs are not common in the input.

The following figures (8.3–8.6) illustrate the distribution of tense, mood and aspect (TMA) markers found in SVCs with two or three verbs.

Most first and second verbs of the two-SVCs are marked with a TMA, as are the few cases of three-SVCs. The data shows children actually prefer either one of the aspect markers *fin* or *pe*. If they mark the first verb with an aspect marker, the same marker is kept on the second or/and third verb. The most frequently occurring TMA combination patterns are listed in Table 8.2.

Note that ø is commonly used to mark *habitualis*, which is expressed in English for instance by the present tense.

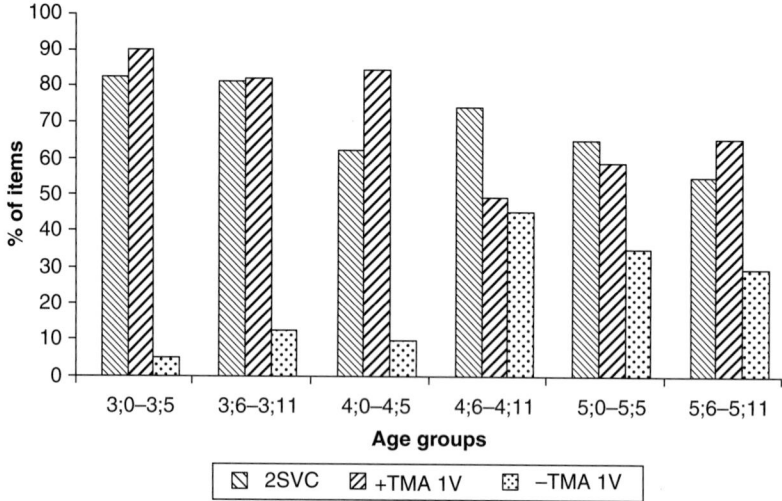

FIGURE 8.3 Two-SVCs with TMA marker on first verb

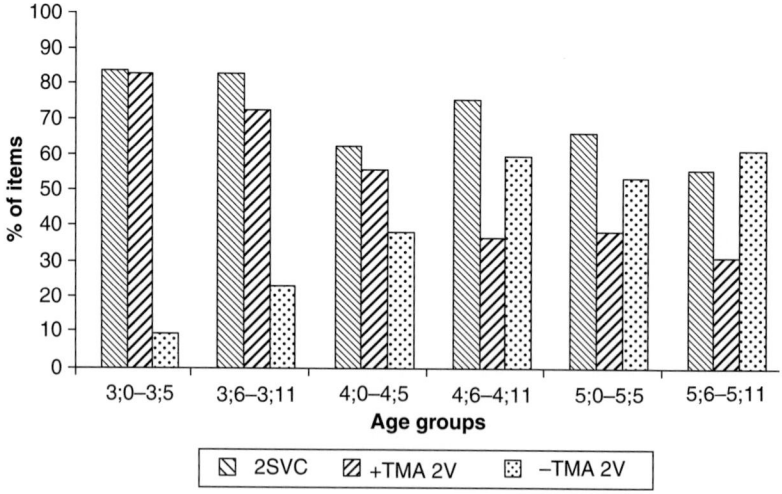

FIGURE 8.4 Two-SVCs with TMA marker on second verb

Though the combinations are limited, children do seem to have a good command of these combinations as most of them are correctly used and combined according to the adult model. Two children used verb reduplications to mark continuation, as seen in examples (44) and (45):

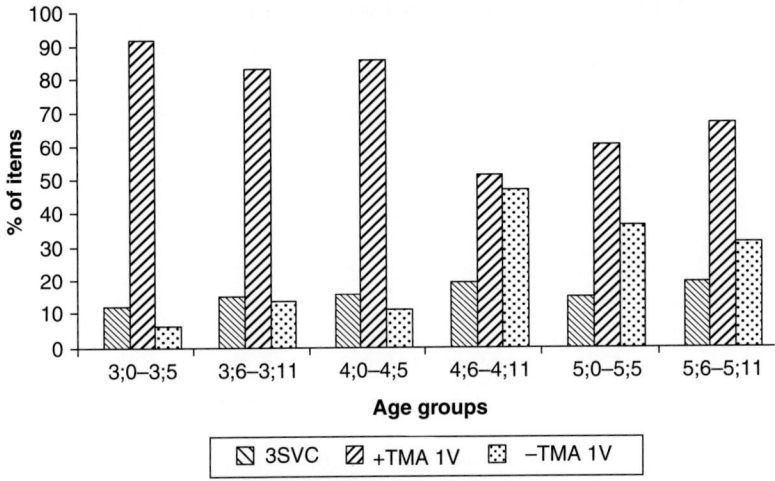

FIGURE 8.5 Three-SVCs with TMA marker on first verb

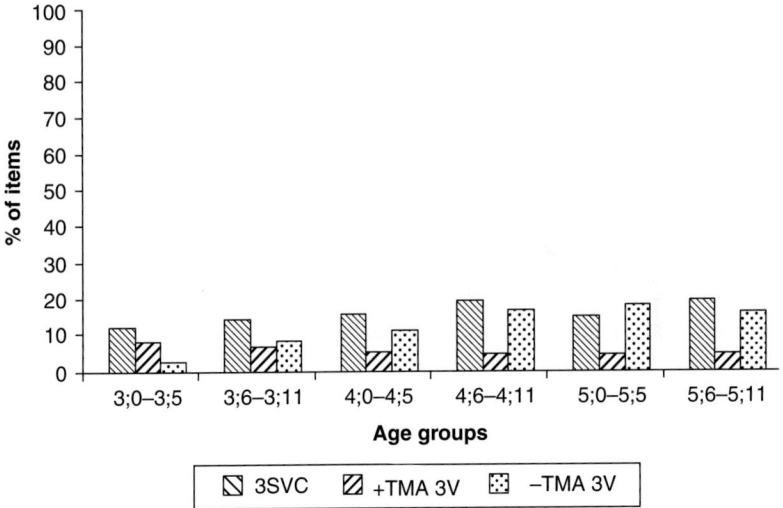

FIGURE 8.6 Three-SVCs with TMA marker on third verb

(44) ti   lisyen pe   mars marse partu   rod   bul
      little   dog   ASP walk REDUP everywhere look ball
      'The little dog keeps on walking everywhere looking for the ball.'
      (Benjamin 4;7)

(45) ti   lisyen pe   turn turne pye   dibwa
      little   dog   ASP turn REDUP tree wood
      'The little dog keeps on turning around the tree.' (Chloe 5;2)

Table 8.2 *Two-SVCs with TMA combinations*

TMA combination
Pe + Pe
Pe + ø
Pe + Fin
Fin + Pe
Fin + ø
Fin + Fin
Ti pe + Ti pe
ø + ø

Only one child uses *tipe*. In contrast to Morisyen-speaking children, it seems that the Seselwa-speaking children use one TMA combination (*tipe*) rather early, (i.e. around 3;0). This finding does not contradict my previous conclusion reached on the acquisition of TMA. In Adone (1994a) I concluded that Morisyen-speaking children seem to acquire the semantics of TMA markers quite slowly. The Seselwa data seem to confirm this observation in that there were no early TMA combinations produced. The near complete absence of TMA combinations in the SVCs, as well as the restriction to the aspect markers in the SVCs, are possibly an artefact of the method chosen (elicited production supported visually).

Children in the age group of 3;6–3;11 produced slightly more SVCs than *pu* constructions, as can be seen in Figure 8.7. Examples (46) and (48) are sentences of contexts with *pu* constructions. Examples (47) and (49) show corresponding sentences without *pu*:

(46) Granper pe kas bilimbi[2] **pu** met dan bol.
grandpa PROG break bilimbi COMP put in bowl
'Grandpa is gathering bilimbi to put in the bowl.'

(47) Granper pe kas bilimbi pe met dan bol.
grandpa PROG break bilimbi PROG put in bowl
'Grandpa is gathering bilimbi is putting in the bowl.' [approx.]

---

[2] Bilimbi is a local fruit.

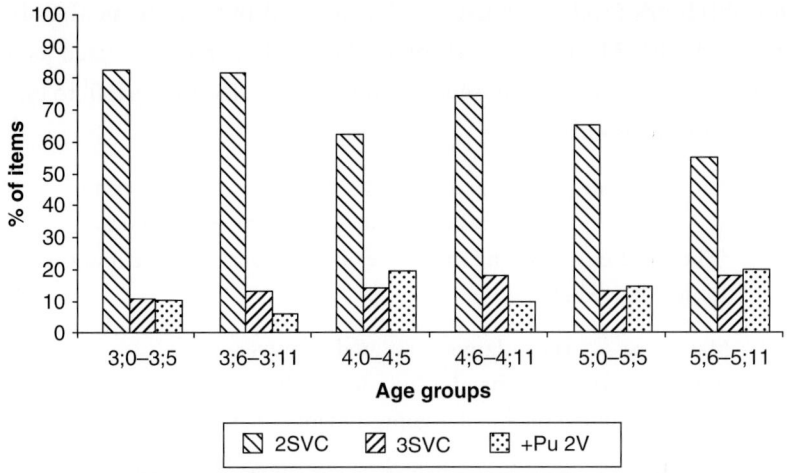

FIGURE 8.7 SVCs and *pu*-sentences

(48) Ban marmai pe   don   tifi balon   **pu**   met   enler lor
     PL   child   PROG   give girl balloon COMP   put   up   on
     miray
     wall
     'The children are giving the girl balloons to put onto the wall.'

(49) Ban marmai pe   **pran** balon   **met** lor   miray.
     PL   child   PROG   take   balloon put   on   wall
     'The children are taking balloons to put them on the wall.'

There were also two cases in which children did not use serial verb constructions. Instead they used conjunctions such as *e* 'and', *pi*, 'after' and *apre* 'after'. This is not surprising given that coordinated structures through conjunctions are well attested in first language acquisition studies. In fact, they represent an alternative to serial verb constructions which are expressions of recursion.

There are also many cases of *al*+verb pattern attested in the data. This confirms the tendency already noted in the spontaneous data of the Morisyen-speaking children (Adone 1994a). It is interesting to note that in all the cases with *al*+verb serial-like constructions, there is no intervening element between *al* and the verb. As such *al* and the verb form a unit. This can be taken as further evidence for children's productive use of *al* as a serial of motion, as already attested with Morisyen-speaking children. *Al* is possibly used as a conjunction to coordinate several propositions. Examples (50) to (52) illustrate the point:

(50) Ban marmai pe   pran butey delo   al don manmi
     PL child   PROG take bottle water go give mum
     'The children are taking the bottle of water to go and give it to their
     mum.' (Rajan 3; 9)

(51) Mami pe   trap lamen al rod   sulyer
     mum PROG   hold hand go look   shoe
     'Mum is holding the hand is going and looking for shoes.' (Fabio 4;2)

(52) Granpapa pe   kas   zariko pe   met dan bol
     grandpa PROG   break bean   PROG   put in bowl
       pe   al met kot so   lakaz.
       PROG   go put at   his   home
     'Grandpa is picking beans, putting them in the bowl and bringing them
     back home.' (Sheryl 4;4)

There are also several cases of causative *fer* 'make' in the SVCs. Here are some examples (53)–(55):

(53) Marmai pe   travay pe   fer   lakaz prop
     child   PROG work   PROG   make   house clean
     'The children are cleaning the house.' (Fabio 4;2)

(54) Tifi pe   pus   sa   tif i pu   fer   tombe.
     girl PROG   push   this girl   COMP make   fall
     'The girl is pushing this girl to make her fall.' (Edrick 4;2)

(55) Mari pe   redi pupet fer   li   kase
     Mary PROG   tear doll make   her break
     'Mary is tearing the doll to break her' (Oneill 5;0)

At this point, it becomes clear that the presence of SVCs in first language acquisition (especially in the Creole data) has to be accounted for. In first language acquisition studies, it is often assumed that the initial state of grammar is lexical, as shown in Roeper (1996). There is accumulating evidence for the proposition that children's initial phrase structure configuration is best described in terms of adjunction[3] (cf. Roeper and de Villiers 1992, Hoekstra and Jordens 1994, Roeper 1996). This means that elements are attached in an adjoined position, instead of being in a complement position. Therefore, case marking and subcategorisation are defined in lexical rather than structural terms. Further support for this claim comes from several other studies. One of these is Tavakolian (1981), which shows the incapacity of children around 3 years of age to distinguish between relative and conjoined clauses. Frank (1992) also shows that children assign a conjoined structure [NP$_1$ V NP$_2$] [e$_1$ V NP$_3$] to structures such as NP1 V NP2 V NP3 as in 'The sheep$_1$ kissed the monkey$_2$ [that e$_1$ tickled the rabbit]'. This means that [e$_1$ V NP$_3$] is treated as an adjunct, showing children's preference for subject control of the embedded subject. This in turn has been confirmed by several other studies, such as de Villiers et al. (1990), Weissenborn et al. (1991) and Adone and Vainikka (1999). These investigations show that children allow subjects of the first wh-questions to have control over the embedded subject. At this point, of the two principles available in the target grammar (i.e. complements and adjuncts), the children start with the adjunction configuration. Remember that there are also sentences with a subject that has V2 (as seen in examples (13), (15) and (16)) which show that children also use complements occasionally. However, the adjunction configuration and subject control together account best for the early serial verb constructions in children's grammar.[4] Currently discussion in the field revolves around recursion as a putatively universal feature of language (Hauser et al. 2002, Arsenijevic and Hinzen 2010).

Both the adjunction configuration and the subject control mechanism make the presence of SVCs plausible. Example (56) in

---

[3] See de Villiers (1991), who argues that the first wh-questions are formed by adjunction to S or IP before CP is built.

[4] Note that Bickerton and Iatridou (1987) propose that SVCs are adjuncts. This means that SVCs are not constituents required by the subcategorisation frames of verbs.

Seselwa provides further support for the fact that children show subject control with *li*:

(56) Madam   i   tir   sulyer dan bwat i   don en tifi
     woman 3SG take shoe   in box   3SG give a   girl
     'The woman takes the shoes out of the box for the girl.'   (Denis 5;8)

The ease with which children produce three-SVCs as well as the amount of innovative constructions in the data can be taken as solid evidence for the fact that children's grammars generate these sentences, instead of an acquisition scenario of the various SVC types on a one-to-one basis. This would further seem to indicate that there must be some serialisation pattern/structure as part of UG that generates a wide range of these structures (cf. Bickerton 1989). If SVCs are indeed part of UG, then there should be evidence for this SVC tendency elsewhere, for example, in acquisition studies of non-serialising languages.

As already presented in the previous section, English acquisition data confirms the NI V1 N2 V2 pattern to some extent. The SVCs found in English are of the causative type with the following verbs (fall, drop, go, come and bring, come and take, come and pull) (cf. Bowerman 1982). Here I repeat some of the examples (57)–(59):

(57)   Go open door.
     (V1 V2 N2)
     (Seth 23 months, Bickerton 1995)

(58)   I did go in the kitchen throw it, dad.
     (N1 AUX V1 PP V2 N2)
     (Seth 27 months, Bickerton 1995)

(59)   Didja sit down tray a give me little pudding?
     (N1 V1 N2 V2 N3 N4)
     (Seth 27 months, Bickerton 1995)

Radford (personal communication) informed me that his English data has quite a substantial amount of SVC-like constructions. Taken together with Bowerman's and Lebeaux's work, the English data show that children of certain language types (those which are potentially able to generate SVCs, e.g. English) go through a stage in which they produce serial-like constructions.

Further convincing evidence comes from sign languages. Serial structures are, for example, well established in some of the sign languages, such as American Sign Language (hereafter ASL) and Nicaraguan Sign Language (cf. Supalla 1982, Senghas *et al.* 1997, Lillo-Martin 1999). The data presented by Supalla makes it clear that ASL has serial verb structures with verbs of motion.

Senghas *et al.*'s study (1997) examining the development of Nicaraguan Sign Language provides very revealing results especially with respect to the emergence of serial verb constructions initiated by children. They develop syntactic and morphological devices to mark argument structure differently from the first generation (adults). In order to examine the changes in the system, Senghas *et al.* devised a four–way classification of the verbs. Class 1 includes verbs with one argument, as in 'A man cries'. Class 2 includes verbs with two arguments of the type 'A woman taps a cup'. Class 3 includes verbs with two arguments that are animate, such as 'A man pushes a woman'. Class 4 includes verbs with three arguments, as in 'A woman gives a cup to a man', with two animate arguments and one inanimate one. Their overall results show that the first generation uses a clear syntax with basic word order to express simple propositions. 'These word orders are consistently maintained, but overall the syntax is very constrained' (Senghas *et al.* 1997: 557). In contrast, the second generation has a new word order and more consistency in the direction of movement. Furthermore, several changes are seen in the grammatical devices used for argument structures. These changes are syntactic and morphological in nature. A sentence expressing two-argument events illustrates the point. The first generation has a rigid word order with the two verbs and the two arguments rigidly interleaved, as in the $N_1 V_1 N_2 V_2$ pattern (MAN PUSH WOMAN FALL). In contrast, the second generation replaces this pattern by the following pattern: $N_1 V_1 V_2 N_2$. The two verbs are still required but are now adjacent as in (MAN PUSH FALL WOMAN). This change in the VP with two separate verbs moving closer to each other, as is the case with serial verbs, is very interesting for a number of different reasons. First, it shows that verbs are pairing up to form a single unit. Second, it shows very clearly that it is children, not adults, who undertake the changes. This change of syntax with the second generation of signers shows a preference for N1 N2 V1 V2 (MAN WOMAN PUSH FALL) or N1 V1 V2 N2 (MAN PUSH FALL WOMAN). So far, these two cases reinforce the view that SVCs are part of the human grammar.

At this point the question to be answered is: how do English children learn that their language is a non-serialising language? In other words, what triggers the restructuring of their grammar? One possible explanation lies in the acquisition of conjunctions and double-object constructions that are abundantly available in English. A look at the Seselwa data shows that there is an increase of double–object constructions with age which seems to correlate with a decrease in the use of serial verb constructions. Older children around 4;5 use more ditransitive verbs in double-object constructions instead of serial verb constructions. This development is explained by children gaining more access to input with double-object constructions rather than serial verb constructions. Children do not get a conventional model in terms of serial verb constructions and as a result, they choose another option that is available in the input.

The fact that Seselwa-speaking children produce innovative constructions highlights the capacity of children to overgeneralise, as Pinker (1999) has already shown in other domains of grammar. Here it means that children fully exploit the V+V pattern in the first place, thereby producing overgeneralisations.

CONCLUDING REMARKS

The existence of SVCs in early child language is clearly a logical result of children's initial grammar because the initial stages of grammar seem to be constrained by recursion and adjunction principles. The fact that children can produce SVCs at an early age can be taken as a strong indication that serialisation is part of UG. Similar to passive constructions, serial verb constructions are rare in the input and thus cannot be regarded as a model for children's serial verb constructions. Further, the fact that children create new verb combinations and overgeneralisations confirms the absence of a model to follow and also highlights children's creativity in acquisition. Interestingly, the correlation between serial verb constructions and double-object constructions shows that in the absence of a conventional model children choose another available construction, ditransitive verbs.

9 Acquisition without a conventional language model

INTRODUCTION

So far, I have investigated how Creole children acquire some complex structures in their first language. At the beginning of the study it was assumed that the input Creole children get is not different from the input children get from established languages. While this assumption is to some extent correct, it has become obvious that the nature of input in the Creole context is different, i.e. there is no conventional language model available. Consequently, this has an impact on acquisition. My goal in this chapter is to summarise the acquisition highlights of the study and to discuss the role of children in acquisition, especially in the absence of a conventional language model. Finally, I explore some implications of these findings for future research.

THE ACQUISITION OF COMPLEX STRUCTURES

The primary goal of this study has been to make a contribution to the field of first language acquisition by discussing the acquisition of four complex structures in two Creole languages.

In the domain of pronouns and reflexives there is evidence for the violation of Principle B, thus confirming a cross-linguistic tendency. Chien and Wexler (1990) have proposed that children violate Principle B because they lack a pragmatic principle, rather than syntactic knowledge, an issue that needs further research. In this study, the youngest children used the pronoun *li* both locally and non-locally, an observation that bears similarity with early Creole grammar where *li* was bound locally and non-locally. Note that the input is variable, as Seselwa adults use *li* to mark non-local and local referents, *li-mem* and *so lekor* to mark local referents only. In the face of these results it is plausible that these children are recreolising the input in the absence of a conventional language model, i.e. they are falling back on the default setting available in UG, thus replicating what Creole learners have done during creolisation.

The findings in the area of double-object constructions show the following picture: children seem to prefer double-object over prepositional ditransitive constructions, thus confirming a tendency seen in English and Dutch acquisition data (Bruyn *et al.* 1999). The Creole data shows clearly that children overgeneralise the DOC pattern to verbs which are usually used in a prepositional ditransitive construction. While so doing, these children definitely regularise their input. The combined results from cross-linguistic acquisition studies and those achieved in this study lead me to speculate that DOC must be a default option in UG, an option that children start with independent of their target language.

In the domain of passive, Creole children as young as 3;5 seem to have some knowledge of adjectival and verbal passive. This result is new in so far as the experiments used here have not previously been conducted with children of that age. Another worthwhile result is that children from an early age seem to have implicit arguments in their grammars, as claimed by Roeper (1987b). Interestingly, the passive produced by these Creole children is similar to the acquisition of English and Dutch passive in that it is without morphology. While the sceptical reader might be inclined to accept this result as natural given that adult Creole passive is without morphology, I find this explanation very unsatisfactory especially against the background that passive is also acquired without morphology in languages with morphology. Again, here it could well be that passive without morphology is a default option in early child grammar that children fall back on when input is not clear. Moving from (–morphology) to (+morphology) passive would then depend very much on the morphological profile of the target grammar (inflectional/fusional, isolating or polysynthetic). For polysynthetic languages such as Inuktitut, language-internal factors such as prolific verbal inflections or head-movement as a word-building strategy definitely have an impact on acquisition (Allen 1996), thus supporting a gradual model of language acquisition in which lexical learning plays a role.

Serial verb constructions are present in child grammar and illustrate recursive patterns in early child grammar. The experimental data shows that children create SVCs quite productively, independent of the input. They overgeneralise the (V+V) pattern to verbs that are not used in a serial verb construction and they generate (V+V+V) patterns. The new combinations of verbs in SVCs show innovations in child grammar. These results fit well with the findings of Senghas and colleagues (1997) with respect to the emergence of serial verb constructions in Nicaraguan Sign Language. These researchers showed that children developed syntactic and morphological devices to mark argument structure in a different way from the first generation of adults.

Overall, the acquisition findings show that children acquire their first language in spite of the variability in the system. Furthermore, the findings throw light on the role of children in acquisition.

GOING BEYOND INPUT: THE ROLE OF CHILDREN IN LANGUAGE ACQUISITION

There is little doubt that the ability to acquire and use language is a species-specific faculty of humans. Although animals can also demonstrate coordination of their behaviour, their communication is limited (cf. Hultsch et al. 1999). It is also uncontroversial that language as a human activity is highly rule-governed. Within the generative field it is generally assumed that humans have a 'language faculty' that is partially genetically determined. This is supported by a number of observations that show language development under disturbances of the external and internal environment of children. A cross-modal examination of case studies reveals that language learning in blind children takes place in a similar way to language learning in sighted children (cf. Andersen *et al.* 1984, Landau and Gleitman 1985). Further studies on the acquisition of signed languages show that these languages are not acquired differently from spoken languages (Morgan and Woll 2002). Studies on Williams Syndrome show that despite heavy impairment of non-linguistic abilities, language development in these children proceeds in a similar way as in normal children, albeit slower at times (Bartke *et al.* 1996, van der Lely 1996, Clahsen and Almazan 1998, Bellugi and St George 2000).

Further evidence for this genetic predisposition for language comes from studies supporting the view of 'a critical period', or most recently 'sensitive periods' for language acquisition. Evidence for this sort of constraint in human language development comes from children who have undergone hemispherectomy, and from feral children like Genie, who did not have exposure to language until the age of 13 (Curtiss and de Bode 2001). All these findings taken together indicate very clearly that complete and successful acquisition depends very much on early exposure to a language model.

In the discussion on input the frequency of linguistic constructions has often been mentioned to play a role. Interesting examples of complex passive constructions acquired by children very early in Inuktitut, K'iche Mayan, Sesotho and Zulu, together with experimental studies conducted by Brooks and Tomasello (1999), are mentioned by Tomasello (2003) to support the claim that frequency plays a key role. Although the argument of frequency might be interesting to pursue, I cannot see how to interpret the development of passive, for instance, in Seselwa in the light of frequency. Passive constructions are not frequently used in adult Seselwa, given that it is a spoken language, and yet children master these passive constructions early.

Let us look at what children do in acquisition. Interestingly, a wide array of empirical studies reveals the human ability to create a system out of inconsistency (French *et al.* 1999). Humans are generally known for being capable of dealing with a so-called 'unstructured environment' in a highly systematic way, in the sense that they are able to learn and modify their knowledge even in the absence of 'environmental systematicity'. Marcus *et al.* (1992), Clahsen (1996, 1999), Clahsen *et al.* (1996), Pinker (1999) all point to one ability of children, namely their ability to generalise and over-generalise. Children generalise rules and overgeneralise structures. It has also been mentioned that overgeneralisations are rare in the acquisition data on English and German. At this point we might ask ourselves why these children apparently rarely overgeneralise. It has been argued that parental correction could be a reason. But it is clear that even if parents explicitly correct errors and revise ill-formed constructions, this cannot be sufficient to constrain chil-dren's overgeneralisations. In many cultures children spend more time with their siblings than with their parents or caregivers, and thus do not get any feedback. In addition, in many cultures parents do not correct, recast or revise ill-formed utterances. Alternatively, another valid reason for the small amount of overgeneralisation might lie somewhere else. It is plausible to argue that overgener-alisations are rare because children have access to a conventional language model that constrains their language use. As a result, there is no 'space' for overgeneralisations. Cases of overgeneralisa-tion in the child's grammar in a way confirm children's creativity and ability to generate rules and to apply them elsewhere and also the open-ended productivity of language as Pinker (1999) observed. This explains why children have forms such as *goed* for a period of time and later acquire the target adult form *went*. By the time chil-dren acquire *went*, they have encountered *went* many times. Pinker argues that the frequency of the form contributes to reinforcing the memory for the correct form 'went'. English-speaking children regu-larise the past tense –*ed*: *breaked, eated*, and also produce *broked, ated* (Pinker 1999). Overgeneralisations, according to Pinker (1999), eventually disappear because of accumulated experience and thus consolidation in memory. Thus, children regularise because they lack a conventional language use. Tomasello (2003, 2010) quite convincingly argues that children regularise irregular past tenses in English, for example, because many more exemplars are required to entrench the irregular form. I would add at this point that English children do get these exemplars which Creole children do not.

Another ability of children is to regularise their input. Singleton and Newport (1987), Singleton (1989), Ross and Newport (1996) and Newport (1999) examined how Simon acquired ASL from his deaf parents who were L2 learners of ASL. Their use of morphology and complex syntax was inconsistent when compared to the morphology and syntax of the native speakers. However, the difference between Simon's morphology and syntax and that of his parents is striking. Overall, Simon surpassed his parents' morphology and syntax by regularising each morpheme he was exposed to and using them in over 90 per cent of the contexts required. Hudson-Kam and Newport (2005) conducted a series of experiments on inconsistent input with adults and children. They were able to show that adult learners, in contrast to children learners, do not regularise their input. Furthermore, adult learners reproduced variability as witnessed in the input whereas children systematised the input. Similar results were achieved in a set of three experiments conducted with both Seselwa adults and children. Adone (2001a) sought to find out if adults and children would regularise novel verbs. When asked to put an ending on a novel verb, adults were more inclined to put an irregular ending than children. More importantly, children regularised the e-ending on novel verbs in 90 per cent of the cases. Adone's (2007) study on children home-signers reveals a similar picture in that children regularised some fifteen gestures from the hearing community, including 'to get drunk', 'to run away', 'nothing', 'get scared', thus making these gestures part of their lexicon. The experimental results in this book together with other similar results reveal that in the absence of systematic input, children are capable of imposing a system on their input and are capable of creating something innovative.

PROSPECTS FOR FUTURE RESEARCH

This study offers a window into the acquisition of some complex structures. In the last forty years there has been a substantial number of cross-linguistic language acquisition studies, yet typological acquisition studies are relatively rare (Slobin 1985a, b, 1997, Pye *et al.* 2007, Stoll *et al.* 2007). Acquisition studies on Creole languages are virtually absent. This study, in contrast to other studies focusing on established languages, shows that there are other variables to be taken into account. Although input is available, there is no conventional language model to guide children. This variability can be accounted for by the lack of literacy in the L1 and by the fact that most Creole-speaking adults are nowadays bilinguals, literate in English and/or in French. In the absence of a conventional language model, Creole children have proved to regularise and surpass their input, thus demonstrating creativity during acquisition.

The investigation of four grammatical domains in this study should be regarded as a starting point; there are many other grammatical domains that remain to be investigated, such as relative clauses, wh-questions, and determiners. Furthermore, studies on bilingual acquisition pairing a Creole language with one superstrate language (e.g. English, French) could be undertaken to address some theoretical issues related to the field of language acquisition at large, language contact, and theories of learning, among others. Although this book has addressed some central issues in the field of first language acquisition such as the contribution of children's innate capacity for language and input, especially the complex interaction between these two factors, there are still other areas open for future studies, including Creole late L2 learners of English, French, effects of literacy in a foreign language on Creole grammar, atypical language acquisition with Creole children (cf. Adone and Vainikka 1999), the effect of a Creole language on the acquisition of a sign language as in the case of Mauritian Sign Language. More experimental data is needed to provide insights into the area of processing. More recently, there has been a growing body of studies revealing the statistical learning abilities of children. Evidence comes mainly from the acquisition of the lexicon (Safran *et al.* 1996, Tenenbaum and Xu 2005, Thiessen 2009). Briscoe (2002a, b) argues persuasively that Bayesian parameter setting is relevant to language acquisition. Although I see no reason to adopt a view of language learning that is completely data-driven, I admit that we should not exclude the possibility of children 'scanning' the input for regularities and making use of a strong inference capacity during the acquisition process. However, future work will have to determine the extent to which statistical learning, a new approach to language learning, plays a role in language acquisition.

Finally, the interdisciplinary approach taken in this study, bringing together findings from first language acquisition, language contact, sign languages, home signing, artificial language and learning theories has deepened our understanding of children's contribution to the language acquisition task, stressing their creativity.

Appendix A Experimental materials on constructions with pronouns and reflexives

Grimshaw and Rosen experiment: sample scenarios and test sentences with the verb *grat/e* 'scratch'

Sentences with *li*

    a. BT-grammatical

Scenario 1 shows that the monkey is scratching the bear.

Krapo says:

(1)   Mo   fin   truv Ti   Zako   pe   fer kitsoz   ek
       ISG ASP see   little monkey PROG do   something with

       Lurs.
       bear

       Ti   Zako$_i$ fin   **grat**   li$_k$.
       little monkey ASP scratch 3SG

       'I saw the monkey doing something to the bear. The monkey scratched him.'

    b. BT-ungrammatical

Scenario 2 shows that the monkey is scratching himself.

Krapo says:

(2)   Mo   fin   truv Ti   Zako   pe   dibut   kot   Lurs.
       ISG ASP see   little monkey PROG stand next bear

       Ti   Zako$_i$ fin   **grat**   li$_k$
       little monkey ASP scratch 3SG

       'I saw the monkey standing next to the bear. The monkey scratched him.'

Sentences with *limem*

    a. BT-grammatical

Scenario 3 shows that the monkey is scratching himself.

Krapo says:

(3) Mo   fin   truv   Ti   Zako   pe   dibut   kot   Lurs.
1SG   ASP   see   little   monkey   PROG   stand   next   bear
Ti   Zako   fin   **grat**   **li**   **-mem**.
little   monkey   ASP   scratch   3SG   -REFL
'I saw the monkey standing next to the bear. The monkey scratched himself.'

b.   BT-ungrammatical

Scenario 4 shows that the monkey is scratching himself.
Krapo says:

(4) Mo   fin   truv   Ti   Zako   pe   fer   kitsoz   ek
1SG   ASP   see   little   monkey   PROG   do   something   with
Lurs.
bear
Ti   Zako$_i$ fin   **grat**   **li**   **-mem**$_i$.
little   monkey   ASP   scratch   3SG   -REFL
'I saw the monkey doing something to the bear. The monkey scratched himself.'

Sentences with *so lekor*

a.   BT-grammatical

Scenario 5 shows that the monkey is scratching his body.
Krapo says:

(5) Mo   fin   truv   Ti   Zako   pe   dibut   kot   Lurs.
1SG   ASP   see   little   monkey   PROG   stand   next   bear
Ti   Zako   fin   **grat**   **so**   **lekor**.
little   monkey   ASP   scratch   3POS   body
'I saw the monkey standing next to the bear. The monkey scratched his body.'

b.   BT-ungrammatical

Scenario 6 shows that the monkey is scratching his body.
Krapo says:

(6) Mo   fin   truv   Ti   Zako   pe   fer   kitsoz   ek
1SG   ASP   see   little   monkey   PROG   do   something   with

Lurs.
bear

Ti	Zako$_i$	fin	**grat**	**so**	**lekor$_k$.**
little	monkey	ASP	scratch	3POS	body

'I saw the monkey doing something to the bear. The monkey scratched his body.'

Sample scenarios and test sentences with the verb *beny/e* 'wash'
Sentences with *li*

a. BT-grammatical
Scenario 1 shows that the monkey is washing the bear.
Krapo says:

(7)
Mo	fin	truv	Ti	Zako	pe	fer	kitsoz	ek
1SG	ASP	see	little	monkey	PROG	do	something	with

Lurs.
bear

Ti	Zako$_i$	fin	**beny**	**li$_k$.**
little	monkey	ASP	wash	3SG

'I saw the monkey doing something to the bear. The monkey washed him.'

b. BT-ungrammatical
Scenario 2 shows that the monkey is washing himself.
Krapo says:

(8)
Mo	fin	truv	Ti	Zako	pe	dibut	kot	Lurs.
1SG	ASP	see	little	monkey	PROG	stand	next	bear

Ti	Zako$_i$	fin	**beny**	**li$_k$**
little	monkey	ASP	wash	3SG

'I saw the monkey standing next to the bear. The monkey washed him.'

Sentences with *limem*

a. BT-grammatical
Scenario 3 shows that the monkey is washing himself.
Krapo says:

(9)
Mo	fin	truv	Ti	Zako	pe	dibut	kot	Lurs.
1SG	ASP	see	little	monkey	PROG	stand	next	bear

Ti	Zako	fin	**beny**	**li**	**-mem**.
little	monkey	ASP	wash	3SG	-REFL

'I saw the monkey standing next to the bear. The monkey washed himself.'

b. BT-ungrammatical

Scenario 4 shows that the monkey is washing himself.

Krapo says:

(10)

Mo	fin	truv	Ti	Zako	pe	fer	kitsoz	ek
ISG	ASP	see	little	monkey	PROG	do	something	with

Lurs.
bear

Ti	Zako$_i$	fin	**beny**	**li**	**-mem**$_i$.
little	monkey	ASP	wash	3SG	-REFL

'I saw the monkey doing something to the bear. The monkey washed himself.'

Sentences with *so lekor*

a. BT-grammatical

Scenario 5 shows that the monkey is washing his body.

Krapo says:

(11)

Mo	fin	truv	Ti	Zako	pe	dibut	kot	Lurs.
ISG	ASP	see	little	monkey	PROG	stand	next	bear

Ti	Zako	fin	**beny**	**so**	**lekor**.
little	monkey	ASP	wash	3POS	body

'I saw the monkey standing next to the bear. The monkey washed his body.'

b. BT-ungrammatical

Scenario 6 shows that the monkey is washing his body.

Krapo says:

(12)

Mo	fin	truv	Ti	Zako	pe	fer	kitsoz	ek
ISG	ASP	see	little	monkey	PROG	do	something	with

Lurs.
bear

Ti	Zako$_i$	fin	**beny**	**so**	**lekor**$_k$.
little	monkey	ASP	wash	3POS	body

'I saw the monkey doing something to the bear. The monkey washed his body.'

Sample scenarios and test sentences with the verb *peny/e* 'comb'
Sentences with *li*

a. BT-grammatical
Scenario 1 shows that the monkey is combing the bear.
Krapo says:

(13)
Mo	fin	truv	Ti	Zako	pe	fer	kitsoz	ek
1SG	ASP	see	little	monkey	PROG	do	something	with

Lurs.
bear

Ti	Zako$_i$	fin	**peny**	**li**$_k$.
little	monkey	ASP	comb	3SG

'I saw the monkey doing something to the bear. The monkey combed him.'

b. BT-ungrammatical
Scenario 2 shows that the monkey is combing himself.
Krapo says:

(14)
Mo	fin	truv	Ti	Zako	pe	dibut	kot	Lurs.
1SG	ASP	see	little	monkey	PROG	stand	next	bear

Ti	Zako$_i$	fin	**peny**	**li**$_k$
little	monkey	ASP	comb	3SG

'I saw the monkey standing next to the bear. The monkey combed him.'

Sentences with *limem*

a. BT-grammatical
Scenario 3 shows that the monkey is combing himself.
Krapo says:

(15)
Mo	fin	truv	Ti	Zako	pe	dibut	kot	Lurs.
1SG	ASP	see	little	monkey	PROG	stand	next	bear

Ti	Zako	fin	**peny**	**li**	-mem.
little	monkey	ASP	comb	3SG	-REFL

'I saw the monkey standing next to the bear. The monkey combed himself.'

b. BT-ungrammatical

Scenario 4 shows that the monkey is combing himself.

Krapo says:

(16) Mo   fin   truv   Ti   Zako   pe   fer   kitsoz   ek
        1SG   ASP   see   little   monkey   PROG   do   something   with
       Lurs.
       bear
       Ti   Zako$_i$ fin   **peny**   **li**   **-mem**$_i$.
       little   monkey   ASP   comb   3SG   -REFL
       'I saw the monkey doing something to the bear. The monkey combed
       himself.'

Sentences with *so seve* 'his/her hair'

a. BT-grammatical

Scenario 5 shows that the monkey is combing his hair.

Krapo says:

(17) Mo   fin   truv   Ti   Zako   pe   dibut   kot   Lurs.
        1SG   ASP   see   little   monkey   PROG   stand   next   bear
       Ti   Zako   fin   **peny**   **so**   **seve**.
       little   monkey   ASP   comb   3POS   hair
       'I saw the monkey standing next to the bear. The monkey combed his
       hair.'

b. BT-ungrammatical

Scenario 6 shows that the monkey is combing his hair.

Krapo says:

(18) Mo   fin   truv   Ti   Zako   pe   fer   kitsoz   ek
        1SG   ASP   see   little   monkey   PROG   do   something   with
       Lurs.
       bear
       Ti   Zako$_i$ fin   **peny**   **so**   **seve**$_k$.
       little   monkey   ASP   comb   3POS   hair
       'I saw the monkey doing something to the bear. The monkey combed
       his hair.'

Chien and Wexler experiment: translated sentences and corresponding pictures.

Binding experiment 1: sentences with girls: two sentences per verb
Verb: montre 'point':

(1) Danielle **dir** Anielle pu bizen **montre li** -mem.
Danielle say Anielle MOD need show 3SG -REFL
'Danielle says that Anielle should point to herself.'

(2) Danielle **dir** Anielle pu bizen **montre li**.
Danielle say Anielle MOD need show 3SG
'Danielle says that Anielle should point to her.'

Verb: tuse 'touch':

(3) Danielle **dir** Anielle pu bizen **tus li** -mem.
Danielle say Anielle MOD need touch 3SG -REFL
'Danielle says that Anielle should touch herself.'

(4) Danielle **dir** Anielle pu bizen **tus li**.
Danielle say Anielle MOD need touch 3SG
'Danielle says that Anielle should touch her.'

Verb: grate 'scratch':

(5) Danielle **dir** Anielle pu bizen **grat li** -mem.
Danielle say Anielle MOD need scratch 3SG -REFL
'Danielle says that Anielle should scratch herself.'

(6) Danielle **dir** Anielle pu bizen **grat li**.
Danielle say Anielle MOD need scratch 3SG
'Danielle says that Anielle should scratch her.'

Verb: tiktike 'tickle':

(7) Danielle **dir** Anielle pu bizen **tiktik li** -mem.
Danielle say Anielle MOD need tickle 3SG -REFL
'Danielle says that Anielle should tickle herself.'

(8) Danielle **dir** Anielle pu bizen **tiktik li**.
Danielle say Anielle MOD need tickle 3SG
'Danielle says that Anielle should tickle her.'

Verb: montre 'point':

(9)   Daniel **dir** Raphael pu   bizen **montre** li   -mem.
     Daniel say Raphael MOD need show   3SG -REFL
     'Daniel says that Raphael should point to himself.'

(10) Daniel **dir** Raphael pu   bizen **montre** li.
     Daniel say Raphael MOD need show   3SG
     'Daniel says that Raphael should point to him.'

Verb: tuse 'touch':

(11) Daniel **dir** Raphael pu   bizen **tus**   li   -mem.
     Daniel say Raphael MOD need touch 3SG -REFL
     'Daniel says that Raphael should touch himself.'

(12) Daniel **dir** Raphael pu   bizen **tus**   li.
     Daniel say Raphael MOD need touch 3SG
     'Daniel says that Raphael should touch him.'

Verb: grate 'scratch':

(13) Daniel **dir** Raphael pu   bizen **grat**   li   -mem.
     Daniel say Raphael MOD need scratch 3SG -REFL
     'Daniel says that Raphael should scratch himself.'

(14) Daniel **dir** Raphael pu   bizen **grat**   li.
     Daniel say Raphael MOD need scratch 3SG
     'Daniel says that Raphael should scratch him.'

Verb: tiktike 'tickle':

(15) Daniel **dir** Raphael pu   bizen **tiktik** li   -mem.
     Daniel say Raphael MOD need tickle 3SG -REFL
     'Daniel says that Raphael should tickle himself.'

(16) Daniel **dir** Raphael pu . bizen **tiktik** li.
     Daniel say Raphael MOD need tickle 3SG
     'Daniel says that Raphael should tickle him.'

Binding experiment 2: girl scenario

Verb: montre 'point':

(1) Mari **ule** Annie montre **li** **-mem** ar so ledwa.
Mari want Annie show 3SG -REFL with 3POS finger
'Mari wants Annie to show herself with her finger.'

(2) Mari **ule** Annie montre **li** ar so ledwa.
Mari want Annie show 3SG with 3POS finger
'Mari wants Annie to show her with her finger.'

(3) Zan **ule** Annie montre **li** **-mem** ar so ledwa.
Zan want Annie show 3SG -REFL with 3POS finger
'John wants Annie to show herself with her finger.'

(4) Zan **ule** Annie montre **li** **ar** so ledwa.
Zan want Annie show 3SG with 3POS finger
'John wants Annie to show him with her finger.'

Verb: tuse 'touch':

(5) Mari **ule** Annie tus **li** **-mem.**
Mari want Annie touch 3SG -REFL
'Mari wants Annie to touch herself.'

(6) Mari **ule** Annie tus **li.**
Mari want Annie touch 3SG
'Mari wants Annie to show her.'

(7) Zan **ule** Annie tus **li** **-mem**.
Zan want Annie touch 3SG -REFL
'John wants Annie to show herself.'

(8) Zan **ule** Annie tus **li.**
Zan want Annie touch 3SG
'John wants Annie to touch him.'

Verb: grate 'scratch':

(9) Mari **ule** Annie grat **li** **-mem.**
Mari want Annie scratch 3SG -REFL
'Mari wants Annie to scratch herself.'

(10) Mari **ule** Annie grat **li**.
Mari want Annie scratch 3SG
'Mari wants Annie to scratch her.'

(11) Zan **ule** Annie grat **li** **-mem**.
Zan want Annie scratch 3SG -REFL
'John wants Annie to scratch herself.'

(12) Zan **ule** Annie grat **li**.
Zan want Annie scratch 3SG
'John wants Annie to scratch him.'

Verb: tiktike 'tickle':

(13) Mari **ule** Annie tiktik **li** **-mem**.
Mari want Annie tickle 3SG -REFL
'Mari wants Annie to tickle herself.'

(14) Mari **ule** Annie tiktik **li**.
Mari want Annie tickle 3SG
'Mari wants Annie to tickle her.'

(15) Zan **ule** Annie tiktik **li** **-mem**.
Zan want Annie tickle 3SG -REFL
'John wants Annie to tickle herself.'

(16) Zan **ule** Annie tiktik **li**.
Zan want Annie tickle 3SG
'John wants Annie to tickle him.'

Boy scenario

Verb: montre 'point':

(17) Zan **ule** Fabio montre **li** **-mem** ar so ledwa.
Zan want Fabio show 3SG -REFL with 3POS finger
'John wants Fabio to show himself with his finger.'

(18) Zan **ule** Fabio montre **li** ar so ledwa.
Zan want Fabio show 3SG with 3POS finger
'John wants Fabio to show him with his finger.'

(19) Mari **ule** Fabio montre **li** **-mem** ar so ledwa.
Mari want Fabio show 3SG -REFL with 3POS finger
'Mari wants Fabio to show himself with his finger.'

(20) Mari **ule** Fabio montre **li** ar so ledwa.
Mari want Fabio show 3SG with 3POS finger
'Marie wants Fabio to show him with his finger.'

Verb: tuse 'touch':

(21) Zan **ule** Fabio tus **li** **-mem**.
Zan want Fabio touch 3SG -REFL
'John wants Fabio to touch himself.'

(22) Zan **ule** Fabio tus **li**.
Zan want Fabio touch 3SG
'John wants Fabio to touch him.'

(23) Mari **ule** Fabio tus **li** **-mem**.
Mari want Fabio touch 3SG -REFL
'Mari wants Fabio to show himself.'

(24) Mari **ule** Fabio tus **li**.
Mari want Fabio touch 3SG
'Mari wants Fabio to touch him.'

Verb: grate 'scratch':

(25) Zan **ule** Fabio grat **li** **-mem**.
Zan want Fabio scratch 3SG -REFL
'John wants Fabio to scratch himself.'

(26) Zan **ule** Fabio grat **li**.
Zan want Fabio scratch 3SG
'John wants Fabio to scratch him.'

(27) Mari **ule** Fabio grat **li** **-mem**.
Mari want Fabio scratch 3SG -REFL
'Mari wants Fabio to scratch himself.'

(28) Mari **ule** Fabio grat **li**.
Mari want Fabio scratch 3SG
'Mari wants Fabio to scratch him.'

Verb: tiktike 'tickle':

(29) Zan **ule** Fabio tiktik **li** **-mem**.
Zan want Fabio tickle 3SG -REFL
'John wants Fabio to tickle himself.'

(30) Zan **ule** Fabio tiktik **li**.
Zan want Fabio tickle 3SG
'John wants Fabio to tickle him.'

(31) Mari **ule** Fabio tiktik **li** **-mem**.
Mari want Fabio tickle 3SG -REFL
'Mari wants Fabio to tickle himself.'

(32) Mari **ule** Fabio tiktik **li**.
Mari want Fabio tickle 3SG
'Marie wants Fabio to tickle him.'

Binding experiment 3: girl scenario

Reflexive sentences:

(1) Mari **dir** Anissa **pu** **bizen** don **li** **-mem** en loto.
Mari say Anissa MOD need give 3SG -REFL a car
'Mari says Anissa should give herself a car.'

(2) Mari **dir** Anissa **pu** **bizen** don en loto **li** **-mem**.
Mari say Anissa MOD need give a car 3SG -REFL
'Mari says Anissa should give a car to herself.'

(3) Mari **ule** Anissa don **li** **-mem** en bul.
Mari want Anissa give 3SG -REFL a ball
'Mari wants Anissa to give herself a ball.'

(4) Mari **ule** Anissa don en bul **li** **-mem**.
Mari want Anissa give a ball 3SG -REFL
'Mari wants Anissa to give a ball to herself.'

Pronoun sentences:

(5) Mari **dir** Anissa **pu** **bizen** don **li** en draze.
Mari say Anissa MOD need give 3SG a lolly
'Mari says Anissa should give her a lolly.'

(6) Mari **dir** Anissa **pu** **bizen** don en draze **li**
Mari say Anissa MOD need give a lolly 3SG
'Mari says Anissa should give a lolly to her.'

(7) Marie **ule**   Anissa   don   en   serviet   **li**
     Mari   want   Anissa   give   a   napkin   3SG
     'Mari wants Anissa to give a napkin to her.'

(8) Marie **ule**   Anissa   don   **li**   en   serviet
     Mari   want   Anissa   give   3SG   a   napkin
     'Mari wants Anissa give her a napkin.'

Boy scenario
Reflexive sentences:

(9) Zan   **dir**   Leeroy   **pu**   **bizen**   don   **li**   **-mem**   en   loto.
    Zan   say   Leeroy   MOD   need   give   3SG   -REFL   a   car
    'Zan says Leeroy should give himself a car.'

(10) Zan   **dir**   Leeroy   **pu**   **bizen**   don   en   loto   **li**   **-mem**.
     Zan   say   Leeroy   MOD   need   give   a   car   3SG   -REFL
     'John says Leeroy should give a car to himself'

(11) Zan   **ule**   Leeroy   don   **li**   **-mem**   en   bul.
     Zan   want   Leeroy   give   3SG   -REFL   a   ball
     'John wants Leeroy to give himself a ball.'

(12) Zan   **ule**   Leeroy   don   en   bul   **li**   **-mem**.
     Zan   want   Leeroy   give   a   ball   3SG   -REFL
     'John wants Leeroy to give a ball to himself.'

Pronoun sentences:

(13) Zan   **dir**   Leeroy   **pu**   **bizen**   don   **li**   en   draze.
     Zan   say   Leeroy   MOD   need   give   3SG   a   lolly
     'John says Leeroy should give him a lolly.'

(14) Zan   **dir**   Leeroy   **pu**   **bizen**   don   en   draze   **li**.
     Zan   say   Leeroy   MOD   need   give   a   lolly   3SG
     'John says Leeroy should give a lolly to him.'

(15) Zan   **ule**   Leeroy   don   **li**   en   serviet.
     Zan   want   Leeroy   give   3SG   a   napkin
     'John wants Leeroy to give him a napkin.'

(16) Zan **ule** Leeroy don en serviet **li**.
Zan want Leeroy give a napkin 3SG
'John wants Leeroy to give a napkin to him.'

Binding experiment 4: the match cases
Name-reflexive:

(1) Sa Mari; Sa Mama Tediber. Eski Mama Tediber pe **tus limem**?
'This is Mary; this is Mama Bear. Is Mama Bear touching herself?'

Name-pronoun:

(2) Sa Mama Tediber; Sa Mari. Eski Mama Tediber pu tus li?
'This is Mama Bear; this is Mary. Is Mama Bear touching her?'

Quantifier-reflexive:

(3) Sa Mari; Sa ban tediber. Eski sak tediber pe tus limem?
'This is Mary; these are the bears. Is every bear touching herself?'

Quantifier-pronoun:

(4) Sa ban tediber; Sa Mari. Eski sak tediber pe tus li?
'These are the bears; this is Mary. Is every bear touching her?'

The mismatch cases
Name-reflexive:

(5) Sa Mari; Sa Mama Tediber. Eski Mama Tediber pu tus limem?
'This is Mary; this is Mama Bear. Is Mama Bear touching herself?'

Name-pronoun:

(6) Sa Mama Tediber; Sa Mari. Eski Mama Tediber pe tus li?
'This is Mama Bear; this is Mary. Is Mama Bear touching her?'

Quantifier-reflexive:

(7) Sa Mari; Sa ban tediber. Eski sak tediber pe tus limem?
'This is Mary; these are the bears. Is every bear touching herself?'

Quantifier-pronoun:

(8) Sa ban tediber; Sa Mari. Eski sak tediber pe tus li?
'These are the bears; this is Mari. Is every bear touching her?'

The match cases
Name-name:

(9) Sa Mama Tediber; Sa Mari. Eski Mama Tediber pe tus Mari?
'This is Mama Bear; This is Mary. Is Mama Bear touching Mari?'

Quantifier 'every'-name:

(10) Sa ban tediber; Sa mari. Eski sak tediber pe tus Mari?
'These are the bears; this is Mary. Is every bear touching Mari?

Quantifier 'all'-name:

(11) Sa ban tediber; Sa Mari. Eski tu ban tediber pe tus Mari?
'These are the bears; this is Mari. Are all the bears touching Mari?'

The mismatch cases
Name-name:

(12) Sa Mama Tediber; Sa Mari. Eski Mama Tediber pe tus Mari?
'This is Mama Bear; this is Mari. Is Mama Bear touching Mari?'

Quantifier 'every'-name:

(13) Sa ban tediber; Sa Mari. Eski sak tediber pe tus Mari?
'These are the bears; this is Mary. Is every bear touching Mari?'

Quantifier 'all'-name:

(14) Sa ban tediber; Sa Mari. Eski tu ban tediber pe tus Mari?
'These are the bears; this is Mary. Are all the bears touching Mary?'

Appendix B Experimental materials on double-object constructions

Adone experiment on double-object constructions

List of sentences:

(1) a.   Chloe   ti   aste   Annie   en   bul
      Chloe   TNS   buy   Annie   a   ball
      'Chloe bought Annie a ball.'

     b.   Chloe   ti   aste   en   bul   Annie
      Chloe   TNS   buy   a   ball   Annie
      'Chloe bought a ball for Annie.'

(2) a.   Marius   ti   kwi   Kenny   en   gato
      Marius   TNS   cook   Kenny   a   cake
      'Marius baked Kenny a cake.'

     b.   Marius   ti   kwi   en   gato   Kenny.
      Marius   TNS   cook   a   cake   Kenny
      'Marius baked a cake for Kenny.'

(3) a.   Marius   ti   amen   Kenny   en   draze
      Marius   TNS   bring   Kenny   a   lolly
      'Marius brought Kenny a lolly.'

     b.   Marius   ti   amen   en   draze   Kenny
      Marius   TNS   bring   a   lolly   Kenny
      'Marius brought a lolly for Kenny.'

(4) a.   Aysha   ti   rand   Nightarra   en   liv
      Aysha   TNS   return   Nightarra   a   book
      'Aysha returned a book to Nightarra.'

     b.   Aysha   ti   rand   en   liv   Nightarra
      Aysha   TNS   return   a   book   Nightarra
      'Aysha returned a book to Nightarra.'

(5) a. Tania ti   deman Zan sulyer.
         Tania TNS ask   Zan shoes
         'Tania asked Zan shoes.'

      b. Tania ti   deman sulyer Zan.
         Tania TNS ask   shoes   Zan
         'Tania asked shoes to Zan.'

(6) a. Tania ti   rakont Zan en zistwar.
         Tania TNS tell   Zan a   story
         'Tania told Zan a story.'

      b. Tania ti   rakont en zistwar Zan.
         Tania TNS tell   a   story   Zan
         'Tania told a story to Zan.'

(7) a. Brandon ti   dir   Marcus en keksoz
         Brandon TNS say   Marcus a   thing
         'Brandon told Marcus something.'

      b. Brandon ti   dir   en keksoz Marcus
         Brandon TNS say   a   thing   Marcus
         'Brandon told something Marcus.'

(8) a. Raphael ti   sant   Elmo en sanson
         Raphael TNS sing Elmo a   song
         'Raphael sang Elmo a song.'

      b. Raphael ti   sant   en sanson Elmo
         Raphael TNS sing a   song   Elmo
         'Raphael sang a song to Elmo.'

(9) a. Christian ti   montre Elmo en portre
         Christian TNS show   Elmo a   picture
         'Christian showed Elmo a picture.'

      b. Christian ti   montre en porter   Elmo
         Christian TNS show   a   picture Elmo
         'Christian showed a picture to Elmo.'

(10) a. Nissa ti   pey   Mitch dis Rupi
         Nissa TNS pay   Mitch ten rupees
         'Nissa paid Mitch ten rupees.'

      b. Nissa ti   pey   dis Rupi   Mitch
         Nissa TNS pay   ten rupees Mitch
         'Nissa paid ten rupees to Mitch.'

(11) a. Anthony ti explik Terryna en portre
     Anthony TNS explain Terryna a picture
     'Anthony explained Terryna a picture.'

   b. Anthony ti explik en porter Terryna
     Anthony TNS explain a picture Terryna
     'Anthony explained a picture to Terryna.'

(12) a. Rye ti don Sherman en draze
     Rye TNS give Sherman a lolly
     'Rye gave Sherman a lolly.'

   b. Rye ti don en draze Sherman.
     Rye TNS give a lolly Sherman
     'Rye gave a lolly to Sherman.'

(13) a. Anissa ti fer Edrick en sandkarsel
     Anissa TNS make Edrick a sandcastle
     'Anissa made Edrick a sandcastle.'

   b. Anissa ti fer en sandkarsel Edrick
     Anissa TNS make a sandcastle Edrick
     'Anissa made a sandcastle for Edrick.'

(14) a. Wilnette ti desin Zan en lakaz
     Wilnette TNS draw John a house
     'Wilnette drew John a house.'

   b. Wilnette ti desin en lakaz Zan
     Wilnette TNS draw a house John
     'Wilnette drew a house for John.'

(15) a. Jean Yves ti avoy Aaron en kado
     Jean Yves TNS send Aaron a present
     'Jean Yves sent Aaron a present.'

   b. Jean Yves ti avoy en kado Aaron
     Jean Yves TNS send a present Aaron
     'Jean Yves sent a present to Aaron.'

(16) a. Raphael ti ekrir Laurent en let
     Raphael TNS write Laurent a letter
     'Raphael wrote Laurent a letter.'

   b. Raphael ti ekrir Laurent en let
     Raphael TNS write Laurent a letter
     'Raphael wrote Laurent a letter.'

Appendix C Experimental materials on passive constructions

List of sentences presented in the same order to Seselwa speakers

Van der Lely experiment:

FIGURE AC.1 Van der Lely test of active and passive sentences

(1) Sa ti garson pe kup sa lelefan
     'The little boy cuts the elephant.' (AT)

(2) Sa loto in bit ek sa kamiyon
     'The car hits the lorry.' (AT)

(3) Sa ti garson in kupe par/ek sa lelefan.
     'The little boy is cut by the elephant.' (FVP)

(4) Sa ti garson pe beny sa tifi.
'The little boy washes the girl.' (AT)

(5) Sa tediber pe kud.
'The teddy is being mended.' (SPP)

(6) Sa kamyon pe bit ek sa loto.
'The lorry hits the car.' (AT)

(7) Sa tediber in kud par/ek sa tifi.
'The teddy is mended by the girl.' (FVP)

(8) Sa pwason in manze.
'The fish is eaten.' (AP)

(9) Sa ti garson pe benye.
'The little boy is being washed.' (SPP)

(10) Sa kamyon in bite.
'The lorry is hit.' (AP)

(11) Sa misie pe manz sa pwason.
'The man eats the fish.' (AT)

(12) Sa tediber pe kud.
'The teddy is being mended.' (SPP)

(13) Sa tifi pe beny par/ek sa ti garson.
'The little girl is washed by the little boy.' (FVP)

(14) Sa lelefan pe kupe.
'The elephant is being cut.' (SPP)

(15) Sa misie in desine.
'The man is painted.' (AP)

(16) Sa tifi in kud.
'The little girl is mended.' (AP)

(17) Sa tifi pe beny sa ti garson.
'The little girl washed the little boy.' (AT)

(18) Sa loto in bite.
'The car is hit.' (AP)

(19) Sa madam in desine par/ek sa misie.
'The woman is painted by the man.' (FVT)

(20)   Sa lelefan in kupe.
       'The elephant is cut.' (AP)

(21)   Sa misie in manze.
       'The man is eaten.' (AP)

(22)   Sa kamyon in bite ek sa loto.
       'The lorry is hit by the car.' (AP)

(23)   Sa madam in desine.
       'The woman is painted.' (AP)

(24)   Sa tifi pe kud par/ek tediber.
       'The little girl is being mended by the teddy bear.' (SPP)

(25)   Sa lelefan pe kup sa ti garson.
       'The elephant cuts the little boy.' (AT)

(26)   Sa pwason in manze par/ek sa misie.
       'The fish is eaten by the man.' (FVP)

(27)   Sa ti garson in benye par/ek sa tifi.
       'The little boy is washed by the girl.' (FVP)

(28)   Sa tediber pe kud sa tifi.
       'The teddy mends the girl.' (AT)

(29)   Sa tifi in benye.
       'The little girl is washed.' (AP)

(30)   Sa pwason pe manz sa misie.
       'The fish eats the man' (AT)

(31)   Sa misie in desine.
       'The man is painted.' (AP)

(32)   Sa loto in bite.
       'The car is hit.' (AP)

(33)   Sa misie in manze par/ek sa pwason.
       'The man is eaten by the fish.' (FVP)

(34)   Sa madam pe desin sa misie.
       'The woman paints the man.' (AT)

(35)   Sa tifi in kud.
       'The little girl is mended.' (AP)

(36) Sa misie in manze.
      'The man is eaten.' (AP)

(37) Sa misie pe desine par/ek sa madam.
      'The man is painted by the woman.' (FVP)

(38) Sa kamyon pe bite.
      'The lorry is being hit.' (SPP)

(39) Sa ti garson in kupe.
      'The little boy is being cut.' (SPP)

(40) Sa loto in bite ek kamyon.
      'The car is hit by the lorry.' (FVP)

(41) Sa ti garson in kupe.
      'The little boy is cut.' (AP)

(42) Sa misie pe desin sa madam.
      'The man paints the woman.' (AT)

(43) Sa ti garson in kupe.
      'The little boy is cut.' (AP)

(44) Sa tifi pe benye.
      'The little girl is being washed.' (SPP)

(45) Sa madam pe desine.
      'The woman is being painted.' (SPP)

(46) Sa tifi pe kud sa tediber.
      'The little girl mends the teddy.' (AT)

(47) Sa lelefan pe kupe par/ek sa ti garson.
      'The elephant is being cut by the little boy.' (SPP)

(48) Sa pwason pe manze.
      'The fish is being eaten.' (SPP)

Verrips experiment:

(1) Get sa serkl fin vire ek/par baton/suri lor la.
     'Look, this merry-go-round is turned around with a stick/a mouse on it'
     (passive causative)

(2) Get Ti Zan fin penn latab ek/par pinso/sez.
     'Look, John is painting the table with a brush/chair'.
     (active transitive)

(3) Get sa papiyon fin atrape ek/par en filet/en muszon.
'Look, the butterfly is caught with a net/a bee.'
(passive transitive)

(4) Get sa ti lisyen pe rule ek/par en balye/en bul.
'Look, this little dog is rolled by a stick/a ball.'
(anti-causative)

(5) Get sa brans fin kurbe ek/par en pom /en lot brans.
'Look, this branch is bent by an apple/another branch.'
(passive anti-causative)

(6) Get Pol fin bwar limonad ek/par en straw/ais.
'Look, Paul drank lemonade with a straw/ice.
(active transitive)

(7) Get sa latab fin netoye ek/par Ti Zan/sifon.
'Look, this table has been cleaned by/with John/a piece of cloth.'
(passive transitive)

(8) Get karusel pe turne ek/par en lapel/en lisyen lor li.
'Look, the merry-go-round is turning by/with a spade/a dog on it.'
(anti-causative)

(9) Get en ros ape geny rule ek/par en lapel/en ti zwazo lor li.
'Look, a rock is being rolled by/with a spade/a little bird on it.'
(passive causative)

(10) Get zoranz fin manze ek/par furset/pom.
'Look, the orange is eaten with a fork/an apple.'
(passive transitive)

(11) Get Pyer pe penn. Sa pu en madam ek lisyen/peinso
'Look, Peter is painting. This will be a woman with a dog/a
paintbrush.'
(zero-copula)

(12) Get Zan pe kupe. Sa pu en bato ek sizo/lawal
'Look, John is cutting. It will become a boat with scissors/a sail.'
(zero copula)

(13) Get en poto pe kurbe ek en lakord/en flag
'Look, a pole is bending with a rope/a flag.'
(anti-causative)

(14) Get Zan pe desine. Sa pu en lakaz ek en krayon/en lema
      'Look, John is drawing. It will be a house with a pencil/a TV aerial.'
      (zero-copula)

(15) Get zerb ape geny kupe ek en masin/ban fler.
      'Look, grass is being mowed with a mowing machine/flowers.'
      (passive transitive)

(16) Get en ti garson ape geny puse ek/par en baton/en aiskrim
      'Look, a little boy is being pushed with a broom/an ice cream.'
      (passive transitive)

Appendix D Experimental materials on serial verb constructions

List of sentences:

(1) Marmay pe   pran   balon   met lor miray.
    children PROG   take   balloon   put on   wall
    'The children are hanging the balloons onto the wall.'

(2) Pyero i   pe   taye atrap balon.
    Pyero 3SG   PROG   run   catch balloon
    'Pyero is running after the balloon.'

(3) Mari   i   pe   ris   tediber   kas   li.
    Mari   3SG   PROG   pull   teddy bear   break   3SG
    'Mari is tearing the teddy bear.'

(4) Ti   lisyen   i   n   pran sulyer in   taye.
    little   dog   3SG ASP   take shoe   ASP   run
    'The little dog ran away with the shoe.'

(5) Lisyen i   pe   marse vire fer letur   pye   dibwa.
    dog   3SG   PROG   walk   turn go   around tree wood
    'The dog is going around and around the tree.'

(6) Ti   garson i   n   penn   en   bwat in   fini.
    little   boy   3SG ASP   paint a   box   ASP   finish
    'The little boy finished painting the box.'

(7) Ti   garson i   pe   tap   bul   al   dan   lakaz.
    little   boy   3SG PROG   kick ball go   in   house
    'The little boy kicked the ball into the house.'

(8) Granpapa in   kas   bilimbi pe   met   dan bol   pe
    Granddad ASP   cut   bilimbi PROG   put   in   bowl   PROG
       amen   lakaz
       bring   home
    'Granddad has gathered bilimbi and put them in the bowl to bring home.'

(9) Mari   in   avoy   so   manze   enler   in   fan/tonb
    Mari   ASP   throw   3POS   food   up   ASP   spill/fall
    ater
    on the ground
    'Mari has thrown her food onto the floor.'

(10) Mari   in   pus   sa   tifi   fer   li   tonbe.
     Mari   ASP   push   this   girl   CAUS   3SG   fall
     'Mari has pushed this girl and made her fall.'

(11) Sa   tifi   in   sorti   dan   lakaz   pe   al dan   lapli.
     this   girl   ASP   come out   in   house   PROG   go in   rain
     'This girl came out of the house and went into the rain.'

(12) Madam   in   pran   marmai   amen   labutik
     madam   ASP   take   children   bring   shop
     'The woman is taking the children to the shop.'

(13) Misie   pe   aste   balon   don   mamai
     man   PROG   buy   balloon   give   children
     'The man bought balloons and gave them to the children.'

(14) Marmai   in   amen   termos   don   mama
     children   ASP   bring   bottle   give   mother
     'The children have brought the bottle to the mother.'

(15) Mama   in   pran   zuzu   in   met   dan   larmwar
     mother   ASP   take   toy   ASP   put   in   wardrobe
     'The mother took the toys and put them into the wardrobe.'

(16) Madam   in   tir   sulyer   dan   bwat   pe   done   Mari
     woman   ASP   take   shoe   in   box   PROG   give   mari
     'The woman took the shoes off the box and gave them to Mari.'

(17) Ban   marmai   pe   balye   netoy   lasam
     PL   child   PROG   brush   clean   room
     'The children have cleaned/tidied up the room.'

(18) Madam   pe   kup   dipen   don   marmai.
     woman   PROG   cut   bread   give   child
     'The woman is cutting bread and giving it to the children.'

(19) Ti   lisyen   pe   taye   swiv   ban   marmai.
     little   dog   PROG   run   follow   PL   child
     'The little dog is running after/chasing the children.'

References

Adone, D. (1994a), *The Acquisition of Mauritian Creole* (Amsterdam: Benjamins).

(1994b), 'Creolization and language change in Mauritian Creole' in D. Adone and I. Plag (eds.), *Creolization and Language Change* (Tübingen: Niemeyer), 23–43.

(1997), *The Acquisition of Ngukurr Kriol as a First Language.* A.I.A.T.S.I.S project report (Darwin/Canberra).

(2001a), 'Morphology in two Indian Ocean Creoles', paper presented at the meeting of the Society of Pidgin and Creole Languages, University of Coimbra, Portugal.

(2001b), 'English in two French-based Creoles: Seselwa and Morisyen', paper presented at the meeting of the International Association of University Professors of English, Bamberg.

(2003), 'Reduplication in Creole and sign languages', paper presented at the meeting of the Society of Pidgin and Creole Languages, University of Manoa, Hawaii.

(2006), 'Interference in bilingual grammar: evidence from Morisyen and French bilingual speakers', paper presented at the meeting of the Society of Pidgin and Creole Languages, annual meeting of the Linguistic Society of America, Albuquerque.

(2007), 'From gestures to Mauritian Sign Language', paper presented at the Current Issues in Sign Language Research Conference, University of Cologne, Germany.

(2009), 'Grammaticalisation and creolisation: the case of Ngukurr Kriol', paper presented at the meeting of the Society of Pidgin and Creole Languages, San Francisco.

Adone, D. and I. Plag (eds.) (1994), *Creolization and Language Change* (Tübingen: Niemeyer).

Adone, D. and A. Vainikka (1999), 'Acquisition of wh-questions in Mauritian Creole' in M. DeGraff (ed.), *Language Creation and Language Change. Creolization, Diachrony, and Development* (Cambridge, MA: MIT Press), 75–94.

Aikhenvald, A. (2006), 'Serial verb constructions in typological perspective' in A. Aikhenvald and R. M. W. Dixon (eds.), *Serial Verb Constructions. A Cross-linguistic Typology* (Oxford University Press), 1–68.

Aikhenvald, A. and R. M. W. Dixon (eds.) (2006), *Serial Verb Constructions. A Cross-linguistic Typology* (Oxford University Press).

Allen, S. E. M. (1996), *Aspects of Argument Structure Acquisition in Inuktitut* (Amsterdam: Benjamins).

Allen, S. E. M. and M. B. Crago (1996), 'Early passive acquisition in Inuktitut', *Journal of Child Language* 23.1, 129–155.

Alleyne, M.C. (1971), 'Acculturation and the cultural matrix of creolisation' in D. Hymes (ed.), *Pidginizationa and Creolization of languages. Proceedings of a conference held at the University of the West Indies in Mona, Jamaica* (Cambridge University Press), 169–186.

Andersen, E. S., A. Dunlea and L. S. Kekelis (1984), 'Blind children's language: resolving some differences', *Journal of Child Language* 11, 645–664.

Andersen, R. W. (1981a), 'Two perspectives on pidginization as second language acquisition' in R. W. Andersen (ed.), *New Dimensions in Second Language Acquisition Research* (Rowley, MA: Newbury House), 165–195.

Andersen, R. W. (ed.) (1981b), *New Dimensions in Second Language Acquisition Research* (Rowley, MA: Newbury House).

(1983a), *Pidginization and Creolization as Language Acquisition* (Rowley, MA: Newbury House).

Andersen, R. W. (1983b), 'Transfer to somewhere' in S. Gass and L. Selinker (eds.), *Language Transfer in Language Learning* (Rowley, MA: Newbury House), 177–201.

Ansaldo, U. and S. Matthews (2007), 'Deconstructing creole: the rationale' in U. Ansaldo, S. Matthews and L. Lim (eds.), *Deconstructing Creole. Typological Studies in Language* 73 (Amsterdam/Philadelphia: John Benjamins), 1–18.

Arends, J. (1993), 'Towards a gradualist model of creolization' in F. Byrne and J. Holm (eds.), *Atlantic Meets Pacific: A Global View of Pidginization and Creolization* (Amsterdam: John Benjamins), 371–380.

Arends, J., P. Muysken and N. Smith (eds.) (1994), *Pidgins and Creoles. An Introduction* (Amsterdam: Benjamins).

Arsenijevic, B. and W. Hinzen (2010), 'Recursion as a human universal and as a primitive', *Biolinguistics* 4, 165–173.

Baggioni, D. and D. de Robillard (1990), *Ile Maurice: Une Francophonie Paradoxale* (Paris: L'Harmattan).

Baker, C. L. (1979), 'Syntactic theory and the projection problem', *Linguistic Inquiry* 10, 533–581.

Baker, M., K. Johnson and I. Roberts (1989), 'Passive arguments raised', *Linguistic Inquiry* 20, 219–252.

Baker, P. and C. Corne (1982), *Isle de France Creole: Affinities and Origins* (Ann Arbor, MI: Karoma).

Baker, P. and A. Syea (eds.) (1996), *Changing Meanings, Changing Forms. Grammaticalisation in Creoles* (London: University of Westminster Press).

Baptista, M. (2002), *The Syntax of Cape Verdean Creole* (Amsterdam: John Benjamins).

Bartke, S., G. F. Marcus and H. Clahsen (1996), 'Acquiring German noun plurals' in D. MacLaughlin and S. McEwen (eds.), *Proceedings of the 19th Annual Boston University Conference on Language Development* (Somerville, MA: Cascadilla Press), 60–70.

Bellugi, U. and M. St George (eds.) (2000), 'Linking cognitive neuroscience and molecular genetics: new perspectives from Williams Syndrome', *Journal of Cognitive Neuroscience* 12.1, 1–107.

Bencini, G. M. L. and V. Valian (2008), 'Abstract sentence representation in 3-year-olds: evidence from comprehension and production', *Journal of Memory and Language* 59, 97–113.

Bever, T. G. (1970), 'The cognitive basis for linguistic structures' in J. Hayes (ed.), *Cognition and the Development of Language* (New York: J. Wiley and Sons), 279–352.

Bickerton, D. (1974), 'Creolization, linguistic universals and natural seman-tax and the brain', *University of Hawaii Working Papers in Linguistics* 6.3, 125–141.

(1981), *Roots of Language* (Ann Arbor: Karoma).

(1984), 'The language bioprogram hypothesis', *Behavioral and Brain Sciences* 7, 173–221.

(1988), 'Creole languages and the bioprogram' in F. J. Newmeyer (ed.), *Linguistics: The Cambridge Survey* (Cambridge University Press), vol. ii, 268–284.

(1989), 'Seselwa serialization and its significance', *Journal of Pidgin and Creole Languages* 4.2, 155–183.

(1990), 'If it quacks like a duck... A reply to Seuren', *Journal of Pidgin and Creole Languages* 5.2, 293–303.

(1995), *Language and Human Behavior* (Seattle,WA: University of Washington Press).

(1996), 'An innate language faculty needs neither modularity nor localization', *Behavioral and Brain Sciences* 19.4, 631–632.

(1998), 'Catastrophic evolution: the case for a single step from protolanguage to full human language' in J. R. Hurford *et al.* (eds.), *Approaches to the Evolution of Language* (Cambridge University Press), 341–358.

(1999), 'How to acquire language without positive evidence: what acquisitionists can learn from Creoles' in M. DeGraff (ed.), *Language Creation and Language Change. Creolization, Diachrony, and Development* (Cambridge, MA: MIT Press), 49–74.

Bickerton, D. and S. Iatridou (1987), 'Verb serialization and empty categories', unpublished manuscript, University of Amsterdam.

Boeckx, C., N. Hornstein and J. Nunes (2007), *Control as Movement* (Cambridge University Press).

Bollée, A. (1977), *Le créole francais des Seychelles* (Tübingen: Niemeyer).

(1993), *Dictionnaire etymologique des creoles francais de l'ocean Indien* (Hamburg: Buske).

Bollée, A. (ed.) (2007), *Deux textes religieux de Bourbon du 18e siècle et l'histoire du creole reunionnais. Philippe-Albert Caulier C. M: Profession de Foy, en jargon des Esclaves Nêgres/Petit Catechisme de l'Isle de Bourbon tourné au Style des Esclaves Nêgres* (London, Maharagama: Battlebridge).

Borer, H. (1984), *Parametric Syntax* (Dordrecht: Foris).

(1996), 'Passive without theta grids', unpublished manuscript, University of Massachusetts.

Borer, H. and K. Wexler (1987), 'The maturation of syntax' in T. Roeper and E. Williams (eds.), *Parameter Setting* (Dordrecht: Reidel), 123–172.

Boretzky, N. (1983), *Kreolsprachen, Substrate und Sprachwandel* (Wiesbaden: Harrasowitz).

Bowerman, M. (1979), 'The acquisition of complex sentences' in M. Garman and P. Fletcher (eds.), *Studies in Language Acquisition* (Cambridge University Press), 285–305.

(1982), 'Reorganizational processes in lexical and syntactic development' in E. Wanner and L. R. Gleitman (eds.), *Language Acquisition: the State of the Art* (Cambridge University Press), 319–346.

(1987), 'The "no negative evidence" problem: how do children avoid constructing an overly general grammar?' in J. A. Hawkins (ed.), *Explaining Language Universals* (Oxford: Blackwell), 73–101.

Brandi, L. and P. Cordin (1989), 'Two Italian dialects and the null subject parameter' in O. Jaeggli and Ken Safir (eds.), *The Null Subject Parameter* (Dordrecht: Kluwer), 111–142.

Briscoe, E. J. (ed.) (2002a), *Linguistic Evolution Through Language Acquisition: Formal and Computational Models* (Cambridge University Press).

Briscoe, E. J. (2002b), 'Grammatical acquisition and linguistic selection' in E. Briscoe (ed.), *Linguistic Evolution Through Language Acquisition: Formal and Computational Models* (Cambridge University Press), 255–300.

Brooks, P. and M. Tomasello (1999), 'Young children learn to produce passives with nonce verbs', *Developmental Psychology* 35.1, 29–44.

Bruyn, A. and T. Veenstra (1993), 'The creolisation of Dutch', *Journal of Pidgin and Creole Languages* 8.1, 29–80.

Bruyn, A., P. Muysken and M. Verrips (1999), 'Double-object constructions in the Creole languages: development and acquisition' in M. DeGraff (ed.), *Language Creation and Language Change. Creolization, Diachrony, and Development* (Cambridge, MA: MIT Press), 239–373.

Burzio, L. (1986), *Italian Syntax. A Government-Binding Approach* (Dordrecht: Reidel).

Byrne, A. (1987), *Grammatical Relations in a Radical Creole: Creole Language Library 3* (Amsterdam: Benjamins).

Cairns, H. and D. McDaniel (1987), 'The status of the binding principles in the grammars of young children', paper presented at the 12th Annual Boston University Conference on Language Development.

Carden, G. and W. A. Stewart (1989), 'Mauritian Creole reflexives: a reply to Corne', *Journal of Pidgin and Creole Languages* 4.1, 65–101.

Chaudenson, R. (1981), *Textes créoles anciens (La Reunion et L'Ile Maurice)* (Hamburg: Buske).

  (1992), *Des iles, des hommes, des langues: essais sur la créolisation linguistique et culturelle* (Paris: L'Harmattan).

Chien, Y. C. and K. Wexler (1987a), 'Children's acquisition of reflexives and pronouns', *Papers and Reports on Child Language Development* 26, 30–39.

  (1987b), 'A comparison between Chinese-speaking and English-speaking children's acquisition of reflexives and pronouns', paper presented at the 12th Annual Boston University Conference on Language Development.

  (1988), 'Children's acquisition of binding principles', paper presented at the 13th Annual Boston University Conference on Language Development.

  (1990), 'Children's knowledge of locality conditions in binding as evidence for the modularity of syntax and pragmatics', *Language Acquisition* 1, 225–295.

Chomsky, N. (1965), *Aspects of the Theory of Syntax* (Cambridge, MA: MIT Press).

  (1980), *Rules and Representations* (New York: Columbia University Press).

  (1981), *Lectures on Government and Binding: The Pisa Lectures* (Dordrecht: Foris) / Reprint (Berlin and New York: Mouton de Gruyter, 1993).

  (1986), *Barriers.* (Cambridge, MA: MIT Press).

(2002), *On Nature and Language* (Cambridge University Press).

Chouinard, M. M. and E. V. Clark (2003), 'Adult reformulations of child errors as negative evidence', *Journal of Child Language* 30, 637–669.

Clahsen, H. (ed.) (1996), *Generative Perspectives on Language Acquisition* (Amsterdam: Benjamins).

Clahsen, H. (1999), 'Lexical entries and rules of language: a multidisciplinary study of German inflection', *Behavioral and Brain Sciences* 22.6, 991–1013.

Clahsen, H., S. Eisenbeiss and M. Penke (1996), 'Lexical learning in early syntactic development' in H. Clahsen (ed.), *Generative Perspectives on Language Acquisition* (Amsterdam: Benjamins), 129–160.

Clahsen, H. and M. Almazan (1998), 'Syntax and morphology in Williams Syndrome', *Cognition* 68, 167–198.

Clark, A. and S. Lappin (2011), *Linguistic Nativism and the Poverty of the Stimulus* (Hoboken, NJ: Wiley-Blackwell).

Clark, E. V. (2001), 'Emergent categories in first language acquisition' in S. C. Levinson and M. Bowerman (eds.), *Language Acquisition and Conceptual Development* (Cambridge University Press), 379–405.

Corne, C. (1970), *Essai de grammaire du creole mauricien* (Auckland: Linguistic Society of New Zealand).

(1977), *Seychelles Creole Grammar* (Tübingen: Gunter Narr Verlag).

(1988), 'Mauritian Creole réflexives', *Journal of Pidgin and Creole Languages* 3, 69–94.

Crain, S. and C. McKee (1985), 'Acquisition of structural restrictions on anaphors' in S. Berman, J. W. Choe and J. McDonough (eds.), *Proceedings of the 16th Annual Meeting of the North Eastern Linguistic Society (NELS)* (Montreal: McGill University), 94–110.

(1987), 'Cross-linguistic analysis of the acquisition of coreference relations', paper presented at the 12th Annual Boston University Conference on Language Development.

Curtiss, S. (1977), *Genie: A Linguistic Study of a Modern-Day 'Wild-Child'* (New York: Academic Press).

Curtiss, S. and S. de Bode (2001), 'Language after hemispherectomy: if neither side nor age matters, what does?' in A. Do, L. Domínguez and A. Johansen (eds.), *Proceedings of the 25th Annual Boston University Conference on Language Development* (Somerville: Cascadilla Press), vol. i, 202–213.

Darwin, C. (1877), 'A bibliographical sketch of an infant', *Mind* 2, 285–294.

DeGraff, M. (ed.) (1999), *Language Creation and Language Change. Creolization, Diachrony, and Development* (Cambridge, MA: MIT Press).

DeGraff, M. (2003), 'Against creole exceptionalism', *Language* 79.2, 391–410.

Demuth, K. (1996), 'Collecting spontaneous production data' in D. McDaniel, C. McKee and H. Smith Cairns (eds.), *Methods for Assessing Children's Syntax* (Cambridge, MA: MIT Press), 3–22.

Deutsch, W. and J. Koster (1982), 'Children's interpretation of sentence-internal anaphora', *Papers and Reports on Child Language Development* 21, 39–45.

Deutsch, W., C. Koster and J. Koster (1986), 'Children's errors in understanding anaphora', *Linguistics* 24, 203–225.

Diessel, H. (2004), *The Acquisition of Complex Sentences.* Cambridge Studies in Linguistics *105* (Cambridge University Press).

Dixon, R. M. W. (1979), 'Ergativity', *Language* 55, 59–138.

(2006), 'Serial verb constructions: conspectus and coda' in A. Aikhenvald and R. M. W. Dixon (eds.), *Serial Verb Constructions. A Cross-linguistic Typology* (Oxford University Press), 338–350.

Durie, M. (1997), 'Grammatical structures in verb serialization' in A. Alsina, J. Bresnan and P. Sells (eds.), *Complex-Predicates* (Stanford, CA: Center for the Study of Language and Information), 289–354.

Eimas, P., E. R. Siqueland and J. Vigorito (1971), 'Speech perception in infants', *Science* 171, 303–306.

Eisenbeiss, S., H. Clahsen, P. Prüfert and J. Cholin (2002), 'Strong stems in the German mental lexicon: evidence from child language acquisition and adult processing' in I. Kaufmann and B. Stiebels (eds.), *More than Words. A Festschrift for Dieter Wunderlich* (Berlin: Akademie Verlag), 91–112.

Elman, J. L., E. A. Bates, M. H. Johnson, A. Karmiloff-Smith, D. Parisi and K. Plunkett (1996), *Rethinking Innateness: A Connectionist Perspective on Development* (Cambridge, MA: MIT Press).

Emmorey, K., U. Bellugi, Friederici, A. and P. Horn (1995), 'Effects of age of acquisition on grammatical sensitivity: evidence from on-line and off-line tasks', *Applied Psycholinguistics* 16, 1–23.

Erbaugh, M. S. (1982), *Coming to Order: Natural Selection and the Origin of Syntax in the Mandarin Speaking Child*, unpublished Ph.D. thesis, University of California at Berkeley.

Feldman, H., S. Goldin-Meadow and L. Gleitman (1978), 'Beyond Herodotus: the creation of language by linguistically deprived deaf children' in A. Lock (ed.), *Action, Symbol and Gesture: the Emergence of Language* (New York: Academic Press), 351–414.

Florigny, G. (2010), *Acquisition du kreol mauricien et du français et construction du discours à travers l'analyse de productions orales d'enfants plurilingues mauriciens. La référence aux entités*, unpublished Ph.D. thesis, 14th December 2010, Université de Paris, Ouest Nanterre la Défense.

Fox, D., Y. Grodzinsky and S. Crain (1995), 'An experimental study of children's passives', *Papers on Language Processing and Acquisition, MIT Working Papers in Linguistics* 26, 249–264.

Frank, R. E. (1992), *Syntactic Locality and Tree Adjoining Syntax*, unpublished Ph.D. thesis, University of Pennsylvania.

French, P., U. Lindenberger and J. Kray (1999), 'Imposing structure on an unstructured environment: ontogenetic changes in the ability to form rules of behavior under condition of low environmental predictability' in A. Friederici and R. Menzel (eds.), *Learning: Rule-Extraction and Representation* (Berlin: De Gruyter), 139–158.

Gazzaniga, M. (1985), *The Social Brain* (New York: Basic Books).

Gerken, L. A. (1996), 'Phonological and distributional cues to syntax acquisition' in J. Morgan and K. Demuth (eds.), *Signal to Syntax: Bootstrapping from Speech to Grammar in Early Acquisition* (Mahwah, NJ: Erlbaum), 411–425.

Gibson, E. and N. J. Pearlmutter (eds.) (2011), *The Processing and Acquisition of Reference* (Cambridge, MA: MIT Press).

Gleitman, L. and E. Wanner (1982), 'Language acquisition: the state of the art' in E. Wanner and L. Gleitman (eds.), *Language Acquisition: The State of the Art* (Cambridge University Press), 3–48.

Goldin-Meadow, S. (1982), 'The resilience of recursion: a study of a communication system developed without a conventional language model' in E. Wanner and L. R. Gleitman (eds.), *Language Acquisition: The State of the Art* (Cambridge University Press), 51–77.

(2003), *The Resilience of Language: What Gesture Creation in Deaf Children Can Tell Us About How All Children Learn Language* (New York: Psychology Press).

Goldin-Meadow, S. and C. Mylander (1984), 'Gestural communication in deaf children: the effects and noneffects of parental input on early language development', *Monographs Of the Society for Research in Child Development* 49.3–4, 372–374.

Goldin-Meadow, S., C. Butcher, C. Mylander and M. Dodge (1994), 'Nouns and verbs in a self-styled gesture system. What's in a name', *Cognitive Psychology* 27, 259–319.

Gopnik, M. and M. Crago (1991), 'Familial aggregation of a developmental language disorder', *Cognition* 39, 1–50.

Gordon, P. (1996), 'The truth-value judgment task' in D. McDaniel, C. McKee and H. Smith Cairns (eds.), *Methods for Assessing Children's Syntax* (Cambridge, MA: MIT Press), 211–231.

Gordon, P. and J. Chafetz (1990), 'Verb-based versus class-based accounts of actionality effects in children's comprehension of passives', *Cognition* 36, 227–254.

Gregoire, A. (1937), *L'apprentissage du langage: les deux premières années* (Liege/Paris).

(1947), *L'apprentissage du langage. La troisième année et les années suivantes* (Liege/Paris).

Grimshaw, J. and S. Rosen (1990), 'Knowledge and obedience: the developmental status of binding theory', *Linguistic Inquiry* 21, 187–222.

Gropen, J., S. Pinker, M. Hollander, R. Goldberg and R. Wilson (1989), 'The learnability and acquisition of the dative alternation in English', *Language* 65, 203–257.

Hakes, D. T. (1980), *The Development of Metalinguistic Abilities in Children* (Berlin: Springer-Verlag).

Hale, K. L. and S. J. Keyser (1987), 'A view from the middle', *Lexicon Project Working Papers 10*, Center for Cognitive Science (MIT).

Hall, R. A. (1966), *Pidgin and Creole Languages* (Ithaca, NY: Cornell University Press).

Hatch, E. and H. Farhady (1982), *Research Design and Statistics for Applied Linguistics* (Rowley, MA: Newbury House).

Hauser, M., T. Fitch and N. Chomsky (2002), 'The faculty of language: what is it, who has it and how did it evolve?', *Science* 298, 1569–1579.

Heine, B. and T. Kuteva (2005), *Language Contact and Grammatical Change. Cambridge Approaches to Language Contact* (Cambridge University Press).

Hicks, G. (2009), *The Derivation of Anaphoric Relations* (Amsterdam: John Benjamins).

Hinton, G. E. (1992), 'Wie neuronale Netze aus Erfahrung lernen', *Spektrum der Wissenschaft* 11, 134–143.

Hirsch-Pasek, K. and R. M. Golinkoff (1996), *The Origins of Grammar: Evidence from Early Language Comprehension* (Cambridge, MA: MIT Press).

Höhle, B. and J. Weissenborn (1999), 'Discovering grammar. Prosodic and morphosyntactic aspects of rule formation in first language acquisition' in A. Friederici and R. Menzel (eds.), *Learning: Rule Abstraction and Representation* (Berlin: Walter de Gruyter), 37–69.

Hoesktra, T. and P. Jordens (1994), 'From adjunct to head' in T. Hoekstra and B. D. Schwartz (eds.), *Language Acquisition Studies in Generative Grammar* (Amsterdam: Benjamins), 119–149.

Hoffmeister, R. and R. Wilbur (1980), 'Developmental: the acquisition of sign language' in H. Lane and F. Grossjean (eds.), *Recent perspectives on American Sign Language* (Hillsdale, NJ: Lawrence Erlbaum Associates).

Holm, J. (1988), *Pidgins and Creoles I: Theory and Structure* (New York: Cambridge University Press).

Holm, J. and S. Michaelis (eds.) (2008), *Contact Languages: Critical Concepts in Language Studies* (London: Routledge).

Horgan, D. (1978), 'The development of the full passive', *Journal of Child Language* 5, 65–80.

Hsu, J. R. and L. M. Hsu (1996), 'Issues in designing research and evaluating data pertaining to children's syntactic knowledge' in D. McDaniel, C. McKee and H. Smith Cairns (eds.), *Methods for Assessing Children's Syntax* (Cambridge, MA: MIT Press), 303–341.

Hudson, J. (1983), 'Transitivity and aspect in the Kriol verb', *Papers in Pidgin and Creole Linguistics 3, Pacific Linguistics A-65* (Canberra: Australian National University), 161–176.

Hudson-Kam, C. H. and E. L. Newport (2005), 'Regularizing unpredictable variation: the roles of adult and child learners in language formation and change', *Language Learning And Development* 1.2, 151–195.

Hultsch, H., R. Mundry and D. Todt (1999), 'Learning, representation and retrieval of rule-related knowledge in the song system of birds' in A. Friederici and R. Menzel (eds.), *Learning Rule Extraction and Representation* (Berlin: Reuter), 89–115.

Hyams, N. (1986), *Language Acquisition and the Theory of Parameters* (Dordrecht: Reidel).

Hyams, N. and S. Sigurjónsdóttir (1990), 'The development of long distance anaphora: a cross-linguistic comparison with special reference to Icelandic', *Language Acquisition* 1, 57–63.

Israel, M., C. Johnson and P. J. Brooks (2000), 'From states to events: the acquisition of English passive participles', *Cognitive Linguistics* 11.1/2, 103–129.

Itard, J. (1806), *The Wild Boy of Aveyron* (translated by J. White, London, 1972).

Jakubowicz, C. (1984), 'On markedness and binding principles', *Proceedings of the 14th Annual Meeting of the North Eastern Linguistics Society (NELS)* (Cambridge, MA: MIT Press), 154–182.

Jusczyk, P. W. (1997), *The Discovery of Spoken Language* (Cambridge, MA: MIT Press).

Kaufman, D. (1984), 'On binding and control', *Linguistic Inquiry* 15, 417–460.

Kayne, R. (1975), *French Syntax* (Cambridge, MA: MIT Press).

(2002), 'Pronouns and their antecedents' in S. Epstein and D. Seely (eds.), *Derivation and Explanation in the Minimalist Program* (Malden, MA: Blackwell), 133–166.

Kearney, G. E. and D. W. McElwain (eds.) (1976), *Aboriginal Cognition* (Canberra: Australian Institute of Aboriginal Studies).

Kegl, J. and G. A. Iwata (1989), 'Lenguaje de Signos Nicaraguense: a Pidgin sheds light on the "Creole"', *Proceedings of the 4th Annual Meeting of the Pacific Linguistics Conference* (University of Oregon), 266–294.

Kriegel, S. (1996), *Diathesen im Mauritius- und Seychellenkreol* (Tübingen: Gunter Narr).

Kuhl, P. and J. D. Miller (1975), 'Speech perception by the chinchilla: voice-voiceless distinction in alveolar plosive consonants', *Science* 190, 69–72.

Landau, B. and L. R. Gleitman (1985), *Language and Experience: Evidence from the Blind Child* (Cambridge, MA: Harvard University Press).

Lane, H. L. (1976), *The Wild Boy of Aveyron* (Cambridge, MA: Harvard University Press).

Lebeaux, D. (1989), *Language Acquisition and the Form of Grammar*, unpublished Ph.D. thesis, University of Massachusetts, Amherst.

Lefèbvre, C. (1998), *Creole Genesis and the Acquisition of Grammar: The Case of Haitian Creole* (Cambridge University Press).

van der Lely, H. K. J. (1996), 'Specifically language impaired and normally developing children: verbal passive vs adjectival passive sentence interpretation', *Lingua* 98, 243–272.

Lenneberg, E. (1967), *Biological Foundations of Language* (New York: Wiley).

Levin, B. (1993), *English Verb Classes and Alternations* (University of Chicago Press).

Levin, B. and M. Rappaport (1986), 'The formation of adjectival passives', *Linguistic Inquiry* 17, 623–661.

Lillo-Martin, D. (1999), 'Modality effects and modularity in language acquisition: the acquisition of American Sign Language' in T. K. Bhatia and W. C. Ritchie (eds.), *Handbook of Language Acquisition* (San Diego, CA: Academic Press), 531–567.

Lumsden, J. S. (1999a), 'The role of relexification in creole genesis', *Journal of Pidgin and Creole Languages* 14.2, 225–258.

Lumsden, J. S. (1999b), 'Language acquisition and creolization' in M. DeGraff (ed.), *Creolization, Diachrony, and Language Acquisition* (Cambridge, MA: MIT Press), 129–157.

Lust, B. C. (ed.) (1986), *Studies in the Acquisition of Anaphora: Vol 1. Defining the Constraints* (Dordrecht: Reidel).

Lust, B. C. (ed.) (1987), *Studies in the Acquisition of Anaphora: Vol 2. Applying the Constraints* (Dordrecht: Reidel).

Lust, B. C., C. Foley and C. Dye (2009), 'The first language acquisition of complex sentences' in E. Bavin (ed.), *Handbook of Child Language* (Cambridge University Press), 237–257.

Manzini, R. and K. Wexler (1987), 'Parameters, binding theory and learnability', *Linguistic Inquiry* 18, 413–444.

Maratsos, M. (1974), 'Children who get worse at understanding passive: a replication of Bever', *Journal of Psycholinguistic Research* 3.1, 65–74.

(1999), 'Some aspects of innateness and complexity in grammatical acquisition' in M. Barrett (ed.), *The Development of Language* (East Sussex: Psychology Press), 191–228.

Maratsos, M., D. E. C. Fox, J. A. Becker and M. A. Chalkley (1985), 'Semantic restrictions on children's passives', *Cognition* 19, 167–191.

Marcus, G. F. S. (1993), 'Negative evidence in language acquisition', *Cognition* 46, 53–85.

(2001), *The Algebraic Mind: Integrating Connectivism and Cognitive Science* (Cambridge, MA: MIT Press).

Marcus, G. F. S., S. Pinker, M. Ullman, M. Hollander, T. Rosen and F. Xu (1992), 'Overregularisation in language acquisition', *Monographs of the Society for Research in Child Development* 57.

Mason, M. K. (1942), 'Learning to speak after six and one half years of silence', *Journal of Speech and Hearing Disorders* 46, 267–273.

Mazurkewich, I. and L. White (1984), 'The acquisition of the dative alternation: unlearning overgeneralizations', *Cognition* 16, 261–283.

McDaniel, D. and H. S. Cairns (1987), 'The child as informant: eliciting linguistic intuitions from young children', unpublished manuscript, City University of New York.

McDaniel, D., H. S. Cairns and J. R. Hsu (1990), 'Binding principles in the grammars of young children', *Language Acquisition* 1, 121–139.

McDaniel, D., C. McKee and H. Smith Cairns (eds.) (1996), *Methods for Assessing Children's Syntax* (Cambridge, MA: MIT Press).

McKee, C. (1988), *Italian Children's Mastery of Binding*, unpublished Ph.D. thesis, The University of Connecticut, Storrs.

McWhorter, J. H. (1997), *Towards a New Model of Creole Genesis* (New York: Peter Lang).

(2001), *The Power of Babel: A Natural History of Language* (New York: Times Books).

Mehler, J., P. Jusczyk, G. Lambertz, N. Halsted, J. Bertoncini and C. Amiel-Tison (1988), 'A precursor of language acquisition in young infants', *Cognition* 29, 143–178.

Meisel, J. (1995), 'Parameters in acquisition' in P. Fletcher and B. MacWhinney (eds.), *The Handbook of Child Language* (Cambridge, MA: Blackwell), 10–35.

Meisel, J., H. Clahsen and M. Pienemann (1981), 'On determining developmental stages in natural second language acquisition', *Studies in Second Language Acquisition* 3, 109–135.

Meisel, J. and M.-J. Ezeizabarrena (1996), 'Subject-verb and object-verb agreement in early Basque' in H. Clahsen (ed.), *Generative Perspectives on Language Acquisition* (Amsterdam: Benjamins), 201–240.

Michaelis, S. (1994), *Komplexe Syntax im Seychellen-Kreol. Verknüpfung von Sachverhaltsdarstellungen zwischen Mündlichkeit und Schriftlichkeit* (Tübingen: Narr).

Mills, A. (1985), 'The acquisition of German' in D. I. Slobin (ed.), *The Cross-linguistic Study of Language Acquisition. Volume 1: the Data* (Hillsdale, NJ: Erlbaum), 141–255.

Morgan, G. and B. Woll (eds.) (2002), *Directions in Sign Language Acquisition* (Trends in Language Acquisition Research 2), (Amsterdam, Philadelphia: Benjamins), 255–275.

Mufwene, S. (1996), 'The founder principle in creole genesis', *Diachronica* 13, 83–134.

(1999), 'On the language bioprogram hypothesis: hints from Tazie' in M. DeGraff (ed.), *Language Creation and Language Change: Creolization, Diachrony, and Development. (Learning, Development, and Conceptual Change).* (Cambridge, MA: MIT Press), 95–127.

(2000), 'La fonction réfléchie en créole', *Langages* 138, 114–124.

Mühlhäusler, P. (1986), *Pidgins and Creole Linguistics* (Oxford: Blackwell).

Muysken, P. C. (1988), 'Are creoles a special type of language?' in J. F. Newmeyer (ed.), *Linguistics: The Cambridge Survey* (Cambridge University Press), vol. II, 285–301.

Muysken, P. C. and T. Veenstra (1995), 'Universalist approaches' in J. Arends, P. Muysken and N. Smith. (eds.), *Pidgins and Creoles. An Introduction* (Amsterdam: John Benjamins), 121–134.

Neumann, I. (1985), *Le créole de Breaux Bridge, Louisiane – Etude morphosyntaxique – textes – vocabulaire.* Kreolische Bibliothek 7 (Hamburg: Buske).

Newport, E. (1982), 'Task specificity in language learning? Evidence from speech perception and American Sign Language' in E. Wanner and L. R. Gleitman (eds.), *Language Acquisition: The State of the Art* (New York: Cambridge University Press), 450–86.

(1990), 'Maturational constraints on language learning', *Cognitive Science* 14, 11–28.

(1999), 'Reduced input in the acquisition of signed languages: contributions to the study of creolisation' in M. DeGraff (ed.), *Language Change: Creolization,*

Diachrony, and Development. (Learning, Development, and Conceptual Change) (Cambridge, MA: MIT Press), 161–178.

O'Toole, B. (1990), 'Community-based rehabilitation: the Guyana evaluation project' in M. J. Thorburn and K. Marfo (eds.), *Practical Approaches to Childhood Disability in Developing Countries: Insights from Experience and Research* (St Johns, Newfoundland: Memorial University Project SEREDEC, 3D Projects), 293–316.

Otsu, Y. (1981), *Towards a Theory of Syntactic Development*, unpublished Ph.D. thesis, MIT, Cambridge, MA.

Perlmutter, D. M. (1978), 'Impersonal passives and the unaccusative hypothesis' in J. Jaeger *et al.* (eds.), *Proceedings of the 4th Annual Meeting of the Berkeley Linguistic Society*, (University of California at Berkeley), 157–189.

Pinker, S. (1984), *Language Learnability and Language Development* (Cambridge, MA: Harvard University Press).

(1989), *Learnability and Cognition: the Acquisition of Argument Structure* (Cambridge, MA: MIT Press).

(1999), *Words and Rules* (London: Weidenfeld and Nicolson).

(2002), *The Blank Slate. The Modern Denial Of Human Nature* (New York: Viking).

Pinker, S., D. S. Lebeaux and L. A. Frost (1987), 'Productivity and constraints in the acquisition of the passive', *Cognition* 26, 195–267.

Plag, I. (1993), *Sentential Complementation in Sranan. on the Formation of an English-Based Creole Language* (Tübingen: Niemeyer).

(1998), 'Letter to the editor', *Journal of Pidgin and Creole Languages* 13.1, 210–212.

Poeppel, D. and K. Wexler (1993), 'The full competence hypothesis of clause structure in early German', *Language* 69.1, 1–33.

Pomerleau, A., G. Malcuit and C. Sabatier (1991), 'Child-rearing practices and parental beliefs in three cultural groups of Montreal: Quebecois, Vietnamese and Haitian' in M. H. Bornstein (ed.), *Cultural Approaches to Parenting* (Hillsdale, NJ: Lawrence Erlbaum Associates), 45–68.

Pye, C., B. Pfeiler, L. de León, P. Brown and P. Mateo (2007), 'Roots or edges? A comparative study of Mayan children's early verb forms' in B. Pfeiler (ed.), *Learning Indigenous Languages: Child Language Acquisition in Mesoamerica* (Hannover: Verlag für Ethnologie, Colección Americana X), 15–46.

Radford, A. (1990), *Syntactic Theory and the Acquisition of English Syntax* (Oxford: Blackwell).

(1996), 'Towards a structure-building model of acquisition' in H. Clahsen (ed.), *Generative Perspectives on Language Acquisition* (Amsterdam: Benjamins), 43–90.

(1997), *Syntax. A Minimalist Introduction* (Melbourne: Cambridge University Press).

(2006), 'Children's English: principles-and-parameters perspectives', unpublished manuscript, University of Essex.

Ravel, J.-L. and P. Thomas (1985), *Etat de la Reforme de l'Enseignement aux Seychelles (1981–1985)* (Paris: Ministere des Relations Exterieures, Cooperation et Développement).

Reinhart, T. (1983a), *Anaphora and Semantic Interpretation* (London: Croom Helm).

(1983b), 'Coreference and bound anaphora: a restatement of the anaphora questions', *Linguistics and Philosophy* 6, 47–88.

Reuland, E. (2011), *Anaphora and Language Design* (Cambridge, MA: MIT Press).

Rizzi, L. (1986), 'On the status of subject clitics in Romance' in O. Jaeggli and C. Silva-Corvalan (eds.), *Studies in Romance Linguistics* (Dordrecht: Foris), 391–419.

(1994), 'Some notes on linguistic theory and language development: the case of root infinitives', *Language Acquisition* 3, 341–393.

(2000), 'Remarks on early null subjects' in M.-A. Friedeman and L. Rizzi (eds.), *The Acquisition of Syntax: Studies in Comparative Developmental Linguistics* (Harlow: Pearson Education Limited), 269–292.

Roberts, J. (1995), 'Pidgin Hawaiian: a sociohistorical study', *Journal of Pidgin and Creole Languages* 10, 1–56.

Roeper, T. (1987a), 'Implicit arguments and the head-complement relation', *Linguistic Inquiry* 18, 267–310.

(1987b), 'The acquisition of implicit arguments and the distinction between theory, process and mechanism' in B. MacWhinney (ed.), *Mechanisms of Language Acquisition* (Hillsdale, NJ: Erlbaum).

(1988), 'Theory and explanation in acquisition', *Papers and Reports in Child Language Acquisition* 27, 162–166.

(1996), 'The role of Merger Theory and formal features in acquisition' in H. Clahsen (ed.), *Generative Perspectives on Language Acquisition* (Amsterdam: Benjamins), 415–450.

Roeper, T. and J. de Villiers (1992), 'The One Feature Hypothesis', unpublished manuscript, University of Massachusetts, Amherst.

Roggoff, B., J. Mistry, A. Goncu and C. Mosier (1991), 'Cultural variations in the role relations of toddlers and their families' in M. H. Bornstein (ed.),

Approaches to Parenting (Hillsdale, NJ: Lawrence Erlbaum Associates), 173–184.

Ross, D. and E. Newport (1996), 'The development of language from non-native linguistic input' in A. Stringfellow, D. Cahana-Amitay, E. Hughs and A. Zukowski (eds.), *Proceedings of the 20th Annual Boston University Conference on Languages Development* (Somerville, MA: Cascadilla Press), vol. I, 634–645.

Safran, J., R. Aslin and E. Newport (1996), 'Statistical learning by 8-month-old infants', *Science* 274, 1926–1928.

Sankoff, G. (1979), 'The genesis of a language' in K. C. Hill (ed.), *The Genesis of Language* (Ann Arbor, MI: Karoma), 23–47.

Savage-Rumbaugh, S., J. Murphy, R. A. Sevcik, K. E. Brakke, S. L. Williams and D. M. Rumbaugh (1993), *Language, Comprehension in Ape and Child (Monographs of the Society for Research in Child Development)* (University Of Chicago Press).

Saxton, M. (1997), 'The contrast theory of negative input', *Journal of Child Language* 24, 139–161.

Saxton, M., B. Kulcsar, G. Marshall and M. Rupra (1998), 'Longer-term effects of corrective input: an experimental approach', *Journal of Child Language* 25, 701–721.

Schlisselberg, G. (1988), *Development of Selected Conservation Skills and the Ability to Judge Sentence Well-Formedness in Young Children*, unpublished Ph.D. thesis, City University of New York.

Schütze, C. T. (1996), *The Empirical Base of Linguistics: Grammaticality Judgments and Linguistic Methodology* (University of Chicago Press).

Senghas, A. (1995a), 'Children's contribution to the birth of Nicaraguan Sign Language', *MIT Working papers in Linguistics*.

(1995b), 'The development of Nicaraguan Sign Language via the language acquisition process' in D. MacLaughlin and S. McEwen (eds.), *Proceedings of the 19th Annual Boston University Conference on Language Development* (Somerville, MA: Cascadilla Press), 543–552.

Senghas, R., J. Kegl and A. Senghas (1997), 'Creation through contact: the development of a Nicaraguan deaf community', paper presented at the Second International Conference on Deaf History, Association of Deaf History, International University of Hamburg.

Siegel, J. (1999), 'Creole and minority dialects in education: an overview', *Journal of Multilingual and Multicultural Development* 20, 508–531.

Sigurjónsdóttir, S., N. Hyams and Y. C. Chien (1988), 'The acquisition of reflexive and pronouns by Icelandic children', *Papers and Reports on Child Language Development* 27, 97–106.

Silverstein, M. (1976), 'Hierarchy of features and ergativity' in R. M. W. Dixon (ed.), *Grammatical Categories in Australian Languages* (Canberra: AIAS), 112–171.

Singler, J. V. (1992), 'Nativization and pidgin/creole genesis: a reply to Bickerton', *Journal of Pidgin and Creole Languages* 7, 319–333.

(1995), 'The demographics of creole genesis in the Caribbean: A comparison of Martinique and Haiti' in J. Arends (ed.), *Creolization: The Early Years* (Amsterdam: John Benjamins), 203–232.

(1996), 'Theories of creole genesis, sociohistorical considerations, and the evaluation of evidence: the case of Haitian Creole and the Relexification Hypothesis', *Journal of Pidgin and Creole Languages* 11, 185–230.

Singleton, J. L. (1989), *Restructuring of Language from Impoverished Input: Evidence for Linguistic Compensation*, unpublished Ph.D. thesis, University of Illinois at Urbana-Champaign.

Singleton, J. L., J. Morford and S. Goldin-Meadow (1983), 'Once is not enough: standards of well-formedness over three different time spans', *Language* 69.4, 683–715.

Singleton, J. L. and E. Newport (1987), 'When learners surpass their models: the acquisition of American Sign Language from impoverished input', poster presented at the biennial Meeting of the Society for Research in Child Development, Baltimore, MD.

Skuse, D. K. (1994), 'Extreme deprivation in early childhood' in D. Bishop and K. Mogford (eds.) *Language Development in Exceptional Circumstances* (Hove/Hillsdale: Lawrence Erlbaum Associates), 29–46.

Slobin, D. I. (1985a), (ed.) *The Crosslinguistic Study of Language Acquisition: Volume 1: The Data* (Hillsdale, NJ: Erlbaum).

(1985b), (ed.) *The Crosslinguistic Study of Language Acquisition: Volume 2: Theoretical Issues* (Hillsdale, NJ: Erlbaum).

(1997), 'The universal, the typological, and the particular in acquisition' in D. I. Slobin (ed.), *The Crosslinguistic Study of Language Acquisition: Vol. 5. Expanding the Contexts* (Mahwah, NJ: Lawrence Erlbaum), 1–39.

Snyder, W. and K. Stromswold (1997), 'The structure and acquisition of English dative constructions', *Linguistic Inquiry* 28, 281–317.

Solan, L. (1983), *Pronominal Reference: Child Language and the Theory of Grammar* (Dordrecht: Reidel).

(1987), 'Parameter setting and the development of pronouns and reflexives' in T. Roeper and E. Williams (eds.), *Parameter Setting* (Dordrecht: Reidel), 189–210.

Squire, L. R. and E. R. Kandel (1999), *From Mind to Molecules* (New York: Scientific American Library).

Stern, C. and W. Stern (1907), *Die Kindersprache: Eine psychologische und sprachtheoretische Untersuchung* (Leipzig: Barth).

Stoll, S., B. Bickel, G. Banjade, M. Gaenszle, E. Lieven, N. P. Paudyal, I. P. Rai, M. Rai and N. K. Rai (2007), 'Free prefix ordering in Chintang', *Language* 83, 44–73.

Stromswold, K. (1996), 'Analyzing children's spontaneous speech' in D. McDaniel, C. McKee and H. Smith Cairns (eds.), *Methods for Assessing Children's Syntax* (Cambridge, MA: MIT Press), 23–53.

Sudhalter, V. and M. D. S. Braine (1985), 'How does comprehension of passives develop? A comparison of actional and experiential verbs', *Journal of Child Language* 12, 455–470.

Supalla, T. (1982), *Structure and Acquisition of Verbs of Motion in American Sign Language*, unpublished Ph.D. thesis, University of California, San Diego.

Suppes, P., R. Smith and M. Léveillé (1973), 'The French syntax of a child's noun phrases', *Archives de Psychologie*, 207–269.

Syea, A. (1985), *Aspects of Empty Categories in Mauritian Creole*. British thesis, supplied by the British Library.

Tavakolian, S. (1981), 'The conjoined clause analysis of relative clauses' in S. Tavakolian (ed.), *Language Acquisition and Linguistic Theory* (Cambridge, MA: MIT Press), 167–187.

Tenenbaum, J. and F. Xu (2005), 'Word learning as Bayesian inference: evidence from preschoolers', *Proceedings of the 27th Annual Conference of the Cognitive Science Society*, Stresa, Italy.

Teng, X. (1989), 'On the acquisition of the passive with instrumental prepositional phrase in English', unpublished manuscript, University of Massachusetts, Amherst.

Thiessen, E. (2009), 'Statistical learning', in E. Bavin (ed.), *The Cambridge Handbook of Child Language* (Cambridge University Press), 35–50.

Ting Ting, R. C. and P. Gordon (1998), 'The acquisition of Chinese dative constructions' in A. Greenhill, M. Hughes, H. Littlefield and H. Walsh (eds.), *Proceedings of the 22nd Annual Boston University Conference on Language Development* (Somerville, MA: Cascadilla Press), vol. I, 109–120.

Thomason, S. G. and T. Kaufman (1988), *Language Contact, Creolisation, and Genetic Linguistics* (Berkeley: University of California Press).

Thornton, R. and K. Wexler (1999), *Principle B, VP Ellipsis, and Interpretation in Child Grammar* (Cambridge, MA: MIT Press).

Todd, L. (1990), *Pidgins and Creoles* (New York: Routledge).

Tomasello, M. (2003), *Constructing a Language: A Usage-Based Theory of Language Acquisition* (Cambridge: Harvard University Press).

(2010), 'Language development' in U. Goswami (ed.), *Blackwell Handbook of Childhood Cognitive Development* (Cambridge: Blackwell).

Vainikka, A. (1990), 'The status of grammatical default systems: comments on Lebeaux' in L. Frazier and J. de Villiers (eds.), *Language Processing and Language Acquisition* (Dordrecht: Kluwer), 83–103.

Vainikka, A. and M. Scholten (1994), 'Direct access to X-theory: evidence from Korean and Turkish adults learning German' in T. Hoekstra and B. D. Schwartz (eds.), *Language Acquisition Studies in Generative Grammar: Papers in Honor of Kenneth Wexler from the GLOW Workshop.* (Amsterdam: Benjamins), 265–316.

Valian, V. (2009), 'Innateness and learnability' in E. Bavin (ed.), *The Cambridge handbook of Child Language* (Cambridge University Press), 15–34.

Van Kleeck, A. (1982), 'The emergence of linguistic awareness: a cognitive framework', *Merill-Palmer Quarterly* 28, 237–265.

Veenstra, T. (1996), *Serial Verbs in Saramaccan: Predication and Creole Genesis*, unpublished Ph.D. thesis, University of Amsterdam.

(2001), *The Syntax of Passives in Saramaccan: Architectural Implications*, unpublished manuscript, Freie Universität Berlin.

Veenstra, T. (2003), 'What verbal morphology can tell us about creole genesis: the case of French-related creoles' in I. Plag and S. Lappe (eds.), *The Phonology and Morphology of Creole Languages* (Tübingen: Niemeyer), 293–314.

Venditti, J. and M. Swerts (1996), 'Prosodic cues to discourse structure in Japanese', in J. L. Morgan and K. Demuth (eds.), *Signal to Syntax: Bootstrapping from Speech to Grammar in Early Acquisition* (Mahwah, NJ: Erlbaum), 287–311.

Veronique, D. (1984), 'Typologie du predicat et formes du passif en mauricien', *Cercle linguistique d'Aix en Provence. Travaux 2. Le Passif*, 53–74.

Verrips, M. (1992), 'Comprehension of passive and anti-causative by Dutch children' in M. Verrips and F. Wijnen (eds.), *The Acquisition of Dutch*. Amsterdam Series in Child Language Development (University of Amsterdam), vol. i, 51–60.

(1993), 'The categorical nature of children's passives' in W. Philip and F. Wijnen (eds.), *Connecting Children's Language and Linguistic Theory*. Amsterdam Series in Child Language Development, vol. v (University of Amsterdam).

(1996), *Potatoes Must Peel*, unpublished Ph.D. thesis, University of Amsterdam.

de Villiers, J. (1991), 'Why questions' in T. L. Maxfield and B. Plunkett (eds.), *UMOP. Papers in the Acquisition of WH* (Amherst: University of Massachusetts Press), 155–173.

de Villiers, J. and P. de Villiers (1973), 'Development of the use of word order in comprehension', *Journal of Psycholinguistics Research* 2, 331–341.

de Villiers, J., T. Roeper and N. Vainikka (1990), 'The acquisition of long distance rules' in L. Frazier and J. de Villiers (eds.), *Language Processing and Language Acquisition* (Dordrecht: Kluwer), 257–297.

de Villiers, P. and J. de Villiers (1974), 'Competence and performance in child language: are children really competent to judge?', *Journal of Child Language* 1, 11–22.

Vincent, L. J., C. L. Salisbury, P. Strain, C. McCormick and A. Tessier (1990), 'A behavioral-ecological approach to early intervention: focus on cultural diversity' in S. J. Meisels *et al.* (eds.), *Handbook Of Early Childhood Intervention* (Cambridge University Press), 173–195.

Weissenborn, J., T. Roeper and J. de Villiers (1991), 'The acquisition of wh-movement in German and French' in T. L. Maxfield and B. Plunkett (eds.), *UMOP. Papers in the Acquisition of WH* (Amherst: University of Massachusetts Press), 43–77.

Wexler, K. (2011), 'Cues don't explain learning: maximal trouble in the determiner system' in E. Gibson and N. J. Pearlmutter (eds.), *The Processing and Acquisition of Reference* (Cambridge, MA: MIT Press), 15–42.

Wexler, K., C. T. Schütze and M. L. Rice (1998), 'Subject case in children with SLI and unaffected controls: evidence for the Agr/Tns omission model', *Language Acquisition* 7, 317–344.

White, L. (1987), 'Children's overgeneralizations of the dative alternation' in K. Nelson and A. van Kleeck (eds.), *Children's Language* (Hillsdale, NJ: Erlbaum), vol. vi, 261–287.

Yip, V. and S. Matthews (2007), *The Bilingual Child: Early Development and Language Contact* (Cambridge University Press).

Zubizaretta, M. L. (1987), *Levels of Representation in the Lexicon and in the Syntax* (Dordrecht: Foris).

Index